Mambo Mupepi

THE LEGENDARY
NEHANDA NYAKASIKANA

Limited Special Edition. No. 12 of 20 Paperbacks

Mambo earned a Ph.D. at Benedictine University, Chicago, and is the founder of Grand Change LLC, a change management organization specializing in building effective capability in varied economies. Mambo's research interests are corporate organization dynamics—organizational knowledge, learning, and change and their mediation/moderation by organizational design choices. Mambo has published numerous articles, books, and book chapters, including the following:

Amplifying the significance of sociotechnical systems thinking: (2018), Situational Dynamics (2018), Effective Talent Management (2017), Punctuating a cultural equipoise of ineptness: (2017), Gender intelligence (2017), The Organization Development of the First Chimurenga (2015), Certain Change: (2014), Re-engineering the Division of Labor: (2014), Unlocking and building effective entrepreneurial capacity in Zimbabwe (2010), among others.

I dedicate this book to Freedom Fighters Sister Doreen Marange Mupepi and Brother Patrick Fungai Mudyiwa Mupepi. They took the African Triumvirate threads to liberate Zimbabwe.

Mambo Mupepi

THE LEGENDARY NEHANDA NYAKASIKANA

AUSTIN MACAULEY PUBLISHERS™

LONDON · CAMBRIDGE · NEW YORK · SHARJAH

A CIP catalogue record for this title is available from the British Library.

ISBN 9781786934666 (Paperback)
ISBN 9781786934673 (Hardback)
ISBN 9781528952040 (ePub e-book)

www.austinmacauley.com

First Published (2019)
Austin Macauley Publishers Ltd
25 Canada Square
Canary Wharf
London
E14 5LQ

Chapter One
Introduction

This is a biography of Nehanda Charwe (c. 1864–1898), arguably the most influential spiritual medium during both the First Chimurenga (1883–1904) and Second Chimurenga (1966–1980). Exploring the life story of one of Zimbabwe's female rulers makes it possible to examine the events that led up to the occupation of Zimbabwe by the British South Africa Company (BSAC), and the subsequent organization and development of the resistance movement. The epistemology used to analyze the life of Nehanda Charwe has been drawn from political discourse and the history of Zimbabwe, with the aim of understanding how the current citizenry's collective sense of identity developed within the Mutapa states and the British Federation of Rhodesia and Nyasaland (1890–1963), now the sovereign states of Malawi, Zambia, and Zimbabwe.

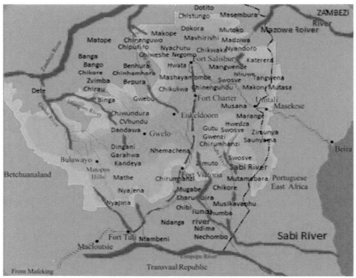

Map 1: Showing the routes of the Pioneer Column

The story of Nehanda begins with the invasion of Zimbabwe by the Pioneer Column 1890 and is dominated by the life history of the Hwata dynasty of which she was the highest priest. The Pioneer Column decided to settle in the Hwata state with invalid documentation signed by Chief Lobengula Khumalo of the Ndebele, who was not any part of the traditional Mutapa authorities (Rudd 1888 and Moffat 1888). The Pioneer Column clashed with the bona fide authorities of Zimbabwe (see Map 1). The Hwata lived among other Zezuru communities such as the Shumba and Nematombo dynasties who were neighbors in the Mazowe and Zambezi valleys. In Mudenge (1974), the word "Rozvi" denotes the Rozvi Empire (1684–1834), under the leadership of Changamire, who brought the whole of present-day Zimbabwe under his control, forming a polity that became known as the Rozvi Empire. The Rozvi Empire was the foundation of what later became the Shona states. The words "Rozvi" and "Shona" are interchangeable, relating to the same culture and emphasizing the distinction between history and current affairs.

The Hwata chiefdom was similar with many others such as Makoni or Shumba dynasties for having originated from the first Chaminuka. They were politically autonomous ethnic groups with a very high degree of self-sufficiency, and a sense of identity. Their totem was the Hwata which is a bird better known as the secretary bird. Its habitat is the savanna grasslands and it can be seen removing teaks from cattle. The Hwata's religion was also co-terminus with a cultural sovereignty originating from the Mutapa. Southall (2010) described ethnicity as a society with characteristics of self-sufficiency. The society also employed appropriate technology and the division of labor to increase output. Southall proposed that the society had its own language, religion and recognized that the family formed the nucleus of its organization.

Punctuating a cultural equilibrium

The mysterious look of the colonists led the indigenous people to describe them as knee-less people. The color of their skin exacerbated the situation leading to another perceived description…spooky. Nehanda Charwe already knew who the colonists were. Pasipamire's oracles had foretold the arrival of the knee-less people and as such encouraged the locals to study the new people, their ways and language. Most of all she wanted them to study the technology they had brought. The four wheels of the wagon, heifers that had names such as *Blackface* or *Charlieworks* could be span and used to pull up to two tons of cargo. All that was new to the local people. The horse too was a new beast of burden. They could be span or ridden by individual riders. The horses looked like the zebra but were short of the stripes. The most amazing technology was that of the self-loading Winchester rifle which could bring down a charging elephant bull to a dead end. It too, could be used to hunt lions and be useful as a military weapon. All these wonders punctuated a cultural equilibrium where the poisoned arrows once made sense in warfare and hunting.

Nehanda wanted her people to embrace all these new things as fast as they could. She knew what the villagers did not know, that the British were in the country to stay. But could not let go the truth lest no one enlisted for the resistance.

Diagram 1: The Pioneer Column 1890 invades Zimbabwe

During the evening of colonial conquest, the local community, prepared foods of all types and presented it to the new comers. They were offered sadza and meat served with wild spinach, boiled pumpkins which were meshed in peanut butter, and wild fruit such as Matamba known botanically as Strychnos spinosa. The tree thrives in the tropics such as those found in Zimbabwe. In Stone (2017), once a piece of fruit such as Matamba, were picked from its tree, it continued to respire, aging slowly until it began to breakdown. Microorganisms then moved in causing the fruit to spoil or ferment. When allowed to ferment the Matamba produced a potent drink akin to a wine or sherry (Stone, 2017). This drink could have appealed to the settlers because it was clear and unlike the brew made from corn and rapoko. The gregariousness of the settler community got accustomed to the local food and drink traditions before they built their own wineries and breweries.

For many, that was the first time they had seen a White person. The Portuguese traders limited their presence to the Zambezi Valley at Masekesa or Sena. When David Livingstone entered Zimbabwe by way of the Zambezi River, he remained on the river and its surrounding chiefdoms such as that of the Sechele (1858) [2010]. The Pioneer Column came with members of clergy whose role was to propagate the Gospel in their new-found land of the future Rhodesia. The problems they encountered was a people who were finding it difficult to change their culture for anything. Livingstone was renowned to have converted only one person, the chief of the Sechele. Chief Sechele was also possessed by the spirit of his ancestor that enabled him to make rain and diagnose illnesses and treat those inflicted. Sechele was akin to hundreds of other traditional authorities such as Nyachuru or Hwata. It took much persuasion and self-study of the bible to have a testimony of Jesus Christ. Livingstone propounded that Sechele had expressed concern that since he was a noted rainmaker and an implicit believer of the RTR, he could not let go the only culture he knew. At first, he could not afford to lose his faith in a religion that gave him his livelihood. He charged the people for making the rain. Sechele could have answered Livingstone that he could not abandon his faith to become a Christian. Sechele like many other indigenous people sustained their livelihoods by ensuring rainfall and curing those who were ill using traditional herbal medicine.

The guardian angel

The Gombwe ("Guardian Angel" in the Shona Language) Nehanda Nyakasikana came to possess Princess Nyanda during the reign of Emperor Nyatsimba Mutota (1430–1450).

This was the beginning of the Rozvi Traditional Religion (RTR), antecedent of the Shona Traditional Religion (STR) of today. The RTR or STR was embraced by the Magombwe ("Angels" in the Shona Language) as a symbol of freedom, offering a sense of identity and belonging. Folklore suggests that "Chaminuka" was a title implying "emperor" or "king", as well as "high priest" among the Shona people. The STR was understood to be—and used as—a symbol of national unity. The religion was created in the courts of the First Chaminuka (1430–1450) and diffused throughout the Mutapa states. The Zimbabwe Bird was an icon of co-constructed meaning and reality, which was translated in the courts of the traditional authorities. At the time of the arrival of the British *en masse*, Nehanda Charwe was one the nation's several experts on traditional customs and practices. Charwe's daughter had been possessed by the Gombwe spirit at the point of conception, while developing as a fetus—in around 1864. Nehanda's mother carried her for a full-term, nine-month pregnancy, when the spirit had already gained access to the baby. The spirit influenced the choice of foods the mother could eat, rejecting some of her favorite dishes. The baby's development was dynamically related to the personality of the mother, whose choices were a *fait accompli* within the Charwe household. The Gombwe Nehanda Nyakasikana controlled where she could go, whether to the fields or to fetch firewood or water. The Gombwe also brought its own preferred rituals into the Charwe household. For example, three ritual ceremonies for Magombwe now had to be performed in Charwe's courtyard. The first ritual was held in January to thank Musikavanhu for new crops. It was a mbira concert, known as "Bira Rekudyazvitswa" (a concert to celebrate new crops). During this shindig, people could eat green pumpkin leaves, known as mubowora, as well as nyeve (spinach) and green mealies. The cooking prowess of the Hwata women, known as vaHera, produced exceptional recipes, including peanut butter to garnish vegetables and many other delicious delights, providing children and adults with a variety of nutritious foods to build their stamina for the frosty Mazowe Valley winters.

The second ritual the Charwe family had to learn about and participate in was the April Bira, held to celebrate the harvest of corn, millet, sweet potatoes, groundnuts, monkey nuts, and other grains; beer was brewed and sadza cooked from the new corn. The ritual was known as *Mishashe.* Mbira drums and leg-worn maracas led the music and dancing. As the Hwata were champion dairy farmers, milk was one of the types of foods celebrated, in the hope of enabling the cows to produce more. Paramount Chief Gwindi sent out emissaries to Chief Mzilikazi in 1866 to stop cattle raids. The raids were resumed when Lobengula succeeded his father Mzilikazi and failed to uphold his legacy.

The last ritual that the Charwe household had to master was the Rukoto ceremony, held in September before the rains were due, to pray to the Magombwe, including Chaminuka, Ganyire, Goredema, Gorejena, and Gwangwadza. This ritual was critical for possible bumper crops to happen. It was intended to request for appropriate rainfall to avert a drought disease free crops.

These were some of the practices that the Charwe family had to embrace, as time went on. The Gombwe Nehanda Nyakasikana was a special defense force. This spirit was not celebrated as described above because it had its own rituals, such as the ritual to prepare for the chief's succession. This Gombwe specialized in warfare and the defense of the Munhumutapa Empire. Emperor Sororenzou requisitioned this Gombwe, sending it directly to Musikavanhu, also known as "Mwari" among the Shona communities. The role of the first Nehanda Nyakasikana Gombwe was to stop the slavery imposed by the Portuguese and Arabs during the early fifteenth century. The Gombwe's responsibilities included securing barter trade with the Indians, Arabs, and Portuguese.

Before he was murdered in 1883, the Emperor Pasipamire Chaminuka foretold the coming of the Pioneer Column. Nehanda Charwe was a young woman then, around 26 years of age. She was born to lead the Zimbabweans in a defense of

13

their territory, against a plan that the British had taken a long time to work out strategically and finally to implement. This strategy to expand British imperialism began in 1890 with the Pioneer Column.

How did the annexation occur?

Different philosophies were used to justify the "Scramble for Africa", or the occupation of African land by the European superpowers of Britain, Belgium, France, Portugal, and Italy, from the early 19th through the beginning of the 20 centuries. The Industrial Revolution in Britain gave the impetus for the need of raw materials. In addition, the population was expanding in geometric progression while food production was unproductive to feed everyone. As part of the British Empire expansion, colonies served as the land Britain needed to settle its people as colonists who could work the land to supply the country with the raw materials as well as food. Thus, the colonies served as a solution for unemployment and the shortage of housing. England and France were home to the Industrial Revolution and political change respectively. The Advances made in these transformations were not new but the series of self-perpetuating and apparently unstoppable developments which were set in motion by the advances made earlier in eighteenth century Britain transformed the life of man and the nature of human society more profoundly and more rapidly than anything that had happened since innovations in agriculture (Moore, 1984).

Britain as a world superpower nation deployed the use of companies and special agents to expand its hegemony of the world. It used Cecil John Rhodes to expand its interests in Africa. Rhodes teaming with Alfred Beit Charles Rudd and Leander Starr Jameson created the British South Africa Company as a vehicle to expand British Imperialism in the land they later called Southern Rhodesia in 1890 (Mupepi, 2015). The British formed the Pioneer Column, a force raised by Cecil Rhodes and his British South Africa Company in 1890, to annex the territory of Zimbabwe. The Pioneer Column administrator, Leander Starr Jameson, promised to the men and women who could reach the heart of Zimbabwe, land upon which they could rekindle their dreams. At that time, the British Isles were in dire economic straits. The administration of Prime Minister Lord Salisbury was contending with housing and welfare reforms. In Steel (2002), Salisbury is credited with the passing of the teacher's remuneration and the first special education legislations. The Elementary School Teachers (Superannuation) Act of 1898 enabled teachers to secure an annuity via the payment of voluntary contributions. The Elementary Education (Defective and Epileptic Children) Act of 1899 permitted school boards to provide for the education of mentally and physically defective and epileptic children. These laws were part of the welfare reform programs the Tory government introduced in the British Isles at the end of 1899. The Tory administration had also supported immigration to the colonies and sustained Cecil Rhodes' application for a royal charter in 1889 which led to the formation of the BASC and subsequently the Pioneer Column 1890.

The data available from 1881 to 1912 on British welfare reforms are based on the records of trade unions that paid unemployment benefits to their members. In 1912, trade unions that paid benefits had 1.4 million members. This means that the unemployment rates for this period are based on a very small segment of the UK population, made up mainly of manual workers (Keynes, 1936). The lowest unemployment rate recorded during this period was 1.4% in 1890 and the highest was 10.2% in 1892 (Keynes, 1936). The population was increasing by massive strides, while the economy was not doing well enough to sustain the increased productivity. As a result, unemployment in the UK was very high. Sustainable jobs became scarce, and the expansion of the British Empire offered hope. State-organized migration to Africa began with the Port Elizabeth settlers in 1820, followed by the 1890 Pioneer Column invasion of Zimbabwe.

According to Samkange (1967), a clash of colonial visions between Portugal and United Kingdom led Lord Salisbury to issue an ultimatum to Portugal, ordering it to leave the Shire-Zambezi Valley territories, which correspond to today's Zambia, Zimbabwe, and Malawi, leaving them free for the United Kingdom. During the following year, the Anglo-Portuguese Treaty of 1891 was signed. The Anglo-Portuguese Treaty was an agreement between Portugal and the United Kingdom of Great Britain and Ireland, which fixed the boundaries of the British Central Africa Protectorate (now Malawi), the territories administered by the British South Africa Company in Mashonaland and Matabeleland (now parts of Zimbabwe), North-Western Rhodesia (now part of Zambia), Portuguese Mozambique, the British South Africa Company-administered territories of North-Eastern Rhodesia (now part of Zambia), and Portuguese Angola (Mupepi, 2015).

The Pioneer Column was created to open the lands north of the Limpopo and Zambezi rivers to further British imperialism. Cecil Rhodes promoted this vision because he could create his own wealth by supporting imperialism. In Von der Heyde (2017), Rhodes is described as having been at loggerheads with the Afrikaners, Dutch, Shona, Ndebele, and other ethnic groups, who did not want to lose their land to pave the way for British capitalism. The Pioneer Column was made up of British subjects and others, who were sworn in at Macloutsie in the British Protectorate of Bechuanaland on June 28, 1890.

What could have been a happy Mazowe Valley for the local community, became a place where the African dreams were thwarted. The locals began to sleep less and less hours each day as they were evicted from their land. Stress increased and they had no choice but to fight.

Strategy and anxiety

Rhodes had received reports from his agents Frederick Selous and Thomas Baines about a new-found land north of the Limpopo River. He was anxious to get to Mashonaland before the Germans, Portuguese, or Boers. His first step was to persuade the Matabele King, Lobengula, in 1888, to sign a treaty giving him mining and administration rights in

Matabeleland, in return for helping the king subjugate the Shona people. Lobengula had dreamed of an Ndebele state among the Mutapa states. He claimed to be the ruler of the Shona people, a role he had achieved through coercion, extortion, murderous raids, and cattle rustling (Macmillan, 2017). Earlier in 1884, Lobengula had been tricked by the missionaries who negotiated on his behalf with third parties to sign the Rudd Concession of 1884. Charles Rudd was instrumental in securing this signed agreement between Rhodes' British South Africa Company (allegedly on behalf of Queen Victoria, although without any official knowledge or authority) and Lobengula. Rhodes then sought and obtained a charter from the British government that allowed him to act although in a limited way, with the government's consent. The next step was to occupy the territory and the Pioneer Column 1890 was created to do just that.

Rhodes and his partners created the Pioneer Column 1890 as a project management organization whose mission was to occupy the land north of the Limpopo and Zambezi Rivers within given budget parameters. The Pioneer Column was made up of engineers, health cadres, clergy and teachers, geologists, military personnel, cartographers, and agronomists, among many others. They were ready to start a new life in what became a Rhodesia paradise. They started to exploit the land using state-of-the-art technology to excavate potential gold mines, create commercial farms, build urban settlements and infrastructure.

Diagram 2: Local knowledge systems were employed to chart the route

A fistful of sterling notes

The Pioneer Column could hire the local people to get to their destination. Many parts of the country were unknown to the Column and there were no maps to refer to except those which were drawn by Frederick Selous. Becker (1979), describes how the Pioneer Column was led by a team comprising Frank Johnson, Frederick Selous, Colonel Edward Graham Pennefather, Star Johnson, and the local cowboys (see diagram 2). In Nyandoro (1995), Bobo Garande a local headman from Chief Makope was one of the local people hired to navigate the route leading to the heart of the Hwata community at a place they named Mt. Hampden.

Garande became the first convert of the Salvation Army who was baptized by Captain Edward Cass in 1892. The *Enterprise* wagon of the Salvation Army had carried a supply of religious materials as well as textbooks to teach the locals how to read and write in English. Shortly, the first school was established at Pearson Farm about 18 miles from Salisbury city center (Nyandoro, 1995). The Pioneer Column knew that the Shona did not have a professional army such as the Ndebele or Zulu had. They then planned to deal with any objection to progress their mission as and when it arose. For example, when they passed through Chief Chibi's land in the lowveld Chibi had maintained a commando unit comprising of at least fifty armed men to buttress his ivory and gold trade with the Portuguese and Boer traders situated at Delagoa Bay. When the Column attempted to negotiate to cross Runde River, they were ambushed. Here the locals had an advantage created by their knowledge of geographical information system (see diagram 1). Alderson (1923) [2017] suggested that the wagons comprising the Pioneer Column 1890 (Column) were forty-five and covered a length of a mile and a half; and when the inevitable occurred this was often drawn out to four to five miles. Thus, the Column could have been too long to defend in case of an ambush. Frank Johnson who had been made the project manager developed and implemented a defense strategy (see figure 1).

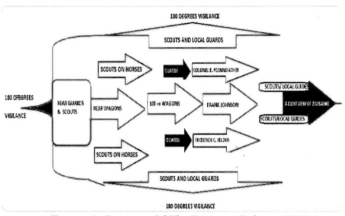

Figure 1: Strategy Of The Pioneer Column 1890

In Becker (1979), Frank Johnson, a 23-year-old adventurer, undertook to deliver the territory that became Southern Rhodesia. Money was not an issue to Cecil Rhodes all he wanted was the delivery of a country which they later named after him. Johnson took his time to select recruits and examining their balance sheets to see if they had the assets to enable the applicants to start a successful enterprise farming mining or any other business. Johnson promised that he could deliver the Column to the required destination within nine months. To accomplish that goal, he recruited 250 men as guards and charged a fee of £87,500 excluding expenses. Frederick Selous, a hunter with an intimate knowledge of Mashonaland, agreed to join the effort as a guide. Selous had travelled to all the four corners of Zimbabwe (Becker, 1979). Frank Johnson published recruitment notices in Kimberley, offering each volunteer 3,000 acres of land and 15 mining claims that covered about 21 acres. On the advice of Cecil Rhodes, most of the recruits Johnson selected were the sons of rich families, so that if they were, indeed, imperiled by Lobengula, their families would be more likely to enlist British government support to rescue them. Johnson's entry strategy comprised a team of scouts and guards who had 360-degree visibility of the Column positioned on the left right rear and front headed towards Zimbabwe (see figure 1). The settlers believed that the Ndebele were the only force they would have to reckon with, even though the Shona were the actual owners of their dream country. The perceptions of the Pioneers and those that followed led to race relations shrined in mistrust (Samkange, 1967). Johnson's column eventually consisted of 180 civilian colonists, 62 wagons, and 200 volunteers, who ultimately formed the nucleus of what became the British South Africa Police. They were recruited for their skill at riding horses and their ability to shoot straight at stationary or moving target (Becker, 1979).

An additional party of 110 men, nearly a hundred wagons, 250 cattle, and 130 spare horses later attached itself to the column. It made the total number of wagons to exceed 150 and that of cattle to be 500. The troopers/scouts were equipped with Martini-Henry and Winchester rifles, revolvers of all makes, seven-pound field guns, and Maxim machine guns, as well as an electric searchlight. They were prepared to defend themselves or attack when it was necessary (see figure 1) (Becker, 1979). The Column was too long and vulnerable to attack by mobile enemies or commandoes of states such as Makoni or Hwata. To effectively defend the Column Colonel Edward Pennefather decided to place scouts or troopers who patrolled the all the sides of the train to give 360 degrees vigilance. Johnson and Selous also employed local guides to avoid treacherous passes and effectively gain speed to reach Mashonaland central by September. They had started their journey in January and at that time the rains were getting less and less and ending in March. At nighttime they formed a laager, one huge structure formed by parking the wagons inside a diamond shaped parking structure to accommodate people livestock and horses. In a laager the women, children and livestock, are placed at the center of a diamond shape or laager. The troopers and scouts provided all night security in three eight-hour shifts (see figure 2). The laager was important for discussing any problems and planning the journey which could start at sunrise or six am and rests at 4pm. It gave the afternoon shift the opportunity to gather firewood to keep the guards, scouts, and troopers warm and hyenas, jackals, and lions at bay.

Progress was made to reach Fort Victoria where some members of the Pioneer decided to stay awaiting further instructions from the Company. The same applied to those who settled at Charter and Enkeoldorn. Those who had travelled via Bulawayo some of them decided to stay in Bulawayo and Essexville where Selous had a farm. Those who proceeded met the Column from Fort Victoria at

Selous (1969) has argued that the British entry into the Mutapa states may have started with the arrival of early hunters, such Bill Hartley and Thomas Baines. The missions undertaken by Frederick Selous collected the data that was interpreted by Rhodes needed to develop a useful annexation strategy. Selous was employed by the British Army, as well as being an agent of Cecil Rhodes. He travelled on fact-finding missions into the Mutapa states. The laager as a resting structure was adapted from the Boer Trekkers that had decided to join the Column. They were interested in search of land to worship and pastures to raise livestock such Merino sheep and Afrikander cattle (see figure 2).

It took Starr Jameson, the BSAC (British South Africa Company) administrator, three months to put together a force to occupy Zimbabwe, drawn from volunteers and former members of the military police in the British Bechuanaland Protectorate. Cecil Rhodes was highly motivated to carry out this act of British imperialism and was aware of the dividends that lay ahead. He had plans to expand mining and agriculture in the lands north of the Limpopo and Zambezi rivers.

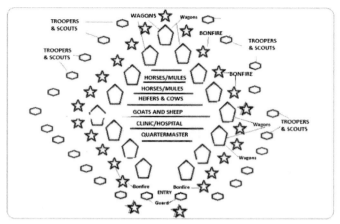

Figure 2: A laager was formed to protect the Column at might

Selous (1969) has suggested that the two columns were quickly put together, one from Fort Victoria and the other from Fort Salisbury. As the storm gathered, the Imperial Government was persuaded to believe that a Matabele invasion of Mashonaland was imminent; it therefore decided to send its own invasion column, comprising the Bechuanaland Mounted Police (BMP) and mercenaries from the Transvaal. The hired mercenary fighters met with the BMP force at Macloutsie and joined the British South Africa Police. The rest of the Pioneer Column was made up of men and women of British and Dutch stock and other selected individuals from European countries and the United States of America. In this way, the Pioneer Column became a crack commando unit, under the leadership of Colonel Pennefather (BSAP, 2017).

Diagram 3: A third shift keeping warm & intruders away

In the Mutapa courts, Nehanda was engaged in civil education and mobilizing forces to resist occupation. In 1884, Lobengula had refused to take Nehanda's counsel, deciding instead to sign the Rudd Concession and Moffat Treaty during that same year (Mupepi, 2015). The Fort Salisbury Column was led by Major Patrick Forbes, and the Fort Victoria Column was under the command of Major Allan Wilson. It was based at Iron Mine Hill before advancing towards Bulawayo. Two battles followed. In the first, Jameson's forces clashed with the Matabele regiment known as the "Ibiza", which numbered about 6,000. During the night of October 24th, they attacked the Column in the Battle of Shanghai River. The Column fought off the attack, with the Matabele suffering large numbers of casualties, due to the superior firepower of the Column. They had made a fatal error in their offensive, attacking at night, when the Column was already in its laager. The Maxim machine gun created such havoc among the Matabele regiments that many of the attackers perished, and the remnant was forced to flee with mounted infantry hard on their heels. For the Matabele army, it seemed the end. Chaminuka foretold Lobengula everything that transpired. Lobengula was attempting to revoke the Moffat and Rudd treaties of 1888, which had led to the occupation of Zimbabwe. As Lobengula had sold out the Shona by claiming to be their king, the Pioneer Column was free to annex everything between the Limpopo and Zambezi Rivers. Some of the tensions that now exist between the Shona and Ndebele have their roots in cattle rustling and kidnapping of women and children, as well as the fabrication of a Zimbabwean kingdom at the beginning of the twentieth century.

Nehanda finally met with the Column as it approached Mupfure River and the Chaminuka city, Chitungwiza. It was about seven years since the death of Pasipamire Chaminuka, who had foretold the coming of the "knee-less" white people. Nehanda encouraged the local people to give them food and water and a place where they could build their homes; thus, Fort Charter was founded. However, Selous had earmarked a place he called Mount Hampden as the center of the Mutapa states. On October 31, 1890, the Column arrived at Mount Hampden, in a region that was under the jurisdiction of Paramount Chief Bungu Mukombami of the Hwata dynasty (White, 1986).

The British had arrived in the heartland of Shonaland. Their hegemony spread from South Africa into Zimbabwe, Zambia, Malawi, Tanzania, Kenya, Sudan, and Egypt, in great strides within a short period of time (1885–1918). The memory landscape of the arrival of the colonists includes the stolen Zimbabwe Bird, the greed that drove Zimbabweans from their homelands, and forced labor—or the reintroduction of slavery in the form of forced labor. These atrocities were carried out everywhere the British went in Africa (Parsons, 1993).

The Column finally reached its destination, a place in the heartland of the Hwata people. They named it as Mt. Hampden in September 1890.

Who was Charwe in the Hwata structure?

Paramount Chief Gwindi was the head of the Hwata dynasty in 1890 (see figure 1). Nehanda Charwe was born in the Mazowe Valley, in Chief Chidamba's village. Her parents were part of the larger dynasty of the Hwata people. Nehanda Charwe was a spirit medium of the *Gombwe* (Royal Mhondoro or Angel) named Nehanda Nyakasikana, which originated during the Zimbabwe Kingdom (1220–1450).

The Hwata dynasty was made up of a society of pastoral farmers and goldminers. They were very gregarious and shared the Mazowe and Zambezi Valleys with other dynasties such as the Shumba who were also hunters, goldminers, as well as pastoral farmers. They were some of the happiest people in Zimbabwe at that time in moment. Their environment invited physical activity such as herding cattle in the mountains and valleys constituting the physical geography of the Zimbabwe plateau. They could enjoy swimming in the crocodile free headwaters of the Mazowe River. They raised corn and rapoko and cattle as sources of beef and milk and cereal and ate very healthy foods. When the Pioneer Column 1890 arrived, these pastoral farmers were engaged in a lucrative barter trade in the Zambezi Valley with the Arabs, Indians, and Portuguese (Mudenge, 1974).

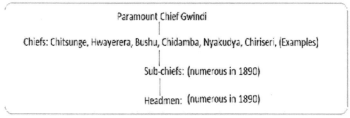

Figure 2:The Organizational structure of the Hwata Chieftainship

The Structure of a paramount chieftainship

The spirit, Nehanda, manifested during the reign of Nyatsimba Mutota, the First Emperor (1430–1450), and continued to possess specific mediums from the Hwata dynasty throughout the Munhumutapa Kingdom (1450–1760), Rozvi Empire (1684–1834), Mutapa States (1834–1890) and in British Central Africa (Northern Rhodesia,

Southern Rhodesia, and Nyasaland, 1890–1964), Rhodesia (1964–1978), Rhodesia Zimbabwe (1978–1979) and the Republic of Zimbabwe (1980–present). As this pattern suggests, Rozvi spiritualism has remained fluid throughout the ancient kingdoms and later in the sovereign southern African states (Mupepi, 2015).

In 1890, when the Pioneer Column arrived, the Gombwe Nehanda Nyakasikana had already possessed the daughter of Charwe, better known as Mbuya Nehanda. This medium teamed up with other Magombwe, including Gumboreshumba, Kaguvi, and Mukwati Chaminuka, to successfully counteract colonization. The three became the African Triumvirate, using the Rozvi Traditional Religion (RTR), a monotheistic belief in one Supreme Being, known as Mwari or God, to advance a co-constructed defense of the Mutapa states. After the conclusion of the Berlin Conference in 1885, the European superpowers of Great Britain, Belgium, France, Italy, Germany, and Portugal flexed their muscles and successfully evicted Africans from their homes, to pave the way for European settlement. The colonists possessed superior firepower and bulldozed their way in, dispossessing Africans and dismantling their customs and beliefs, while attempting to replace the latter with Western ideas. This effort worked: more than 90% of the Zimbabwean population is Christian (The Catholic Church in Zimbabwe, 2015). According to Mupepi (2015), the Pioneer Column was made up of engineers and many other craftsmen. It also included clergymen, whose role was to pacify the local community to ease European colonization.

In addition to drafting mutual agreements, the colonizers agreed to define a modus operandi for colonizing the Africans. In these chronicles, the participating Europeans agreed not to meddle in each other's business, but to support each other in the case of possible rebellions. The Atlantic slave trade in the British colonies had ended in 1833 and two independent African states had been created in West Africa. The state of Sierra Leone was founded by Great Britain in 1847 to resettle freed slaves. Earlier, in 1787, the Americans established the state of Liberia, building the first urban settlement to have a university in Monrovia. The two states of Sierra Leone and Liberia were created from West African empires, including Ghana, Mali, and Songhay, then known as the Sahelian kingdoms. At that moment in time, the sun never set on the British Empire.

During the period of colonization, in 1884–1885, nearly all important matters within the British Empire were decided in London, England. The same administrative support systems also existed in British settlements in South Africa in 1795–1820. London was growing fast, after having been destroyed by fire in 1666 (Hanson, 2001). The government was grappling with welfare issues, such as housing, education, and food. The Education Act of 1880 mandated that a student could leave school upon reaching the required standard of reading, writing, and calculating, which varied according to the school board in charge (for example, the Welsh Joint Examination Board or the London Associated Examination Board). Making it compulsory for students to stay in school up to the age of 16 was a burden on taxpayers. The government had to balance the purse on welfare, as the people's working and living conditions also needed upgrading. Arrow (2004) postulates that Thomas R. Malthus (1766–1834) realized that population growth would outpace food production in a geometric progression. Food production is assumed to increase in accordance with the arithmetic mean, all things being equal. The British government sought to address this phenomenon by encouraging immigration and reviewing ways to increase industrial productivity. It took the government a long time to recognize the effectiveness of classical economic theories, such as Adam Smith's principles governing the division of labor and David Ricardo's premise that specialization would develop a lucrative international market (Buchan, 2006). However, the colonists wasted no time in building consumer economies based on classical economic ontology, wherever they went. They took calculated risks by imitating each other. They also made effective research and development part of their organizations, in order to produce increased crop outputs with a surplus for the export market. Britain was a ready-made import market for foodstuffs from all over the world. Land was scarce in the British Isles and the opportunity to produce food at an affordable price was lucrative for the colonists. Trade from South Africa, India, the Americas, and the Far East was instrumental in building commerce and industries in the British Isles. The colonists invested the proceeds from this investment to build vibrant consumer economies in the colonies.

The British had naval and light infantry forces that took as little as two weeks to sail around the world (Newitt, 1995). Much later, the Rhodesians invested in agricultural research and became the world's best tobacco producers, when their colony was at its peak. All the colonies, however, became killing fields of inequality. Separate economic development plans became the modus operandi of colonial administrations. The all-white inclusive government implemented a systematic process to deprive all other races of every advantage. There were no equal opportunities in any aspect of life.

In the heart of southern Africa, the Chaminuka family, led by Tofara, had founded the Munhumutapa Kingdom, which was later consolidated by Tofara's grandnephew, Emperor Nyatsimba Mutota (1430–1450) (Mupepi, 2015). Chaminuka Murenga and Nehanda Nyakasikana, the Magombwe (plural) of the Chaminuka Mutota, were steadfast; they continue to be revered among the people of the fluid Mutapa and Rozvi empires. It is compelling for Southern Africans to read this history and important for them to draw some lessons to progress toward a better future.

This biography is informed by African novels and folklore, as well as by scholars, such as Mutswairo (1956), Mudenge (1974), Samkange (1967), White (1986), Vera (1993), Beach (1994), Baldick (1997), Ehret (1998), Doumba and Doumba (2004), Keller (2005), Mavhunga (2003), Mudenge (1988), Mupepi, 2014) and Mupepi (2015), among many others. It begins by tracking the leadership of the

Mutapa and Rozvi empires, and bringing them out of the dimly lit background into the spotlight of the Republic of Zimbabwe, where they be precursors to a growing democracy and vibrant economy with plentiful jobs.

The local people knew that Mbuya Nehanda had the ability to engage in a beneficial dialogue with Mwari.

The Development of the Chimurenga

A "Chimurenga" is a struggle for political freedom. It combines physical fighting, characterized by hit-and-run tactics, with biological warfare, in the form of poisoned darts, arrowheads, and spears. It is a concept developed from the tactics invented by the second Emperor Murenga Chaminuka (1450–1480). For example, in the First Chimurenga the BSAC (1896-7) reported that many troopers of the British South Africa Police were killed by injuries caused by arrows. The list of those killed included Captain Edward Thomas Cass of the Salvation Army and Telegraph Operator John Leonard Blakeston. The BSAC (1896/7) report mentioned that more than 500 settlers had perished in Mashonaland alone up to the arrest of the African Triumvirate in 1897. Murenga combined local knowledge, for example, of geographical systems, with intensive military endurance training. He viewed local knowledge as a system that could be used to increase the effectiveness of an army, when advancing a military campaign. The geography, biology, and botany of any locality could be used to support military defense or a strategy for conquering an enemy. For example, Murenga developed a poison by mixing Makonde tree latex with Black Mamba venom. The mixture was used to paint the heads of spears or arrows, where it formed a white resin. This resin dissolved when it entered the body, passing into the blood stream and impacting the central nervous system. The concoction was composed of potent neurotoxins that caused the fast onset of symptoms, such as difficult breathing or dizziness and led to death in a matter of minutes unless an antidote was applied immediately. In the savanna grasslands that were punctured by granite hills and valleys, geographical information about saddles or treacherous mountain passes could be incorporated into military maneuvers in out witting enemies.

Another example of local knowledge system is analyzed by Eckstein (2009), who discusses the Carthaginian General Hannibal, who, in his military campaign, failed to cross the snow-covered Alps. He had neglected to assess the capacity of his transportation system, based on elephants and donkeys, which had strength but no speed or agility. The Alps are characterized by alpine cliffs and gorges, which the heavy-footed animals could not negotiate successfully. Once he had come up with a solution—to attack Rome in the summer rather than the winter—he was able to surprise the Romans and to beat them thoroughly on their own territory. Army commanders can arrive at rational solutions, with the aid of deputies who are experts in various aspects of military campaigns that are successful when put together. Eckstein (2009) has argued that Hannibal lost his only siege engines and most of his elephants to the cold temperatures and icy mountain paths. In the end, he could defeat the Romans in the field but not in the strategically crucial city of Rome; this left him unable to win the war.

Alliances that made the difference

In the work of Mutswairo (1956) and Gelfund (1959), Nehanda Charwe is portrayed as a heroine of the occupation of Zimbabwe by Europeans. She is credited for uniting the freedom fighters, co-constructing a shared vision of freedom, and motivating villagers to actively support the resistance. She delivered orations in nearly all the major villages throughout the Mutapa states. Gelfund (1959) views her role as effective, when it was supported by experienced traditional authorities, such as Gumboreshumba Kagubi, who was also assumed to be the medium of the Gombwe Murenga Chaminuka. Gelfund has suggested that the spirit of Nehanda came originally from the Chaminuka; as a result, the mediums of Nehanda could also be possessed by the Chaminuka at any time.

The local people felt that they had been unlawfully conquered. There was no provocation, but just shear arrogance. At home in the Mazowe Zambezi valleys, the war effort surpassed those of all other regions, because the Pioneer Column had pierced right into the heart of the region, with its base at Mount Hampden and Salisbury. The chieftainships impacted directly included those of Hwata, Makope, Negomo, Mashayamombe, Swosve, Mangwende, Nhohwe, Makoni, Mupepi Nyachuru, Mapondera, Chipuriro, Chingowo, Mavhirivhi, Dokora, Chihota, Madziwa, Chinhamora, Rusike, Chikwaka, Seke, Chinengundu, and Nyamweda, among many others. They were assisted by Magombwe Nehanda Charwe, Gumboreshumba Kagubi, Mukwati Chaminuka, Ganyire, Goredema, Gorejena, Vamande, Shiripinda, Bvukupfuku, Shamhuyemunhanzwa, and Dzivaguru, among many others. These authorities raised an army that could collaborate, depending with the enemy. For example, Mapondera, Chipuriro, Nyachuru, Negomo, and Makope fought as a group to stop the expansion of the BSAC into the Centenary, Mvurwi, Mt. Darwin, and Sipollilo districts (Beach, 1979).

In the Mrewa area, Nehanda was supported by Chiefs Mangwende Nhohwe, Magombwe Vanyamita, and Biri, among others. In the eastern area, Chiefs Mutoko, Makoni, Tangwena, and Nyamaropa were among those sustained by Magombwe Nehoreka, Dzivaguru, Nyanhewhe, and Nerutombo. Magombwe Nyarutswa, Sakureba, Karuwa, and Mukungurutse teamed up with the chiefs in what is now the Mutare district or Manicaland South, an area that included Zimunya, Mutasa, Marange, Mutambara, and Mutema, among many others.

In Hwedza, Paramount Chief Swosve brought with him his son, Prince Nyangombe, an expert elephant hunter and trader who had set up shop at the confluence of the Mazowe and Zambezi Rivers. Nyangombe brought about a hundred of his commandos, who were trained to use both types of rifle (zvifefe in Shona). They took the war seriously and invited all the chiefs to go to the Swosve foundries at Hwedza, where the

Chimurenga was officially commissioned and soldiers were issued with spears, arrowheads, and pellets mixed with gunpowder for the musket rifles. Artillery production was coordinated in three places: Penhalonga Mine, where copper was smelted to make bullets; Buchwa mine, where iron ore was refined to make arrowheads; and Mazowe, at what colonists called the Iron Duke Mine. These mines and their foundries made all the weapons used by the resistance army. In 1896, the resistance got more supplies from the Transvaal, where local people were angry about the Jameson Raid, organized and supported by Cecil Rhodes. In Mozambique Dambukashamba, an alliance of Mapondera managed to secure some weaponry from the Portuguese who had also been impacted by Lord Salisbury's ultimatum in 1890. Many of the chieftainships in northern Zimbabwe had been short-changed in the creation of the border between Mozambique and Southern Rhodesia. Rhodes had been advised erroneously by Lobengula; the villages in Mozambique were part of the Mutapa states. Rushinga and Nyamapanda were part of the same chieftainships. Mutasa's land was separated from that of Tangwena by the Pungwe River, all the way to the Indian Ocean. A "gentlemen's agreement" between Rhodes and Prince Lourenco Marques had taken land from Zimbabwean traditional authorities (Newitt, 1995).

The task that lay ahead for Nehanda was to coordinate the resistance. Her cousin, Gutsa Hwata, Gombwe Mukwati Chaminuka (as the First Gombwe), and Chaminuka Mukwati lived on Matopos Hill, outside kwaBulawayo. Mukwati arrived when the resistance started to offer assistance to Nehanda Charwe. Many folk stories suggest that Mukwati was possessed by the Gombwe Chaminuka long before the assassination of Pasipamire in 1883. The death of the King of the Mutapa States triggered the collective imagination of Africans to resist colonization. The leadership of the Gombwe Nehanda Charwe involved dual responsibilities (see Figure 1). The first set of duties related to the office of the highest priestess in the religious order of her ancestors, established in 900 [AD] (Pikirayi, 2011).

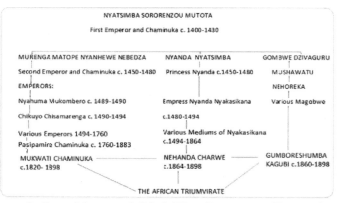

Figure 3: From Mutota c. 1430–1450 to Pasipamire Chaminuka c. 1760–1883

Her second responsibility was to preside, as legal counsel, over the Chaminuka inner cabinet office. She had a seat on the courts of all of the paramount chiefs of the Mutapa states. This dyad is revisited to appreciate the dynamics of the African Triumvirate that organized the First Chimurenga (1883–1904), and to prepare for the rise of African nationalism and the subsequent Second Chimurenga (1966–1980). The religiosity and structure of civil society during the pre-and post-Mutapa periods are analyzed to understand how the resistance to colonization was strategized and implemented under the guidance of the African Triumvirate (AT), an indomitable leadership comprising *Magombwe:* Nehanda Charwe (c.1864–1898), Gumboreshumba Kagubi (c.1860–1898), and Mukwati Chaminuka (c.1840—c.1904) (Mupepi, 2015) (see Figure 3)

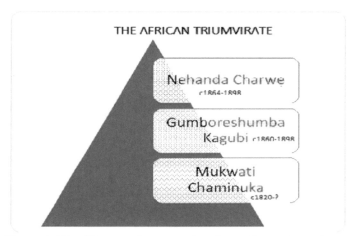

THE AFRICAN TRIUMVIRATE

Nehanda Charwe
c1864-1898

Gumboreshumba
Kagubi c1860-1898

Mukwati
Chaminuka
c1820-?

Figure 4: The AT created to control and coordinate the resistance
(Mupepi, 2015).

Overseeing traditional leaders during the colonial era were the so-called "native commissioners". There was really nothing native about them in the early days because they came from Europe or South Africa to occupy these very powerful positions in the colonial administration. Their view of African traditional leaders was appalling. The native commissioners underrated the local people and considered it out of the question to develop amicable relations. Native Commissioner J.D. White was responsible for the district of Mazowe, extending from the border between today's Mount Hampden and Mount Darwin in the north, Chipuriro in the west, Salisbury in the south, and Goromonzi in the east. Madzivanzira (2017), presents a genealogy of the Hwata dynasty, complete with the dates and names provided by traditional Hwata dynasty authorities, such as the spirit mediums of Goredema, Mutsahuni, Nematombo, and Ganyire. The records of the native commissioner chronicle the origins of the Hwata dynasty and provide a catalogued Charwe (c. 1864–1898) was held in high esteem. Apart from having a direct relationship with the Hwata dynasty, she also presided over the Shumba dynasties of Dema, Makope,

Mutoko, Nerwande, and the Nyachuru and Nematombo Mapondera dynasties among numerous others, throughout the Mutapa states. The counsel to the Hwata chieftainship at the time of the arrival of the Pioneer Column in 1890 was Gombwe Nehanda Charwe. Chiefs on the plateau and throughout the Mutapa states had been informed of the impending colonization by Nehanda Charwe's oracle. It was a real threat, and it is inspiring to learn how Nehanda dedicated her life to free Zimbabweans.

Nehanda was a well-born daughter of the nobility, as her parents were part of the Hwata dynasty and directly related to Paramount Chief Gwindi. They lived in a village under the jurisdiction of Chief Chidamba. Nehanda, popularly referred to as Mbuya Nehanda or simply *Ambuya* was skillful and passionate about knowledge pertaining to religion and the government of the Rozvi. As a girl growing up in the Mazowe Valley, Nehanda may have been a tomboy. She looked after her father's herd of cattle and other flocks, such as goats and sheep. As a baby, she forced her mother to change many things she had always taken for granted, including her diet. Chavunduka (1980) presents various arguments about this fact, given that pregnancy often influences the behavior of African women, for example, by changing their diet and tastes. For expecting mothers, the baby in the womb often influences the taste of food. Such changes in taste can create a preference for certain foods over others. A mother's diet could change drastically if she was expecting a child chosen by the ancestral spirits to be their medium. In addition, the community had expectations for Nehanda's future that compelled her parents to reinvent and reorganize the socialization of their daughter as she grew up and interacted with other children. During the 20th century, the arrival of the settlers into Zimbabwe had been foretold by the oracles of Pasipamire Chaminuka and others (Mupepi, 2015). The concern of most villagers was that the state, with all its renowned hunters and fighters, did not have the capacity to defend their territory. After the death of Pasipamire Chaminuka in 1883, nothing could be taken for granted until

Nehanda Charwe was an adult and could hold oracles to determine the way forward.

Gelfund (1959) has suggested that the ancestral spirits selected their mediums beginning with the character and disposition of the parents. It can therefore be assumed that vaCharwe (Mr. Charwe) and his wife were an honorable couple among the Hwata, worthy of being selected to raise a child whose destiny would elevate her to the second most powerful position in the empire.

This discussion re-constructs aspects of Zimbabwe's past to appreciate how *Ambuya* could have developed a strategy for resisting colonization. Physically, the freedom fighters were defeated in all respects. Their weapons were no match for Maxim machine guns, Hotchkiss automatic rifles, and explosives made of dynamite. The British Empire was designed to be aggressive and to expand by conquest, not unlike the Munhumutapa Empire, in some respects. Technology made the difference, enabling the British to expand in great strides, to the point where the "sun never set" on their conquered lands. However, the freedom fighters won the hearts of Zimbabweans, helping to build a foundation for African nationalism from 1898 onwards.

Although annexation was inevitable, Ambuyaensured that it would not happen without a fight. She explored the ways in which the emotions of her people could be aroused and contrasted with STR beliefs. She also considered how the cooperation of the Mutapa states could be harnessed to create the synergy needed to defend Zimbabwe. The Shona could collectively respond—both militarily and psychologically—to defend their values. However, this was an enormous challenge. Nothing like this had been attempted since the defeat of the Portuguese in Zambezi Valley in 1630, during the barter trade wars, when Emperor Kapararidze triumphed (Jones, 1998). Kapararidze's empire had controlled present-day southern Angola, with bases in Mavinga, the southern Congo, Zambia, Mozambique, Malawi, Tanganyika south of Mount Kilimanjaro (southern Tanzania), Zimbabwe (including the Transvaal up to Mutiusina zita in the Rand),

Botswana, and Namibia. Kapararidge and his predecessor, Mavura, had deployed traditional authorities as rulers in given localities. They had done this to empower the chiefs to defend the Mutapa Empire. Other authority figures who presided over large districts included chiefs, subchiefs, and headmen. They included the Paramount Chiefs Mutsahuni, Mutoko, Nerwande, and Chinengundu in fifteenth century and Paramount Chief Hwata in 1890. The Mutapa states were a close-knit community, sharing the same values and beliefs, as well as defending each other in times of conflict. They were thinly divided, allowing intermarriages and supporting each other in the face of external threats, such as the arrival of the knee-less people. The Shona community had fertile land, cattle, gold, and everything that Mwari (the Lord) had created for Zimbabweans to prize.

Ambuya's mission as a Gombwekadziguru (a guardian angel spirit possessing a woman) focused on the welfare of the Rozvi. In this role, she had a special responsibility for national defense, food and health, and biological warfare, including medicinal weeds, herbs, and anything that could be used to enhance the strength of warriors. She worked tirelessly with her spiritual father, Murenga Chaminuka. Mudenge (1988) explains how Nehanda Nyakasikana and Murenga, the Second Chaminuka, coordinated the defense of the Rozvi against the Portuguese and secured the Mutapa Empire (1450–1480). This caused a crisis of sovereignty because the Portuguese longed to control the lucrative Mutapa gold and ivory trade. They also wanted to buy slaves to feed what became the Atlantic slave trade. Emperor Mavura Mhande (1629–1652) signed the Treaty of Vassalage with the Portuguese, allowing them to create the commercial farms they referred to as *Prazos* (Stewart, 1989). In 1652, the Rozvi took control of the trade, and for once enjoyed the position of a monopolistic supplier; they owned the most productive gold mines and had some of the best local ivory hunters, such as Prince Nyangombwe Swosve. The Portuguese too were a monopoly, being the only providers of European goods on the market. They brought guns and gunpowder, cloth, agricultural tools and implements, and many other goods that were sourced all over Europe. The memories of the Portuguese in the Zambezi Valley and the plateau were passed on from one village to the next until African scholars such as Mutswairo (1956) and Chakaipa (1959) incorporated some of the stories about what life was like in the historical past into their books. Mediums acted as the main repository for community history, and often reviewed the past in public sessions, or confirmed facts relating to highly contested chieftainships. The royal spirits of the Magombwe had numerous mediums. Charwe Kagubi and Mukwati were the *Magombwe* or *Royal Mhondoros* and the African Triumvirate (AT) when the Pioneer Column came marching into Great Zimbabwe in 1890 (see Diagram 1).

The plans of the African Triumvirate (AT) revealed the most sophisticated awareness of what was going on in the country at that time. They acknowledged the truth that they were on the verge of losing the country. Nehanda Charwe is famous for her response to a crowd that asked how Mwari was going to protect them against the rapid fire of the Maxim machine guns. Her reply was that Mwari was going to turn those bullets into water. She had no time to think or consult Kagubi, but had to provide an answer that would help to recruit freedom fighters. In the actual fight, the local people had no chance against European firepower, which was far superior to that sourced from the Portuguese.

Although there were no modern roads or communication technologies, the villagers managed to advance the resistance in a unique way. Families were the nucleus of the dairy and beef industries for which the Hwata were renowned (Madzivanzira, 2017). They provided food to the freedom fighters and those who had been made destitute by the colonists during the struggle. During those years, people lived in villages separated by cornfields, thick forests, and grazing pastures. They discussed current affairs while watching their flocks or working in the fields. They washed their laundry in local rivers. From all of these meeting places, the information exchanged through social intercourse travelled far and wide.

Rumors too originated in such venues and were quickly diffused.

The Charwe family was part of these interactions; everyone valued traditional authorities, including the Magombwe and traditional healers. In terms of wealth, the land of the plateau offered the most gold, ivory, and iron and copper ores, in comparison with the land north of the Zambezi and Okovango rivers. The local communities owned dairy and beef cattle, later called "Mashona-type" cattle by the English settlers. They gave them that name because the cows were resistant to draught and immune to the bite of the Tsetse fly, which caused a sleeping sickness among infected animals. The Mashona cattle were crossbred with the Sanga cows of South-central Africa and developed over thousands of years to be thoroughly adapted to the local environment (Hodder-Williams, 1983). Their resistance to elevated temperature, ticks and flies, and their ability to maintain reproductive efficiency in the semi-arid African climate molded their unique characteristics. The Hwata, Shumba and other dynasties raised Mashona cattle for food and as a medium of exchange. During the Chimurenga, freedom fighters received milk and other foods that made all the difference in the fight for liberation.

Cattle formed part of the marriage ritual in many ways. Lobola or roora, a bridal price, was/is assessed and determined as a number of cattle, goats, or sheep. People who were convicted of civil or criminal offences had to pay fines assessed and translated into numbers of cows, goats, sheep, or chickens to the court of Chaminuka (Gelfund, 1966). The number of cattle charged as a fine depended on the gravity of the offence. In civil matters, the plaintiff paid a fee of chickens or a bag of cereal to get the court to hear his grievances. If found guilty, the accused was required to pay the court and compensate the plaintiff in both criminal and civil proceedings. Civil and criminal proceedings could be heard concurrently and cattle were the main currency for paying fines and compensatory damages. Nehanda acted as a prosecutor in most of the paramount chieftainship courts in the plateau and Zambezi Valley. At the end of many proceedings, she was sometimes given one or more cows. Nehanda amassed a herd of cattle on behalf of her family, as a result of her official duties. In the civic affairs of her people, she acted as an ambassador to the Matabele people, with whom she negotiated the second truce between the Ndebele and Hwata peoples. In 1856, she introduced diplomatic relations between the Mzilikazi and Shona communities and between Nehanda Charwe and Prince Gwindi Nherera, the son of the Paramount Chief Nherera (White, 1986).

At the age of nineteen or thereabouts, Nehanda was asked by the chiefs, in the wake of Pasipamire Chaminuka in 1883, to persuade Lobengula Khumalo to refrain from involving the Mutapa states in his dubious deals with Cecil John Rhodes. For this role, she was paid handsomely by the chiefs and asked to organize what became the First Chimurenga of 1883–1904. Her father, Charwe, and her siblings may have inherited Nehanda's wealth after her death in 1898 (Mupepi, 2015).

After the Chaminuka in 1884, the AT were assigned numerous responsibilities by a council of paramount chiefs that acted as the overall authority after the death of Pasipamire. Nehanda was made responsible for leading all of the freedom fighters, with support from Kagubi and Mukwati. Her brother, Gutsa, was put in charge of recruitment and logistics, along with members of the Shona dynasties and many others. There were three key responsibilities: national security, governance, and health. Nehanda was the top government officer and legal advisor for all the Mutapa paramount chieftainships or states. Collectively, they were responsible for national security and health. Nehanda held her clinics in two places. The first was in the Hwata villages, although the patients did not give her much time to travel outside her village. She had other Mhondoros, whose roles were directly linked to the health needs of the Hwata people. She also visited a second major group of clinics at Nyota, in the courts of Negomo, and at Nzvimbo, Nyakudya, Nyangoni, and Shutu. The Magombwe were also responsible for rituals concerning rainfall and providing traditional health services.

They had to ensure that the rains arrived on time, so that people could grow enough food. In addition, they were involved in an ad hoc planning team focused on the resistance. This task entailed travelling and canvassing for supporters. The RTR required rituals for many things, including rainmaking, and life and death celebrations.

Before 1883, Nehanda Charwe was consulted by numerous chiefs, including the Ndebele king, Lobengula Khumalo. At this point in her life, the medium earned the Shona title, Mhondoro spirit, which gave her the power to make rain, cure ailments, change weather patterns in time of war, and create advantages for people who knew the local territory and other knowledge systems. Mbuya Nehanda had additional responsibilities as the trustee of the paramount chiefs and the chief advisor to Chief Hwata.

Diagram 2: The Pioneer Column hoist the Union Jack, the British flag

When the Pioneer Column entered Zimbabwe, it was successful because of many people such as Frederick Selous or Bobo Garange. In the Hwata realm, Mbuya was responsible for gold mining and trading. This job could have entailed visiting the areas where gold was mined. In this role, she came into confrontation with the 1890 Pioneer Column, which came across her territory with no permits. The local people's most forceful objection to Christian traditions arose from the fact that custodians of the Gospel were responsible for the poverty and diseases that were manifesting among the people. They were also blamed for forced labor that ensued. Although slavery had been banned in British colonies in 1833 because of the William Wilberforce human rights advocacy, the evils of slavery in forced labor and child labor persisted in one form or another. According to Newitt (1995), the Jesuits built monasteries using forced labor and slaves. Cecil Rhodes invited them and the Catholic Dominican communities to join the Pioneer Column in 1890 (See Diagram 1). Subsequently, when the Pioneer Column entered Zimbabwe, it included members of the Salvation Army and their entourages and wagons, known as the *Enterprise* (Murdoch, 2015). Numerous other churches and church-related organizations were represented in the first Column and among those who arrived in 1891. The Prime Minister Lord Salisbury and Queen Victoria blessed the adventure and issued a royal charter, on the understanding that the BSAC was going to protect the Shona people from the threatening Ndebele. Stott (2012) suggested that slavery could have been done away with sooner if the architects and builders of the British Empire had considered much earlier the concept of the principles of the division of labor propounded by Adam Smith. In his proposition Adam Smith suggested that a slave was not productive at all because he or she was preoccupied by how he/she was going to escape rather than how the job at hand was going to be done. In Mupepi (2016), the Pioneer Column were driven by the need to fulfill their own entrepreneurial aspirations. Any opportunity to increase output by lowering costs was welcome. The Mutapa authorities did not participate in slavery because the RTR promoted the fact that the death of a slave created a Ngozi or evil spirit that would haunt the slave-master and his family forever. In addition, the Gombwe Nehanda Nyakasikana came to protect the Munhumutapa Empire from the slave trade promoted by the Arabs and Portuguese. In Macmillan (2017), Paramount Chief

Lewanika of the Lozi people of Barotseland did not engage in the slave trade and refused to sell any of his subjects to Arab and Portuguese traders who had fairs or markets in the Lozi territories. Macmillan proposed that although slavery had been abolished serfdom or other forms of slavery where essential features of production among the settler communities in what became Northern Rhodesia, Southern Rhodesia and Nyasaland. Therefore, slavery in its various formats could be found in the colonies in Africa and fluid British Empire in those times.

The strategy to annex the Mutapa states included converting the Africans from their traditional beliefs and practices to those of the Christian faith. The first assignment given to Frederick Selous by the British Government was to find out about the structure and governance of the Mutapa states (Selous, 1969). Various maps depicting governance, political boundaries and geographical features were drawn and presented to Cecil Rhodes who put them into the scheme for effective colonization. Rhodes sent his agents to various chiefs in Mutapa states and were met with mixed successes and failures. For example, Frederick Selous obtained a gold mining concession from Kadungure Chivaura Mapondera:

The Selous Exploration Company of Cape Town was floated in mid-1889, with Frank JOHNSON of the Bechuanaland Exploration Company as a prime mover. SELOUS, hired take a prospecting party to the Mazowe River for the Bechuanaland Company, sailed from England on 3rd

May 1889 and from Port Elizabeth to Durban in mid-June. The party arrived at Vicenti on the lower Zambezi 25th July, and the agent of the African Lakes Company furnished boatmen to take them to Tati, where they waited for porters. In the area of the upper Mazowe, on 25th September 1889, SELOUS obtained a concession for the Selous Exploration Company from the Korikori chiefs Mapondera and Temaringa. The B.S.A. Company offered 100 square miles in the area in return for the concession, but it was sold to W. A. LIPPERT c. January 1890. However, the Colonial Secretary would not admit its validity and Lippert's claims (Tabler, 1972).

Colonization of the Mutapa states took different formats. There were numerous negotiations conducted between agents of Rhodes or the British government. For example, Frederick Selous while doing other assignments found time to make his own deals.

Another colonization strategy was to build the infrastructure such as roads, bridges, and urban development. In 1890 A. R. Colquhoun was given concessionary rights by Chief Mutasa to establish Fort Umtali which later became Mutare City. The building of the railways from Beira into Umtali resulted from a separate concession beginning with the Portuguese authorities. In Winchester (1938), the construction of the Birchenough Bridge over the Sabi River was made possible by agreements made between the BSAC and Chiefs Mutema and Mutambara and funding from the Beit Trust to make commerce and trade possible.

Diagram 5: King Khama and John Smith Moffat (1895) (G. W. H. Knight-Bruce, 1895).

The photograph above (Diagram 2) was taken by G. W. H. Knight-Bruce, a member of the Pioneer Column, who was subsequently appointed the First Bishop of Mashonaland in 1894. Father Alphonse Daignault and Pope Leo XIII had asked the Jesuit Order to start a mission in the African interior, the vast area beyond the Limpopo, extending north and south of the Zambezi. The establishment of this mission coincided with the adventure of the Pioneer Column in 1890 (Dominican Missionary Sisters, 2015). The attempts at setting up a mission, some centuries earlier, had failed for a variety of reasons, one of which was a lack of follow-up missionary services. The Pioneer Column expedition proposed by Cecil Rhodes seemed to offer a new opportunity. Thus, the Catholic Church continued to subjugate local people in commercial farms, monasteries, and schools. They became part of the imperial and colonial governments. Earlier, in 1820, as part of the British Government's efforts to promote the colonization of Africa, the Port Elizabeth Settlers were organized by Prime Minister Robert Banks Jenkins, who landed at Delagoa Bay and founded Port Elizabeth in South Africa (Burman, 1984). Robert Moffat set out from England to settle in Griquatown, in what became the Transvaal, South Africa, to establish a mission at a place he called Kulumani. From there, the Gospel spread to Mutapa Khama, in what is now Botswana (see Diagram 2). The Moffat family's arrival in South Africa coincided with the Great Mfecane (1815–1845), in which many people were evicted from their homes in what became the Natal Orange Free State and Transvaal Boer republics and the Mutapa states. Matabeleland was created as a result of this upheaval. At that moment in time, poverty and diseases of all types began to appear among the local African communities dispossessed of their land (Mupepi, 2015).

Mbuya provided a clear overview of what the villagers had to do: "Go forth and take a black cow and give it to the knee-less people and say, this is the relish we give you as our gesture to welcome you." (Mutswairo, 1957:3). This instruction gave villagers the opportunity to enter the homes of the colonists to search for work and sell food. They also gathered intelligence about settler technology and manpower, identifying farmers who had chosen to settle deep in the valleys, in places such as Centenary or Trelawney. In these outskirts, the settlers were vulnerable to attack but stayed on because they liked the sparse land. There was nothing like it in the United Kingdom. There were traders too, who went further into the woods of the Eastern Highlands, in Chimanimani and Melsetter. These isolated spots became targets in both the First Chimurenga (1883–1904) and the Second Chimurenga (1966–1980).

The African Triumvirate (AT), under the direct command of Mbuya Nehanda, was an ad hoc team dispersed across the nation states. Their purpose was to create the necessary state of public awareness and resentment needed to resist the colonizers. By encouraging people to feel the need to resist, they created a militancy to oppose colonialism. The arrival of the colonists shifted the paradigm for the traditional authorities. As the BSAC evicted local people and seized their land, the traditional authorities were replaced by native commissioners. The Pioneer Column had punctured the cultural equilibrium of the dual-structured authority. The chiefs derived the authority to preside in the village courts from the Chaminuka. They were the second highest order of priests from the Chaminuka, and could hear civil and criminal cases. The village headman acted as the prosecutor; usually, a Gombwe or royal spiritual medium acted as the advisor to the chief. The AT was made up of Nehanda, who is/was the highest priestess, and Kagubi and Mukwati who were the highest priests and officers in the government of the Mutapa states. The Pioneer Column punctured this cultural equilibrium that had been in existence for centuries. There was pandemonium and worry about how the people were going to defend themselves against the sophisticated ballistics of the Pioneer Column.

The result was a complete crisis in the lowlands, ruled by Chiefs Chibi, Nyajena, Charumbira, Chirimhanzi, and others.

According to Thompson (2006), the Pioneer Column had hired local personnel to help plan effective fighting routes and other logistics (see Diagram 3.) The British South Africa Police (BSAP) were the Pioneer Column's first line of defense. The BSAP, and later the Rhodesia Light Infantry and Rhodesia King's Rifles, took part in a number of campaigns in their role as the defense forces of Southern Rhodesia, Northern Rhodesia, and Nyasaland. They were called for duty in the following conflicts: the Matabele War (1893), the Matabele Rebellion (1896), the Mashona Rebellion (1896–1897), the First Shona Chimurenga (1883–1904), and the Anglo–Boer War (1900–1902).

During the First Chimurenga (1883–1904), the BSAC built a telegraph road joining South Africa to Rhodesia. It connected Mafeking in South Africa to Salisbury in the newly conquered lands of Southern Rhodesia, Lusaka in Northern Rhodesia, and Blantyre in Nyasaland. The telegraph road was completely destroyed by commando forces under the direction of Chiefs Chibi, Nyajena, and Ndanga, and others (Jacobsen, 2012). In Chapter Two, Nehanda Charwe leads the traditional authorities in commemorating the death of Pasipamire. A strategy was developed during the wake of Pasipamire Chaminuka and popular phrases, including *vaPambi vepfuma* (those who suck Zimbabwe's wealth), *mwana wevhu* (a child of the local soil), and *chave Chimurenga varume* (it is now a fight for liberation), may have originated from here. The AT handled its complex responsibility to advance civil education among communities dispersed within a radius of 10–300 miles (see Figure 2).

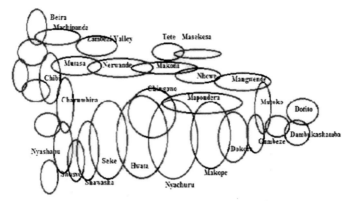

Figure 5: A sociogram showing how the distances between villages varied within a radius of 5–500 miles

The AT raised awareness about the Chimurenga in a multicultural community dispersed across the modern-day provinces of Mashonaland, Matabeleland, Manicaland, and Masvingo. The RTR made it possible to apply this new strategy, which evolved around the Rozvi Traditional Religion (RTR) and continued to exist in tandem with the transference of government to the Shona Traditional Religion (STR) of today.

The biggest challenge lay in forming an army linked to Lobengula's mawuto. Like it or not, they had to extend the hand of fellowship and invite Lobengula to fight with them. A few traditional authorities, such as Chingayira Makoni, Nyangombe Swosve, Chihuri Nyachuru, Chivaura Mapondera, Mashayamombe, Chingowo, and Mangwende, among others, had private militias that they used to promote trade and protect their livestock from Ndebele cattle rustlers.

Some of the members of the Pioneer Column had seen action during the Basuto Gun War (1880–1881), First Boer War (1880–1881), and Anglo Zulu War (1879). According to Von der Heyde (2017), the British colonists triumphed in most of these conflicts. The colonists tried to stop local people from acquiring rifles for any purpose. The empire was able to expand through conquest from Tanganyika to Namibia. It encompassed all of the lands that are now Northern Mpumalanga, Swaziland, Botswana, Malawi, Mozambique, Namibia, Tanzania, Zambia, and Zimbabwe. Von der Heyde has discussed some of the sieges that led to the takeover of African empires during the last two centuries, exploring in detail the historical contexts in which they occurred, day-to-day military actions, and the conditions faced by both soldiers and civilians while defending their territory against hostile forces. The siege descriptions are told as human-interest stories, gleaned from diaries, letters, and eye-witness accounts, while longer features focus on the practical aspects of siege warfare, including artillery, medicine, food, and the psychological effects of besiegement.

The Chaminuka used his religious philosophy to unite all of the different ethnic groups and restructure the government, as part of the STR. Thus, conquered chiefs were reincorporated into the Shona government and society. The Chaminuka's government was decentralized. The chiefs were responsible for issuing hunting and gold prospecting licenses and for the sales tax revenue accruing from traders. This money was receipted in the form of goods, such as guns, gunpowder, cloth, and beads. Decentralization encouraged competition among chiefs, especially those whose regions had more natural resources than others. For example, the feuds between the Shawasha and Rozvi in the mid-1800s were related to gold and other resources. In these particular disputes, women were also a bone of contention, as each ethnic group sought to strengthen and expand its manpower base.

Nyatsimba Mutota was known for having prayed to the Lord, known as Mwari in the Shona Language, to deliver a Gombwe, royal Mhondoro, or angel that could consolidate the fast-growing realm. "Chaminuka" is a title that implies an emperor or king. The discourse raises the following questions, underlining the relevance of the RTR in the organization of pre-colonial and post-colonial Zimbabwe: Who was Nehanda Nyakasikana? If Nehanda Nyakasikana was a spiritual leader what type of leadership did she employ?

Nehanda Nyakasikana (c.1450–1480)

What did the Gombwe Nehanda do to avert Portuguese hegemony? When the Portuguese discovered Southern Africa in the 14th century, they posed a threat to the Munhumutapa Empire (also known as the Mutapa Empire). As mentioned earlier, landmarks such as Mavinga City in Angola, Mutiusina Zita (Tree with no name), and Mapungubwe or the Mandamambwe Ruins in Mpumalanga, South Africa, remain as reminders of the architectural knowledge of the Rozvi in Southern Africa. The Portuguese were very adventurous; alongside the Spaniards, they regularly sailed to the African continent in the company of quasi-military sailors, whose role was to strengthen trade. According to Besenyo (2010), the first Spaniards arrived in western Africa towards the end of the fourteenth century. During their "Journeys of Discovery", the Portuguese wanted to control those parts of Africa they thought they had conquered through discovery. Basenyo has argued that some of these claims were highly contested by the Spaniards and later by the British.

In the Shire-Zambezi Valley, the Portuguese made claims during the latter half of the 20th century, to the colonies of Nyasaland, Southern Rhodesia, and Mozambique. They lost those claims because the British argued that they had actually occupied those territories with the Pioneer Column in 1890. Trade in the Zambezi Valley with the Mutapa chiefs proved too lucrative for the Portuguese to let go. According to Basenyo (2010), the ruling House of Bragada supported the merchant navy as well as the Prazo merchants. The ruling classes were capitalists and they sought to expand markets by venturing into Africa. It can be argued that the Portuguese were successful in creating a niche in the Atlantic Slave Trade and breaking the Munhumutapa Empire by re-labeling ethnic groups, such as the *Machikunda* in the Zambezi Valley, who assisted them in finding slaves (Mupepi, 2015). They seconded their own military personnel to support the Machikunda in subjugating the local population. Mbuya Nehanda is reportedly said to have fought slavery as well as colonialism. She was successful in keeping both the

Machikunda and their Portuguese masters away from the plateau and containing them within the Zambezi Valley.

The Mutapa Kingdom (c. 1220–1450) was transitioning into an imperial power, derived from the Mapungubwe Kingdom (c. 1075–1220) and the Zimbabwe Kingdom (c. 1220–1450), when Bartholomew Diaz reached Africa in 1488 (Davidson, 1966). Nyatsimba Mutota moved his capital city from Great Zimbabwe to Zvongombe on the confluence of the Mazowe and Zambezi rivers for two reasons. The first was that he wanted to be closer to trade in the Zambezi Valley. The Portuguese sailing caravels and Arab dhows could make their way into the interior of the Mutapa Empire from the mouth of the Zambezi River, sailing up to the confluence of the Mazowe and Zambezi rivers. Beyond that point, there were cataracts. It was possible to journey into the interior via waterways by taking the Mazowe River up to present day Bindura. The second reason involved taxation. The Mutapa positioned his trade stations near Bindura and at Zvongombe to allow effective tax and excise duty collection. Hunting permits were issued by the local authorities and all foreigners had to pay for licenses to hunt specific animals. It was a strategy to maximize national income from the country's interface with foreigners. At Zvongombe, the militias were able to monitor the arrival of traders and hunters. Zvongombe was strategically positioned to capture the lucrative international barter trade, in which the Africans, Arabs, Indians, and Portuguese, were key players. The barter deals frequently led to disputes about fair exchange. In the barter business, the traders who were aware of the prices in alternative markets tended to benefit the most, a situation that continues to apply today.

Because of such disputes, the Portuguese often wished to politically control the African market. Knowing this, many African chiefs, including Chingowo and Makope, created their own militias, whose role was to support their own interests. Their business interests included ivory and gold and the dispensation of law and order. The key to the success of the militias was good leadership and the possession of appropriate fighting technologies, such as musket rifles. According to Mupepi and Mupepi (2006), the emperor and his high counsel (Nehanda, Nyakasikana, and Murenga) had to develop schemes to end slavery and grow wealth. They co-constructed their world around the resources that could be found in the empire, such as ivory, gold, and people. The emperor shared defense plans detailing the realities of colonization with his traditional authorities through story-telling. Among the many problems Mbuya Nehanda faced, one was the difficulty of telling the villagers about colonialism. She had to tell them that the colonists were coming to take their land away. It was a way to start a political commotion, nurture anger and negative attitudes about the colonizers, and develop a strategy to defend their turf.

Based on implicit mental modeling (Mupepi and Mupepi 2006), leadership (Mupepi et al. 2007), and the traditional principles of Rozvi society (Mupepi 2015), leaders were nominated and appointed by the Chaminuka. He designed the governance and religion of the state as a single structure, with dual responsibilities. Those chiefs who were annexed had to toe the line to maintain their status. Their authority had to be sanctioned by the Chaminuka; otherwise, it would fall away. Some of the stories indicate that the Machikunda were an ethnic group that became disgruntled with Mutapa rule and decided to defect to the Portuguese. The Shona trained the chiefs to defend their own turf. Preconceptions about what to do under threat and attacks became lesson plans, contributing to oral history Chibanda, 1966) Cognitive schemata or defense strategies were reflected in the design of traditional weapons, such as poison-laced arrowheads. Tactics to mislead the enemy, such as sending them through treacherous passes in the mountains, may have constituted basic leadership lesson plans in the Rozvi forecourts. Mental models and defense structures were deployed to the nation. The strategy of the African Triumvirate (AT) varied, in accordance with the situation and environment in which things were happening. The AT sought to simplify the objectives of the Chimurenga and to ensure the participation of all. The AT were experts on indigenous knowledge systems on such matters as health, trade, gold mining, and hunting. The villagers did not have in their immediate memories any experience of having participated in a war. The Shawasha gold wars and Seke Dema land disputes occurred in the late 1790s and few of the villagers could remember those events (Thompson, 2006). However, some of the oracles, including Ambuya's could traverse antiquity with precision. Those conflicts were recalled as acts of chivalry among the Hwata. Of course, Nehanda's oracles focused on explaining the Hwata's cause, as this was their main totem.

During the Rozvi Empire, Portuguese traders teamed up with the local opposition who were also angling to take over the gold trade, of which the Mutapa had a monopoly. They defeated Emperor Siti Kazurukamusapa (1663–1692) and installed Emperor Kamharapasi Mukombwe in 1694 (Stewart, 1989). After reorganizing themselves, the Rozvi defeated the Portuguese in 1695 (Beach, 1990). The European imperial powers continued to want to occupy Africa at all costs. The Dutch landed at what they called the Cape of Good Hope (Afrikaans: Kaap Goeie die Goeie Hoop; Dutch: Kaap de Goede Hoop; and Portuguese: Cabo da Boa Esperança), in 1652, under the leadership of Captain Jan van Riebeeck of the Dutch East India Company. The station was meant to be a supply center for the BSAC's ships, travelling from Europe to India (Chichester, 1966). Today, these European languages are part of Zimbabwe's culture.

Ndebele Raids

According to Dodds (1998), the Ndebele Raids started around 1840, instigated by the European settlers in Natal and around Delagoa Bay (now Maputo in Mozambique). The Matabele epic began around 1822, when Mzilikazi of the Khumalo, an Ndwandwe clan that was part of the Nguni ethnicity made a claim on the Zulu throne. The Ndebele were sent to attack the Swazis and rob them off their women, children, and cattle. Mzilikazi succeeded in capturing a large number of Swazi cattle, rashly deciding to keep some of them instead of sending them all to Shaka (Dodds, 1998). Realizing that the Zulu king was not likely to look kindly on this sort of thing, he went into hiding in the Drankensburg Mountains. Eventually, the Zulus found him, took him by surprise, and scattered his followers. Mzilikazi and a few hundred others escaped across the Drakensberg Mountains, onto the High Veldt of the future Transvaal (Dodds, 1998). Here, they encountered scattered groups of Sotho, Tswana, and other peoples, many of whom were already impoverished by Nguni or Afrikaner encroachment, and whose traditional fighting methods were no match for the Zulu-style tactics of the newcomers. Town (2003) has shown that Mzilikazi's people continued to pursue their new vocation of cattle rustling. They soon made themselves rich at the expense of the local Sotho and Tswana tribes, many of whose survivors were incorporated more or less willingly into their ranks, in the same way as the Zulus had done to the Ndwandwe. This was the beginning of the class system which characterized their society during the second half of the century. The "amaZansi" or "those from the south" (the original Ndwandwe families) constituted the aristocracy (Towns, 2003).

Diagram 6: The Impis before the Rudd Concession (1884)
(Dodds, 1998)

Later, when they moved north of the Limpopo River, the local Shona and Karanga tribes were incorporated under the name "Holi". It was about this time that the name Matabele (or Ndebele) first came into use. Among various theories about its origins, the most appealing argues that it meant something like "They disappear from sight", referring to the way in which the warriors took cover behind their great Zulu-style shields.

The Ndebele raids were all about cattle rustling and the kidnaping of women and children. They happened during the early hours of the morning. The Ndebele were technically the first terrorist group, followed by the Pioneer Column, who intruded into the lives of the Zimbabweans, who were and still are the rightful owners of the land between the Limpopo and Zambezi rivers. The situational comprehensiveness of their political leadership varied. Within the African Triumvirate, the strategy was designed to reflect the oracles. Consultations with the royal Mhondoros were a continuing practice. In some cases, these oracles were accurate, enabling people to plan for their defense. In the Masviswa Hills in the Mazowe Valley, there are caves on the steep granite hill slopes, whose entrances are covered in tall elephant grass, and thickets used to trick the raiders. Other schemes were designed locally by the chiefs, as they distributed information about the Chimurenga to villagers. Throughout the country, people were profoundly motivated to defend the territory.

The paramilitaries were trained to effectively use musket rifles and bows and arrows in combat. The rifled musket was a type of firearm made during the mid-19th century in England. Originally, the term referred only to muskets that had been produced as smoothbore weapons, where the barrels had later been replaced with rifled barrels (Rothenberg, 1978). The role of the AT was to develop and implement defense plans; most of the chiefs supported the plans by providing funding and other much-needed resources. The musket known in Shona as the chifefe was expensive and could only be purchased outside the country. It was available at the BSAC's Quartermaster ordnance stores, which were controlled by the native commissioners. These officials were permitted to sell arms and ammunition to registered hunters, traders, and chiefs (Von der Heyde, 2010). The sale of firearms was not restricted to the settler community; guns were also sold to indigenous people. The Delagoa Bay Tete Masekesa and Beira Trading Fairs (in present day Mozambique) and Messina and Johannesburg in South Africa, were some of the fairs where guns and gunpowder could be sourced. By the time the chiefs were ready to hire a full-time military organization, Pasipamire Chaminuka had been dead for almost a year. The oracles had predicted this defeat long before his death. All members of the AT were aware of their destiny. They knew that they were going to die violent deaths. The situation compelled all three Magombwe to work tirelessly towards uniting the people, with Mbuya leading the deliberations. At the Chaminuka's wake, one of the resolutions was to create a paramilitary organization and allocate logistical responsibilities to the villagers.

A prayerful myth

The narratives in Mutswairo's first Shona novel *Feso,* published in 1956, show that Chaminuka asked Mwari for a powerful Gombwe or angel that could put a formidable defense strategy in place. This wish was granted and Nehanda Nyakasikana was born in around 1430. She was the child of a dreadful relationship between Nyanda and her half-brother, Murenga. The emperor had requested a Gombwe that could guide and defend the nation. This Gombwe needed to possess innate characteristics, as well as supernatural powers, to manage the responsibilities associated with the defense of a huge empire that was growing pretty fast. In this mythical story, the two half-siblings, Nyanda and Murenga, each lived with their maternal grandparents, who were royalty in their own right. Nyanda was raised by Paramount Chief Swosve in Hwedza, while Murenga grew up with his grandfather Paramount Chief Bunde in Southern Angola. At that point, both chieftainships fell under the jurisdiction of the Chaminuka. It can be assumed that the informal education systems in which they were raised included leadership and cultural studies.

The Hwata chieftainship has been analyzed in relation to the Rozvi dynasty and its genealogy (White 1986), exploring how the Chaminuka developed a form of government that was intertwined with the people's religion (RTR). The Rozvi Traditional Religion (RTR) was invented by the First Chaminuka (1430–1450), in tandem with the government of the multi-ethnic Munhumutapa states. White (1986) discusses the way in which the Nehanda Gombwe or Angel continued to be part of the legal counsel and the highest priestess in the Mutapa and Rozvi states; the book delves into the traditional system of government both before and after colonization to understand how the RTR was instrumental in the genesis of African resistance and nationalism. Throughout this discourse, the Hwata culture is analyzed in relation to the organizational development of the Mutapa states and the metamorphic development of the Second Chimurenga (1966–1980).

The structure of the RTR

Membership of the Rozvi was offered to ethnic groups that were annexed to the Munhumutapa Empire (1430–1450) and many others who joined much later. Paramount chiefs, including Mapondera, Makope, Mutoko, Nerwande, Nyachuru, and Nyashanu, have genealogies that directly relate to the beginning of the Munhumutapa Empire. The Munhumutapa Empire was evolving among Southern African communities, whose nucleus were the Hwata, or collectively the vaKaranga, including vaManyika and vaZezuru, among many others. Nehanda Nyakasikana was only a step away from the Chaminuka and two steps away from Mwari or the Lord. This religion was characterized by ancestor veneration and rituals. Its worship practice was based on traditions and stories, as opposed to scriptures. Both Chaminuka and Nehanda were Magombwe and had direct contact with Mwari. The chronicles assert that the Magombwe obeyed Mwari's instructions, granting everything they were asked to provide. Mwari is the Supreme Being, in the world of the Rozvi (now Shona), and is perceived as being somewhere in heaven or the cosmos. This structure also shows how traditional authorities evolved into the hereditary chiefs, diviners, and healers who exist today, in the fluid Mutapa states (see Map 3).

Defining the terms used in this discussion can enhance our understanding of the political and historical construction of the First Chimurenga (1883–1904). The challenges faced by the AT were numerous, included illiteracy and a lack of military know-how. Technical knowledge was scarce and the AT had to engage with Afrikaners in the Transvaal and Delagoa Bay to source rifles, such as the Winchester Martini-Henry. Ammunition was difficult to find once the British had taken over. Many years later, African nationalism picked up the threads from Nehanda Charwe to advance the Second Chimurenga (1966–1980).

According to Gelfund (1959), the Gombwe viewed the Chaminuka as the ultimate authority in the Mutapa Empire. The Chaminuka was a position and title first held by Mutota, the founding father of the Mutapa Empire. He came from Tanganyika in East Africa. Tanganyika is a Shona word that means "the beginning of the world". The Chaminuka founded the Rozvi Traditional Religion and the Mutapa Kingdom; his family formed the nucleus of Rozvi, which evolved into the Shona of today (Chivaura, 2009). In religious terms, he was the highest priest as the founder of the religion. Gelfund (1959) has argued that he was a step away from Mwari, as well as being the head of state. When Nehanda Nyakasikana assumed her duties, she became the highest priestess in the kingdom, reporting to the Chaminuka with responsibilities in both government and cultural affairs. A Gombwe is a divine angel that possesses an individual at the point of conception, causing that person to become a medium. A child possessed by a Gombwe is often raised differently from others. For example, his or her diet may differ from that of other children. The plural for this word is Magombwe. A person possessed by a Gombwe is also a spiritual medium because the angel comes to possess the individual in spirit form. Kazembe (2011:4) has argued that a medium could be possessed by three or more spirits at the same time. The Chaminuka, Murenga, and Nyanda were also possessed by Magombwe spirits, and Kazembe has suggested that the Chaminuka Gombwe possessed the AT at the same time. According to Gelfund (1959:11), the Magombwe had superior powers to heal the sick, make rain, defend the nation, and even to command wildlife. Stories are told of Murenga being able to hypnotize lions or poisonous snakes and to render them harmless. Frederick Selous, one of the early visitors to the court of Pasipamire Chaminuka, reported that wild animals and reptiles, such as lions and pythons, rested quietly outside the king's home (Selous, 1969).

According to Kazembe (2011), there were two or three Magombwe at most. These were the guardian angels that communicated directly with Mwari. After the fall of Pasipamire Chaminuka, Mukwati was believed to be the next Gombwe Chaminuka. Ranger (1999) points out that the Matopos Hills were and are regarded as sacred shrines. In travelling the kwaBulawayo route, the Pioneer Column had to pass through the Matopos Hills along the Mangwe Pass. All travelers had to descend into Manyami's Kraal and to wait there for the Lobengula's permission to proceed into his capital city. Thomas Bains, the environmentalist and artist, passed through the Matopos Hills en route to Lobengula, seeking permission to paint and hunt wildlife. Baines's pictures have shaped perceptions of Zimbabwe among those who view them in the London Museum in Kensington and in other museums around the world.

The Jesuit Missionaries, who entered Zimbabwe by way of Matabeleland through the Matopos in 1879, saw it as their role to bring Christianity to a people who were already aware of Mwari (the Lord) and had their own way of worshipping Him. Their Mwari lived in the granite of the Matopos Hills. Summaries of letters written home by Fathers Depelchin and Crooneberghs implied that the Africans were sunk low in sin and degradation (Roberts, 1979). The missionaries became aware that the Matopos was a center for African Traditional Religion, and that Chaminuka was the highest priest reporting to Mwari.

The Chaminuka designed the functionality of the government and its agents. The agents were traditional authorities, including Mhondoro spirits and chiefs, who ruled as a court within the structure of a village. Kazembe has suggested that matters involving religion and the state were dealt with concurrently, when justice was dispensed in the Mutapa states. A person who was not in tune with his or her own ancestral spirits would be found guilty of violating the practices that were needed to mediate a better life for his or her family. The RTR is more than just the indigenous beliefs and practices of the Rozvi, precursors of the Shona. It is the religion that developed as a result of acknowledging and practicing the traditions of the ancestors of modern-day Shona. The term "tradition" implies indigenous aboriginal or foundational customs and beliefs, passed on from one generation to the next in narratives, proverbs, parables, or drawings and art. Although the RTR is an inheritance from the past, it is not treated as a piece of historical antiquity, but as a bond that connects the past with the present and the present with eternity. The RTR is not a "fossil" religion, a thing of the past, or a dead religion. It is a religion that is practiced by living Zimbabweans, wherever they are in Africa, Zimbabwe, or the Diaspora (Kazembe, 2011).

At the Chaminuka wake, the RTR offered the traditional authorities an opportunity to thwart the imminent European invasion. The religion was, and is still, a window onto the world of health, prosperity, sickness, and work. It uses rituals, ancestral spiritualism, and totems to create ethnic identity, and a common language to make its belief system corporeal. The totem identity was a practice that promoted environmental ethics, with each ethnic group rising up to protect the animal that was its totem. Thus, the Hwata protected the secretary bird from extinction; the Shumba dynasties saw the lion as their emblem. When the Rozvi first emerged, Chaminuka probably gave totems to groups that were acculturated into the empire and used them to carry out various types of census. Each chief was required to collect a tithe from the villagers, and a totem was affixed to the accounting folio. The same technique was used to count the number of militias. The Chaminuka designed the RTR as a structure in which the common value was ancestral worship. But the national census first counted people by their village of origin, and then categorized them, first by ethnic group and later by totem. The village elders who belonged to a chief's court were responsible for memorizing the census in their own areas. Thus, a chief could ask these individuals, "How many men do you have with the same totem as yours?" The Chaminuka unified all of the traditional practices, such as lobola (roora in the Shona Language), the dowries usually paid to brides' parents in cattle, goats, or sheep. This practice is still in force in Sub-Saharan Africa, although it is debatable whether making money is still the main motive.

The Chaminuka philosophy was very pluralistic in many aspects. In governance, a quorum of chiefs and the elders dispensed justice. The religion was co-constructed with the chiefs and spiritual mediums as stakeholders. Talented individuals were always recognized and given responsibilities in the community, reflecting the types of work that they could do better than others. The chiefs participated in the barter trade on the basis that some natural resources were found in their districts. The villagers, responsible for producing food, instigated a division of labor to increase productivity. For example, boys and girls had specific roles to play within peasant life. Girls and boys in certain age groups were selected to herd the village livestock. In the home, girls spent more time helping their mothers process and prepare food. The importance of learning their adult roles was taken seriously from an early age. Girls developed the competencies needed to be good mothers and housewives. Boys were raised to fend for their families. Men were responsible for putting meat on the table, an expectation that is still prevalent in many societies in Africa, and particularly so in Zimbabwe. The trades of mining and ironmongery were practiced by certain ethnic groups that had special talents in these areas. These were the types of trades that a father could hand down to a son. At the Chaminuka wake in the Mazowe, all of those roles were used to build a bulwark for the Mutapa states. Boys and girls and men and women were enlisted in the biggest clash the country had ever seen.

Issues related to role conflict and identity arose in many instances. For example, males who were inclined to identify themselves as female represented an issue that was addressed seriously by the entire village and viewed as the influence of or possession by an evil spirit. Traditional healers consulted with spiritual mediums to find a way to drive the evil spirit away. According to Evaristo (2014), the community viewed homosexuality as a disease brought by the Portuguese, during the Discovery Age in the 14th century; they believed that the inclination to choose one's gender was introduced by the Europeans in Africa. Many countries in Africa have now accepted the choices people make to be who they want to be, as reflected in the equality laws. However, the debate that apportions blame for everything the Europeans did in the history of Africa should avoid the gender issue, as this is a universal practice with its roots in antiquity.

The Magombwe aimed at developing an empire in which the people could prosper. They defined the ways in which people should live in the new society. The emperor continued to focus on the development of practices that made the Rozvi unique in many respects. During those times, the economy mattered to the Chaminuka because an increased population meant increased revenue in the form of tax and hunting permits. A large population also provided available manpower to work in the gold mines, grow food, and provide for the defense of the country. The Chaminuka family brought the totem system into the Savanna grasslands at the beginning of time. The totem system created many different ethnicities, as each tribe identified itself with the emblem of their chosen animal or bird. The totems can be described as spirit beings, sacred objects, or symbols that served as the emblems of particular groups of people, such as families, clans, lineages, or tribe. The Hwata totem, for example, is a secretary bird, while that of the Shumba is a lion. Regardless of how that animal was distinguished, it remained *Panthera lea,* to use the Roman name. A totemic symbol may serve to remind a kinship group of its ancestry. The Chaminuka deployed this knowledge to ensure that there were no more intra-marriages, which, in those days, could have caused children to be born with inherited illnesses that could lead to pediatric deaths. Instead, the people were differentiated by totem, a practice that could at least ensure the birth of healthy babies.

To organize the military and national defense, the Chaminuka constructed fortresses, such as those which can be seen in the Great Zimbabwe Ruins and the design of the Mapungubwe Fortress in northern Mpumalanga in South Africa. One of the towns founded by the Chaminuka is Mavinga in Southern Angola, which was built as a garrison to stop Portuguese traders from moving into the interior of the empire after they took control of Luanda in the early 15th century. At this time, the Chaminuka needed a formidable defense strategist to protect his interests.

The introduction of Christianity among the Rozvi was carried out by missionaries, such as Father Gonçalo da Silveira and Father Bernard Mizike, who paid a great price for their beliefs. The Gospel continued to spread in Southern Africa because of the Mizike and da Silveira martyrdoms (Chadwick, 1910). According to Kazembe (2011), Christianity brought changes to Zimbabwe that speeded up the process of civilization among the Rozvi. The evolution of traditions and the co-construction of the Rozvi Languages, such as Manyika or Zezuru, led to the creation of the Shona Language (Carter, 1956). Although the Ndebele Language has been adapted in Zimbabwe, it has retained its Nguni identity and the customs of Zululand, where it is still spoken as one of South Africa's top local languages (Nordhott et al. 2013). All of the traditional norms and practices were disrupted by the cultural equilibrium introduced by colonization. Ancestral veneration has continued to co-exist alongside Christianity because traditional customs are interwoven with family customs and do not prohibit anyone from believing in the Son of Mwari, Jesus Christ, as leader of all the Magombwe (Kazembe, 2011).

The Chaminuka at the time of Father Gonçalo da Silveira was Negomo Chirisamhuru (1560–1589) who was granted a Coat of Arms by the King of Portugal, Sebastian 1st (1554–1578). Chadwick (1910) describes how Father Gonçalo da Silveira was appointed to a mission in Southern Africa. According to the Europeans, the area that Father Silveira was assigned to was unexplored. He was going into an unknown territory at a point in time when much of the continent was unknown. The Mutapa Empire was very large, probably covering the whole area of the Southern African states, excluding the Cape, Free, Mpumalanga, and Natal provinces of South Africa. When da Silveira arrived in 1560, he proceeded into the heartland of the Zezuru and Korekore, at the confluence of the Musengezi and Zambezi rivers. He embarked on an ambitious and fruitful Gospel instruction program, whose outcomes were very positive for the Christian faith. He baptized Chief Gamba of the Karanga and his entire kraal of more than 500 families. That tradition has been sustained throughout the centuries and Christianity is the faith of 98% of the population.

Chikanga is a Manyika name for the king. Chikanga Nyangombe (1807–1813) founded the Buhera Kraal as a hunting station on the banks of the Sabi River. Prior to Nyangombe, Chikanga Nyarumwe (1796–1807) was the founding father of the Makoni dynasty and possibly the ancestor of Chingayira Nyamanhindi Makoni (Cahoon, 2015). Chioko Dambukashamba (1887–1902) was one of a group of three freedom fighters, along with Gumbeze and Chivaura Kadungure Mapondera during the First Chimurenga 1883–1904 (Beach, 1988). There were numerous others, whose names have not been recorded in history books, although an oral tradition continues to thrive. At the wake of Pasipamire, the traditional authorities wept over their loss. However, it was also an opportunity to design a strategy, even though the AT knew that they would face a death as cruel as Pasipamire's assassination.

A surviving story about the religiosity of the Mutapa involves the Gombwe Nehanda Nyakasikana. The chronicles suggest that a request had been made to Mwari or the Lord by Chaminuka Mutota for a divine and powerful angel or *Gombwe* who could help in to consolidate an empire that was growing pretty fast during those times.

Duality in structure

The theory of duality of structure was developed by Giddens (1979), who argued that the dyadic organization centered on the relationship between agency and principal. In this dichotomy, the agency has much more influence on the principal than vice versa. The key to Giddens's explanation is that it focuses on the knowledge, ability, and skillfulness of the agent or his capacity to execute contractual obligations on behalf of the principal. The RTR existed as a dual structure made up of the national government and religion. This duality existed at all levels, from the family Mhondoro and the regional Magombwe, to the heads of state affairs and the Chaminuka. From a functional point of view, the family Mhondoro (a traditional midwife) had a dual purpose: delivering babies as part of a state job using African traditional medicine. Both birth and death required notification of the local authority. The chief also had two functions; he was a trader on one hand and a chief on the other. He led a defined ethnic group, whose values and beliefs had been incorporated into the RTR at the moment of annexation.

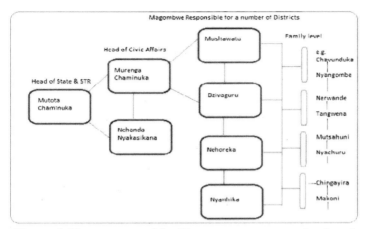

Figure 6: The structure of the Mutapa government and cultural affairs (Mupepi, 2015)

Another example of the division of responsibility can be seen in the case of a chief and his elders, who constituted the Mhondoro counsel, and the appointed village or tribal elders who were responsible for civic affairs in the sub-regions of the Nuanetsu-Runde and Sabi-Limpopo valleys. The same pattern can apply to the Mutsahuni and Nerwande Shumba dynasties (see Figure 1). Giddens (1979:3) has argued that agency cannot be analyzed independently from structure. A structure has properties, referred to as modalities, that are useful for enhancing dual perspectives. In much more recent research, Mupepi (2010) has argued that structures such as those shown in Figure 2 were bound to succeed because the Chaminuka and his people had the resources to sustain them. The diagram can also be viewed from the perspective of what it represents—a man-made religious organization. The model is useful in analyzing the organization's effectiveness and efficiency, although additional data is needed. According to Mupepi (2010), the duality of the RTR reflects its role as both a government system and a religious entity, with measurable outcomes, such as national security, pride, and threats.

The RTR and the state had specific rules and regulations created to control the international barter trade that existed among the Mutapa chiefs and Indian, Arab, and Portuguese traders. No matter what the Chaminuka did to protect the empire, he could not effectively defend it from European attacks. The Mutapa and some of his chiefs had militias to protect their interests in the Cuando-Zambezi, Mazowe-Zambezi, and Shire-Zambezi river valleys. The traditional African customs constituted civil and criminal procedures that the local chiefs were able to enforce to maintain law and order. The structure had both rules and constraints that enabled equitable practices to prevail at the village, district, and regional levels.

The standardization of Rozvi customs and practices led to the creation of a new language referred to as Shona. According to Mutswairo (1956), the Shona Language became a written standard language with an orthography and grammar that was codified during the early 20th century and has been in use since the early 1950s. The first novel written in the Shona Language was *Feso* by Mutswairo, which was published in 1956. The language has a literature based on the Karanga, Manyika, and Zezuru dialects and is constantly changing to reflect socio-economic developments in the fluid Mutapa states, where more than 19.1 million people speak it (Carter, 1986).

How different is the RTR from the ATR? The African Traditional Religion (ATR) is not very different from the RTR. The two religions share a common basis in practice. As Baldick (1997) and Doumba and Doumba (2004) have explained, ATR can be understood as the traditional beliefs and practices of many different groups of people in Africa and its diaspora. The RTR is prevalent among the people of Southern Africa; those who were part of the Munhumutapa and Rozvi empires, in particular, share similar religious values and practices. The diversity in African culture makes it difficult to label or narrowly define the ATR. However, some characteristics, such as rituals and the veneration of ancestors, appear in both ATR and RTR. In addition, they are oral rather than scriptural religions, involving the belief in a supreme creator known as Mwari. This, in addition to a belief in spirits and other divinities, the veneration of ancestors, and traditional medicine, form the main pillars of ATR.

Structuralism is a theory in organizational development that the foundations of human culture should be implicit in the relationship people and some larger, overarching system or structure, such as an organizational structure, that can reveal a hierarchical structure of jobs and their reporting structure. The theory uncovers the structures that underlie all of the things that humans do, think, perceive, and feel. Blackburn (2008) has argued that structuralism is the belief that the phenomena of human life are not intelligible, except through the explicit interrelationships offered by a community. These relationships constitute a structure, and behind local variations in the surface phenomena lie the constant laws of abstract culture.

What is a Chimurenga?

This word is an adjective as well as a noun, derived from the Second Chaminuka Murenga (see Figure 2). A chimurenga is a fight for freedom. The conflict took the form of guerrilla fighting using tactics that included ambushes and hit-and-run attacks. It differed from conventional warfare because there were no conventions to guide the behavior of the two opposing sides. For example, as Grebler (1940) has pointed out, the Treaty of Versailles, a peace accord at the end of World War I, ended the state of war between Germany and the Allied Powers. The other Central Powers on the German side of World War I were dealt with in separate treaties. Although the Armistice, signed on November 11, 1918, ended the actual fighting, it took six months of negotiations at the Paris Peace Conference to conclude the peace treaty. Thus, the Versailles agreement is the convention that ended World War I. In a Chimurenga, those who end up as victors are usually the underdogs (Nyerere, 1967).

The characteristics of a Chimurenga

A Chimurenga is a fight for political freedom. It can be argued that a Chimurenga existed soon after the Portuguese landed on the Atlantic coast, during their Voyages of Discovery in the late 14th century. In a Chimurenga war, the conflict is akin to brawls, such as the Mau Mau (1952–1962) in Kenya, the Maji Maji Uprising (1905–1907) in Tanzania, Umkhonto we Sizwe (MK) in South Africa (1961–1990), the Maritz or Boer Rebellion of 1914 in South Africa, the Jameson Raid of 1895–1896 into the Transvaal and many other skirmishes. These conflicts were motivated by a need to control resources belonging to other countries. In King Chung (2006), "Chimurenga" is a word in the Shona Language implying "revolutionary struggle". In specific historical terms, it refers to the Ndebele and Shona uprising against imminent colonization. The First Chimurenga (1883–1904) was triggered by the assassination of Pasipamire Chaminuka at the hands of Lobengula's warriors, assisted by agents of Cecil John Rhodes and his business partners. It became a political struggle that went underground after the death of one of its champions, Kadungure Mapondera, in 1904. The Chimurenga re-surfaced in 1966 with the Zimbabwe African National Union (ZANU) and Zimbabwe African Peoples Union (ZAPU) at the apex of their struggle.

The Chimurenga against BSAC rule continued during the period 1890–1923. It consisted of hit-and-run attacks and sabotage, aimed at destroying the settler regime. According to King Chung, the war fought between Black Nationalist guerrillas and the predominantly white Rhodesian government during the 1960s and 1970s—the Rhodesian Bush War—is also classified as the Second Chimurenga (1966–1980), which started with the Battle of Chinhoyi in 1966. The concept is occasionally used in reference to the land reform and the Africanization programs undertaken by the Government of Zimbabwe since 1980. Proponents of land reform and the indigenization of industry regard it as the final phase in the liberation of Zimbabwe through economic and agrarian reforms intended to empower Zimbabweans.

Emphasis on local knowledge

Chaminuka Murenga deployed local knowledge techniques to trick and conquer his enemies. He emphasized the importance of local knowledge systems, such as the geography of the territory, and ways of using different plants to produce both medicines and poisons that could be used to design lethal arrowheads and homemade gunpowder. Mavhunga (2003) has suggested that the transfer of firearms technology from South Africa to Zimbabwe had been underway among the Dutch and traditional authorities in the southern-eastern part of the country as early as 1870. In the late 19th century, Africans used firearms purchased from the Dutch and Portuguese traders to achieve various social outcomes, including their effective participation in the First Chimurenga of 1883–1904. The firearms were intended for use in managing the Gonarezhou international wildlife sanctuary in South Eastern Zimbabwe, a rich wildlife habitat now incorporated into the Great Limpopo Transfrontier Park, which is the largest single wildlife conservation area in the world. Mavhunga (2003) describes how plans were created during the Boer Republic of the Transvaal (1856–1902) and the Portuguese Colony of Mozambique (1836–1926) and implemented in 1870. The planned area covered more than 100,000 square kilometers of what was to become Southern Rhodesia in 1890 (Zimbabwe), South Africa, and Mozambique. Frank Johnson from the Transvaal was a young man of 23, who was hired by Rhodes to lead the Pioneers because he knew the area as a hunter and trader. As a trader, he exchanged firearms for ivory and gold. Training in the use of firearms was part of the transaction. During this period, trade with the South Africans and Portuguese was recorded; it is thought to have existed since the 14th century (Mudenge, 1974).

Figure 7: A rough diagram of the genealogy of the Hwata Chieftainship (Madzivanzira 2017)

Of all the traditional leaders, the Hwata knew more about succession planning than anyone else in the country at that moment in time. They were also expert marksmen and good at using bows and arrows. According to Mudenge (1974), trading records kept by the Portuguese showed who the ultimate authority was in the Mutapa Empire during all of the years they did business with traditional authorities.

The Portuguese kept trading accounts to advance their own interests and not to share with anyone else. Their records do not accurately reflect what was going on politically, nor do they give a clear indication of how the dissolved Mutapa states were being structured. It was an empire that stretched from the Atlantic to the Indian Ocean, covering northern

Transvaal and Southwest Africa; Southern Angola extended through Zambia and Southern Tanganyika (Cahoon, 2015).

Map: 2 Southern Africa (Mupepi 2015)

Their main trading partners were the African chiefs and other prominent individuals within the traditional authority structure. The Hwata chieftainship was the leading trade partner with Portugal from 1760 onwards. Other chiefs were responsible for mining and hunting in the Zambezi Valley. Hwata governance extended to large tracts of land on the plateau, excluding the Zambezi Valley. In the latter half of the 14th and early 15th centuries, the Chaminuka family founded the Mutapa Empire under Nyatsimba Mutota, who hailed from Guruswa (present day Mpumalanga Province) in South Africa (see Map 1).The leaders of the Empire were responsible for barter trade from the 15th century to colonization in 1890, in the areas under their jurisdiction. The region had natural boundaries, such as rivers, mountains, grazing pastures, and hunting grounds.

The debut of Matabeleland

In Hunt, et al. (1997), Southern Angola and Southwest Africa (now Namibia) are shown as having been parts of the Mutapa Empire; the Kunene and Kavango rivers and Mavinga were the only Shona names in the area (see Figure 4). People's names, such as "Ndapona", (meaning "I have been cured") from the Kraal of Chief Ovambo (1915–1921), also have meaning in the Shona Language (Hunt et al. 1997: 46). It can be argued that, as it was being established, Matabeleland incorporated many ethnic groups that lived in the Kavango, Kunene, Okavango, and Zambezi river valleys, which included the garrison town of Mavinga. The original concept of Matabeleland has been highly debated; accounts are drawn from Mupepi (2015), Chanaiwa (2000), Rotberg (1988), Keppel-Jones (1983), Hunt, Liu, and Quataert (1997), among many other scholars.

Sibanda et al. (1992) discuss the reign of King Tshaka of Zululand in South Africa and the arrival of European settlers at Port Elizabeth, Delagoa Bay; in early 1810, the entire eastern coast of southern Africa instigated the great rebellion of African people referred to as the Mfacane of 1815–1845. Among the Zulu kingdom's main leaders and military commanders were Mzilikazi and Sotshangan, who had been forced to leave Natal in 1823. Rotberg (1988) has argued that a peace treaty was agreed between the British and Mzilikazi and Sotshangan in 1836. The ambition of the British was to colonize the entire African continent. Rotberg asserts that Rhodes was merely confirming what had been planned for decades. According to Strage (1973), Rhodes' dream was to build a business empire within the British colonies in Africa. He specifically wanted a railroad from Cape Town to Cairo and that became a reality after his death in 1902. Corporations such as Consolidated Goldfields, De Beers Diamonds, and the

Anglo-American Corporation have continued to be key players in sustainable economic development in Africa.

Sibanda et al. (1992) have argued that, in 1836, the Mfacane inertia generated by the Boer Voortrekkers moving away from British rule in the Cape dethroned the Nguni tribes of Mzilikazi and Sotshangan, compelling them to lead another migration north across the Limpopo River into Zimbabwe in 1838. Cahoon (2015) has alluded to the likelihood of Mzilikazi settling at a place he named kwaBulawayo, after his mother. It still exists today and is known as Bulawayo. Sotshangan trekked southeast during the same year and settled at a place he called Gazaland, within the Chimanimani Mountain range. Cahoon (2015) has described how Nguni under Sotshangan became a formidable force, designing and implementing a successful campaign to control the eastern coastal region, beginning in 1839 or thereabouts. According to Mupepi (2015), the Rudd Concession and Moffat Treaty of 1888 and the defeat of Lobengula in 1894 finally led to the creation of Matabeleland as a region separate from the rest of the country, and the control of Zimbabwe by the British South Africa Company. Keppel-Jones (1983; 78) has argued that the lack of signatures from the members of Lobengula's council of elders casts doubt on the validity of this treaty. Nevertheless, it was the basis for launching the Pioneer Column, which subsequently occupied Zimbabwe.

The region that became Matabeleland was demarcated by rivers, including the Gwaai, Mzingwane, Shashani, and Shashe, which enclosed the parcels of land that the Matabele occupied, forcing the Kalanga and Tswana people further south of the Limpopo River. Although these lands were not well drained, they could be modified for commercial farming by applying irrigation technology, something the settlers championed. This region became the breadbasket for all countries north of the Zambezi River.

The Ndebele continued to harass the multicultural community of Zimbabwe, disregarding the Hwata-Mzilikazi Peace Treaty of 1860. Their raids put pressure on Tete Minge, then the second Acting Paramount Chief Hwata (1820–1837), before Kamuteku Hwata was crowned (see Figure 1) (White, 1986). The Hwata lineage had another powerful female ruler, Minge, who rebuffed the cattle rustlers soon after they entered Zimbabwe. The conflict interfered with the Hwatas' dairy farming and mining industries. They were very innovative in preparing food, creating dishes such as sun-dried beef with peanut butter, flavored with onions and tomatoes and served with green pinto beans and ground corn. The wide range of vegetables and flavors were a benefit of the barter trade among the Mutapa kings and Arab, Indian, and Portuguese merchants. The legacy of the Hwata women (vaChihera), passed on to the Zimbabweans of today, includes food sharing and village organization. The popularity of the vaChihera goes back to the proverbial Wasp Path (Mutunhu usina mago), a route that passed somewhere between Buhera and Wedza, its name likely coming from the time when Shayachimwe Mukombami (1775–1820) left the upper Sabi Valley to settle on the plateau, where the grass was always greener around 1770 (Weinrich, 1971). Nehanda Charwe was a great lawyer and strategist in all respects. The succession and crowning of the chiefs was her specialty because the traditional rulers derived their authority from Nyatsimba Mutota, the First Mutapa, who was her spiritual grandfather as well as the First Chaminuka and the First Emperor. It was the responsibility of Nehanda and the other Magombwe to confer the right to rule upon nominated chiefs.

It has been suggested that, after the Ndebele and Nguni raids escalated on the plateau in 1856, Paramount Kamuteku Hwata sent his younger brother Nherera Gwindi (1860–1886) to negotiate a successful truce with Mzilikazi in 1860 (Keppel–Jones, 1983). This truce was honored until the death of Mzilikazi in 1868. When Lobengula was crowned the king of the Ndebele he failed to honor his father's treaties, particularly those with the Shona authorities, who included the Hwata chiefs. When Nherera Gwindi became the 6th Hwata in 1860, his realm enjoyed relative peace and economic progress until 1866. The Hwata were successful beef, corn, and dairy farmers. They were also the best gold producers in the region, once they took over the Chishawasha gold mines. They discovered new sources of alluvial gold on the Mazowe, Murodzi, and Ruya rivers. Frederick Selous was given a mining concession by Chief Chivaura Kadungure Mapondera, one of the first freedom fighters. The Mapondera and Hwata were related; they changed totems to all peripheral areas to strengthen the defense strategy (Mupepi, 2015).

Chivaura's death signified the end of the First Chimurenga (1883–1904). As Galvao (1961) has discussed, Africans were forced to meet at forums such as at Nhimbe (a collective gathering of the Shona in a member's field to weed the corn) and Chibharo. Galvao has argued that the chibharo was a form of forced labor or slavery, which was used to develop the infrastructure of the new colony. The difference between slavery and a chibharo was that the villages who provided labor for the latter would return home at the end of their day's work. By contrast, slaves were taken away permanently; they never returned home. However, forced labor continued in all colonial settlements. It was omnipresent under colonial rule. Vickery (1999) describes how employees of the Rhodesia Railways went on strike in 1945 because they wanted better working conditions. Although they refused to accept rations of beans and cornmeal in lieu of pay, they had to take the food rations or face starvation. The administration urgently needed cheap resources to build up the infrastructure to enable effective transportation and communications. Rockel (2014) has argued that, while much of the involuntary labor force was used to transport goods that they literally carried on their shoulders, the colonial period is characterized by a shift towards road construction and road maintenance, the erection of public buildings, and the upkeep of drainage systems. Although none of this development benefitted the local people directly, it did help them indirectly. They were able to travel easily within the country and some were offered full-time employment on road- and bridge-maintenance crews. However, the colonists were extremely arrogant—they failed to incorporate the traditional authorities into their administration scheme.

Hwata's limited fortunes

The colonists built a viable economy in the country, which they re-named Southern Rhodesia. They did so at the expense of Africans. In addition to the Hwata Mufakose or Mutenhesanwa, Shumba Simboti, Shumba Nechinanga, and Nematombo dynasties that lived on the plateau and enjoyed relative prosperity, until the first Ndebele raids began around 1835–1845, Zimbabwe continued to be a popular land of opportunity for missionaries, hunters, prospectors, and farmers.

During his reign, Paramount Chief Kamuteku Hwata the 4th (1847–1855) faced a new era of attacks from Mzilikazi warriors. Pasipamire Chaminuka had ceded part of Gwanda and what would become Bulawayo to create Matabeleland. From his headquarters in Chitungwiza, Pasipamire had inherited what had remained of the Rozvi Empire. According to Stewart (1989), Emperor Dehwe Mapunzaguta (1740–1760) died before the land was apportioned among some of the chieftainships, such as the Chibi, Nhema, Mapondera, Makoni, and Hwata dynasties. Other dynasties, including the Shumba and Makope, were already firmly established on the plateau and in the valleys facing the Limpopo, Sabi, and Zambezi rivers. The Hwata knew more about succession planning than anyone else in the country at that moment in time. According to Mudenge (1988), trading records kept by the Portuguese indicated that the Hwata community was a trading partner of the Portuguese. Records preserved in stories about the Hwata concur on the traditional boundaries that separated their gold mining and hunting areas. The Portuguese kept their own trading accounts and their records mention that the Hwata, Shumba, and Nematombo dynasties inhabited the plateau as well as the Zambezi Valley. Their main trading partners were the Portuguese, Indians, and other African chiefs.

The chiefs were the leading trade partners of the Portuguese and Indians from the 17th century onwards. The Hwata's area of governance extended to large tracts of land on the plateau, which included the Zambezi Valley. In the latter half of the 14th and early 15th centuries, the Chaminuka family founded the Mutapa Empire under Nyatsimba Mutota, who hailed from Tanganyika (present-day Tanzania). They were responsible for barter trade between the 15th century and colonization in 1890 in the areas under their jurisdiction. The region had natural boundaries, such as rivers, mountains, grazing pastures, and hunting grounds. The area that became Matabeleland was marked off by rivers, including the Gaye, Mzingwane, Shashani, and Shashe, which enclosed the parcels of land the occupied by the Matabele. They forced the Kalanga and some of the Karanga, Venda, and Tswana communities to move further south of the Limpopo River. The new lands were not well drained but could be modified for commercial farming by using borehole water technology, a strategy that the settlers improved upon.

The Ndebele continued to harass the multicultural community that made Zimbabwe at that time. The Ndebele raids could have stressed Tete Minge then Acting Paramount Chief Hwata 2nd (1820–1837) before Kamuteku Hwata was crowned (see Figure 1). The conflict interfered with the businesses of the Hwata people, including those who lived on the plateau and in the Zambezi Valley. They had successful food and foundry industries.

During her campaign in 1884–1898, Nehanda Charwe encouraged the indigenous communities to study the ways of the colonists. She urged them to seek employment as a way of getting closer to the colonists and learning to understand them. The Hwata, Shumba, Nematombo, Nechinanga, and many other dynasties were landowners. Nehanda Charwe was born during a period when the Hwata were successful miners, farmers, and hunters. They were great fighters too, having defeated the chiefs Chishawashas and Harare soon after the Mutapa Empire had dissolved in 1760 (White, 1986).

Authority derived from the Chaminuka

The history of the Mutapa Empire in the late 14th century was mentioned by Portuguese merchants in their business records; however, these offer few accounts of the transaction sociology of the African people during that time. The situation was exacerbated by the illiteracy of the Rozvi villagers, who stored all of their traditions in their memories. Those memories, containing the knowledge, practices, and customs of the Rozvi, were handed down from one generation to the next in narratives. Obviously, some material is bound to be lost when facts are transferred from one person to another verbally. Words can have dual meanings. According to Kazembe (2011), the Gombwe spirit often possessed two or three mediums at a time. The Chaminuka Gombwe could therefore have possessed Nehanda Charwe, Gumboreshumba Kagubi, and Mukwati Chaminuka during the First Chimurenga.

A child with many names

Mbuya Nehanda is referred to as "Nyanda" in most early history records. Other families, whose genealogies were branches of the Hwata Dynasty, included the Mhembere, Jemwa, Mufuka, Katambarare, Mabvurambudzi, Meda, Warambwa, Garwe, Kanengoni, Chivero, Mandaza, Goredema, Muringai, Chiverere, Ndewere, Chakuchichi, Mandizha, and Mutambirwa families. These families told different stories to explain who Nehanda Nyakasikana was, and used different names to refer to this great Gombwe. When Nehanda Charwe was sentenced to death by the Southern Rhodesia Supreme Court, she bequeathed all her ritual authority and artifacts to Mandaza, who was the grandson of Hwata Shayachimwe's fourth son, Kamuteku. Mandaza's descendants are the Goredema, Muringai, Chiverere, and Ndewere families, who live in the Chiweshe, Dande, Guruve, and Zvimba communal lands—the former African Tribal Trust Lands (Chief Native Commissioner, 1901).

The genealogy of the Hwata dynasty is drawn from Madzivanzira (2017), who has explained how the elders gave the Hwata paramount chieftainship a detailed succession plan. In his capacity as the Native Commissioner for Mazowe District, White gathered data about people of the totem of Hwata or Mufakose (Madzivanzira 2017). In Hwata folklore,

Nehanda Charwe is also known as Mbuya Nehanda; in other literature, she is referred to as Nyanda. Nehanda Charwe was a Mhondoro (svikiro) of the Hwata Zezuru people. She was a spirit medium to God the Highest, known as Mwari in the Shona or Zezuru tradition. The Hwata did not believe in Christianity, although they acknowledged the existence of God. They came to understand Christianity during and after the period of colonization.

When Mbuya Nehanda was executed, the story is told that she refused to be baptized before she faced the gallows (Charumbira, 2008). Her will was confirmed in her last words. It included a request to pass on her ritual equipment to Mandaza Goredema, a descendant of the fourth Mambo Hwata Kamuteku, and son of Goredema Mazarura who had been crowned as Chief Hwata Chief earlier on but died in 1890. Goredema Mazarura was the ancestor of the Goredema, Mandaza, Mazarura, Ziwange, Muringai, Kupara, Chiverere, and Ndewere families (White, 1986)).

The Hwata genealogy is important for locating the domicile of the medium, as well as the Gombwe Nehanda Charwe. Mbuya Nehanda could only be appeased by the Goredema Hwata people, although members of the Makope, Nematombo, Nyachuru, and Mutenhesanwa dynasties were close to Nehanda Nyakasikana, Murenga Chaminuka, and Pasipamire Chaminuka through their connection to the founding fathers of the Shona. However, they were responsible for their own ethnicities within the Rozvi, Mbire, and Zezuru communities. They venerated their own individual Magombwe, who were directly responsible for expanding their own traditions. For example, in the Nyachuru dynasty, Magombwe Mutsahuni and his son Ganyire Nyachuru, were directly responsible for the paramount chieftainship of the Shumba Simboti dynasty. Thus, Mbuya Nehanda provided the *esprit de corps* in the struggle for liberation of Africans in the fluid Mutapa states (Stapleton, 2006).

Chapter Two discusses the wake of Pasipamire Chaminuka, who had been dead for a year in 1884. The looming threat of British imperialism caused the African Triumvirate to discuss future strategies when they met for this important ritual activity. Pasipamire was the King of the Mutapa Empire; he was the Chaminuka, the highest priest in the RTR. He was only one step away from Mwari. The purpose of the wake, in the Rozvi Traditional Religion, was to invite the spirit to return to the village to take care of the families left behind. The returning spirits are those that are venerated. This wake was taken by the traditional authorities, led by the African Triumvirate: Nehanda Charwe (Mbuya Nehanda), Gumboreshumba Kagubi, and Mukwati Chaminuka. They used the opportunity to develop and advance a strategy to defend the Mutapa kingdom.

Chapter Two
The 1884 Chaminuka Wake

The Rudd and Moffat Agreements were still new when the Shona, in accordance with their laws, were required to perform the rite to allow the spirit of Pasipamire to return to look after the relatives he had left in the City of Chitungwiza in 1883. The wake was held in 1884, soon after the May harvest. This chapter focuses on re-constructing the wake, as one of the most important rituals of the Rozvi Traditional Religion (RTR). The wake is a rite for a king or a chief; it concludes by nominating a new chief. It is a rite that has survived the test of time, from the 14th century to the present. It is a celebration of the individual's life, often carried out a year after he or she was buried. It is an element of ancestor veneration and a universal cultural proposition among Africans, wherever they are situated, sociologically or geographically.

The wake was held at Paramount Chief Nyachuru's Pagomba, a venue that overlooked a series of shrines and hideout caves in the Shavarunzi Mountains. Chief Nyachuru was merely a caretaker for the sacred places in his region. They included the Masviswa Hills, Shavarunzi Mountains, and Tsungubvi Hills. All of the shrines were highly prized artifacts of the Rozvi and Shona. Legend has it that some of the caves, such as those at the Nyamasviswa Hills on Ndire Mountain had openings onto the banks of the Zambezi River. They were jealously guarded by spiritual mediums; all the cattle herders knew about these sites. The Chaminuka rite was a special occasion among the Rozvi. The King Pasipamire Chaminuka was only one step away from Mwari, the Lord.

Lavish preparations were made to recognize Pasipamire's status and the respect he commanded during his time on earth. This once-in-a-lifetime occasion was attended by royalty from different states, including Barotseland, Basutoland, Mavinga (now part of Angola), Maravi, Tanganyika, Sena, Machikunda, Tonga in the Zambezi Valley, Mutiusinazita, Nambiya, and many others north of the Zambezi and south of the Limpopo. They all shared one thing in common: their royalty was created by the Chaminuka; they were the barons of the Mutapa Empire.

In Zimbabwe, nearly all of the chiefs whose authority was derived from the Chaminuka were present. Invitations had been transmitted by word-of-mouth as the villagers carried out their day-to-day chores and herded their flocks. Special envoys were sent to far away chieftainships, to invite the leaders to attend this special ceremony that would end by nominating a successor to the Zimbabwean throne, known as the Chaminuka. When Changamire Dombo led the Rozvi campaign to conquer Zimbabwe in 1684, he created military structures and changes that allowed the Rozvi Empire to become the strongest empire south of the Sahara. Dombo changed his title from Chaminuka to Changamire because he felt that the structure of the empire could not be led by a defeated leadership. Changamire managed to expel the Portuguese from Mutapa and Manyika (Shillington, 2005). Special messengers were dispatched to traditional authorities situated within and outside the periphery of the fluid Mutapa states to attend the Chaminuka rite in May 1884 (see Figure 4).

Pasipamire Chaminuka was not only the king of the Mutapa states, he was also an extraordinary rainmaker, healer, and the highest authority in the RTR. The wake held in his honor brought together many of the Rozvi traditional leaders, including chiefs, hunters, healers, diviners, spiritual mediums, and herbalists. The wake was a rite of passage that enabled the leader's spirit to rise up and return to the village where he had lived during his time on earth. RTR rituals were characterized by animal sacrifices, music and dancing, feasting and celebration. Different types of foods from all over Rozviland were prepared. The rites for the Chaminuka were very different from others in many ways. This was an occasion where the leaders of the states could gather to discuss matters issues related to the governance of the states. On this occasion, the debate centered on the succession to the throne and the worrisome behavior of Lobengula Nkumalo. There were rumors of war and invasion, at a time when the Mutapa states were losing the ability to defend themselves. The states could not match the fighting technology of the British colonists. The Mutapa states did not have a coordinated defense. Each chief had his own private security guards, but Pasipamire had performed nearly all of the functions of government, including fending off Nguni and Ndebele intruders. Pasipamire had died leaving even his own family defenseless. Mbuya Nehanda considered these facts each time she sat quietly by the firesides of her siblings and other vaChihera women. However, the spirit that possessed her was reassuring, projecting a vision of success, at least in the long run.

An opportunity to strategize

The rite for the Chaminuka provided a forum for the leaders of the Mutapa states to discuss and agree on the succession and national defense. Today, writing is critical in the design and implementation of strategic plans; the twentieth century lordships did not have that technology. They relied on narratives, metaphors, and stories to create meaning and convey ideas. Thus, each chief and his entourage discussed what had transpired at Pagomba. They shared the story to implant it in the memories of their subordinates and families, so that plans to implement the agreed strategy could be assessed, corrected, and perfected. The narrative argument can be described in terms of open systems theory. In this case, its main concepts were communities separated by boundaries, languages and beliefs, and totems from their environment and related to them through adaptation. The conceptual framework can be characterized using a knowledge creation process in which the construction of practices that are useful to one community can become an impediment to another. The purpose of the gathering at the wake was to co-construct the practices they all perceived as useful in the defense of the nation, since the Chaminuka had done most of the strategic planning in his court, creating a substructure of the Rozvi Traditional Religion and Mutapa state.

Before they could define their different perspectives, they had to define each proposition. They used group discussions to arrive at shared meanings, including ways to defend the nation against intrusions such as the imminent Pioneer Column, which every oracle saw on its horizon. The Roman statesmen Cicero argued that every discussion of anything should begin with a definition in order to clarify the subject under dispute. Frederick Selous, a member of the British military, served as a scout and agent for the BSAC. He arrived in Zimbabwe in 1879 and went to Pasipamire's court in Chitungwiza to ask permission to hunt. Although this was granted, he turned out to be a spy, gathering information to prepare for the Pioneer Column invasion ten years later. Selous lived among the Manyika and Zezuru ethic groups and became polygamous by marrying local women. It was considered acceptable for a white man to have a relationship with as many black women as he could afford to pay the dowries (lobola) for. However, it was unacceptable for a black man to have any sort of relationship with a white woman— never mind marriage. Selous lived among the Ndebele in a place later known as Essexville; he married three of the Ndebele women. Living in this way enabled him to have both etic and emic perspectives, on the dynamics of the Shona and Ndebele communities. He obtained detailed information about the capability of the Matabele Army, and made the following information available (Dodds, 1998):

Ingubo, "The Blanket": Formed by Lobengula as his bodyguard, hence the name, implying that it accompanied him everywhere (Dodds 1998:3)

Imbizo, "Drafted": Also created by Lobengula, by drafting aristocratic Zansi boys from smaller regiments formed by Mzilikazi. Regarded as elite. This regiment could move fast to strike any place. Legend has it that it reached as far as Tanganyika rustling cattle and kidnapping women and children

Insuga, "Stand Up": A young regiment with a very distinguished record in the war of 1893.

Inzimnyama, "The Black Ones": An elite Holi regiment, formed in Mzilikazi's reign. Guarded the main entry point to Matabeleland at Mangwe Pass. The name may imply that they carried black shields.

Inyati, "Buffalo": A favorite of Mzilikazi's, probably founded before 1840 but reinforced with younger drafts since. Inyati veterans were still guarding his grave in 1893.

Amahlogohlogo, "Golden Weaver Birds": Lobengula and his cousin Mtshane Kumalo both served in this unit in their youth, and the latter was commanding it in 1893. The name refers to the source of the feathers in the warriors' headdresses.

Zwangendaba, "Here is the News": An elite unit which rebelled against Lobengula in 1870 and was consequently destroyed. The survivors were incorporated into the evocatively named Amabugudwana, "Swimmers in Blood". (Dodds, 1998:3)

Selous travelled into the Zambezi Valley in the hope of meeting a Shona military contingent. The Shona did not have a mabuto or military as such, but certain chiefs, such as Chivaura Kadungure Mapondera, had militias. Others had built fortresses in places like Dlodlo Khami and Naletali to defend against attacks. Mapondera had built a military, complete with alliances in the Zambezi Valley, where he did business with the Portuguese. The same applied to Chingayira Nyamanhindi Makoni, Mutsahuni Shumba, Mutoko Shumba, Chinenguwo Shumab, Nerwande Shumba, Chipuriro Chingowo, Makope Nechinanga, and Nyandoro Kunzvi Nyamasviswa, among many others in the interior and lowveld. Through his nationwide travels, Selous assessed the striking capability of the Mutapa states. He wanted to know the types of weaponry they had and who supplied the weapons. The Portuguese and Afrikaners did not see eye-to-eye with English for many reasons, including the loss of the Cape Colony, Natalia, and the Transvaal to the English. The Portuguese had lost their claim to the Munhumutapa Empire, which included southern Angola and Manica in Zimbabwe.

The members of the Pioneer Column were well informed before they left Bechuanaland. They recruited guides from the Tswana, Zulu, Swati, and Ndebele communities, knowing very well that no Shona would accept the job.

The life of a Chaminuka

According to his written report, Selous (1969) arrived in the court of Pasipamire Chaminuka to learn who the king of the Mutapa Empire was. He was welcomed into the courtyard by guards, who told Selous the purpose of his visit. Selous was very surprised that his host had read his mind correctly. In the courtyard, Selous saw a giraffe grazing in the thickets outside the house of Pasipamire. He saw a lion and a python guarding the entrance to the house. Selous convinced himself that this was either black magic or Pasipamire had some sort of superior power, different from that of the Lobengula. Selous was doing a job for which he was paid handsomely by Rhodes. It was important for him to take positive news to Rhodes. He had to find a way to get rid of Pasipamire and make Lobengula the king of the Shonaland. He could not kill the king directly but felt that, if resources were given to Lobengula, his plan could succeed (Steere, 1973).

Ranger (1982) has suggested that most of the history of Southern Africa has suffered from the fact that very little information was written down—much of it was orally communicated. The case of Pasipamire, medium of Gombwe Chaminuka, is very different. Frederick Selous (1969) wrote about the death of Pasipamire. In 1878, Selous had heard from elephant hunters, including Thomas Baines and Bill Hartley, about an old man who was the King of the Shona. He was told that if he wanted to hunt or prospect for mineral wealth he had to obtain permission from this king. Other Shona chiefs were the victims of continual depredation but Pasipamire had accumulated a considerable amount of cattle, gold, and ivory. Selous confirmed that Pasipamire's city was called Chitungwiza, and that it was situated between the Manyame and Munyati Rivers. He studied rain patterns to learn when the rivers flooded and when there would be less water to facilitate the easy crossing of wagons.

Thus, the Pioneer Column had long been on Rhode's mind as strategy to invade Zimbabwe. The Pioneer Column were modeled as the Port Elizabeth Settlers 1820 at a time when the British economy was experiencing serious unemployment issues. In Burton (1971), the argument that the welfare state in Great Britain was still under construction and the Robert Jenkinson Tory administration encouraged its citizens to immigrate to the colonies as a solution to the welfare problems. Burton propounded that out of 90 000 applications only 4000 were approved to be colonists at Port Elizabeth.

Selous was also told that Mzilikazi Khumalo, the father of Lobengula, had failed to conquer Chaminuka. Because of a truce negotiated between Mzilikazi and his Gombwe Mlimo and Nehanda Nyakasikana Gombwe (not Charwe), Chief Nyajena made land available by to create KwaBulawayo, at the site of the present-day David Livingstone Mission outside Heaney Junction in Matabeleland South. Other oral histories may differ depending with the story's origin village.

According to Mutswairo (1983), the life of Gombwe Nehanda Nyakasikana should be seen through the lens of the Gombwe Chaminuka. Mutswairo offers an etic perspective on the Gombwe Nehanda Charwe, having been born and raised by his patriarchal grandparents, who were related to the Hwata and Shumba dynasties in the Mazowe Valley. Mutswairo has claimed that most of what he knew about Shona traditions was passed on to him in the fore of narratives—embedded in African stories, riddles, and proverbs. The written story of Chaminuka was offered to Mutswairo through documents once owned by Reverend Arthur Shearly Cripps of the Anglican Church, who worked at St. Augustine's Mission, Penhalonga, in Zimbabwe. Cripps was born in England, and came to the Mutapa states as Father Cripps, an Anglican missionary, in which role he carried out research on the life of Prophet Chaminuka.

According to Mutswairo (1983), Cripps conducted ethnographical studies of the Prophet and King Pasipamire Chaminuka, asking Mushaninga and his brother Murambiwa what life was like under this much-revered traditional authority. The two brothers were born around 1790 and 1795 respectively. They remembered their own childhood, when the City of Chitungwiza was bustling with traders and hunters who came to pay homage to the Chaminuka. The rituals of Thanksgiving were held twice during the year: first to give thanks for the crops, and later to give thanks for fruits and wildlife. The Shona community performed these rituals with great dedication each year.

The great offerings

Gelfund (1959) has suggested that it was a Rozvi tradition not to appoint a successor to a fallen chief until a full year had passed, following the chief's death. In the case of Pasipamire, each of the leaders, including his successor, contributed a black heifer to the offering for the late Pasipamire. These animals were slaughtered to appease and show respect for the Gombwe Chaminuka. The Rozvi offering of food and the lives of the animals served a higher purpose as an act of propitiation, for the Chaminuka, who was a divine being only one step away from Mwari. The Chaminuka was a guardian, a divine angel, or Gombwe whose mission was to provide for the children of Zimbabwe. The Chaminuka made rain whenever he saw fit to do so. It provided a bumper harvest of crops year in and year out. However, the Matabele had been cursed before Pasipamire died in 1883. The curse affected the land, causing it to receive less rainfall than anywhere else on the plateau. The Matabele looked to the land on the plateau for food, as well as sustainable employment, because farming, mining, and other industries were very productive. Pasipamire literally gave the Matabele the information they needed if they wanted to kill him. He did this because the oracles had predicted that Nehanda Nyakasikana and the Chaminuka would die the most barbaric deaths (Kazembe, 2011). Zvayi (2008) and Nehanda Radio (2012) have expressed the same sentiments, suggesting that the traditions of leadership of the Magombwe led to mediums dying the most gruesome deaths in Lusaka and Maputo before independence.

The role played by food in the Rozvi story

The sharing of food characterized nearly all Rozvi rituals. Attendance at these functions was usually by invitation. A death or birth was and still is celebrated with feasting. Success at hunting or barter trade was celebrated with all kinds of jubilation, with participants drinking beer and wine and sharing snuff tobacco. The invited dignitaries at this rite became a special group, focused on solving one of the most pressing problems the country had ever seen: colonization. The Shona people were very anxious after the death of Pasipamire. They were left with no apparent heir to the Mutapa throne. The feasting offered invited guests the opportunity to review and evaluate the while eating, drinking, and dancing. After all death, was meant to be celebrated even when those elderly dancers did so with tears on their cheeks, discordantly singing favorite songs, such as "Ndashaya wandidenha" (I'm looking for a fight).

Food was always part of the Shona story. There were all types of dishes and recipes, including rice and sadza served with roast beef or chicken. The Shona gathered to eat sadza with beef or game meat; wild smoked spinach served as the vegetable. The centricity of communal life involved sharing almost everything, including work and food. The meals prepared for rituals were designed to help guests forge relationships, bury anger, and celebrate the lives of those loved ones, who were long gone. This provoked much laughter as well as tears.

The story of the Mbire ethnic group, within the Shona tradition, is illuminated by their gift for cooking. The women of the Mbire were referred to as Mwenewazvo, a name derived from the Mwenemutapa Murenga Chaminuka (1430–1450). The story is that when the Murenga had conquered the Mbire they gave him a woman named Chikombo. He in turn offered her to a paramount chieftaincy, known today as Swosve. This story is highly contested by other chieftaincies within the Mbire ruling class and envious authorities (Gelfund, 1959).

The vaChihera women prepared wild green vegetables, such as cleome gynandra or nyeve in Shona. These greens were flavored with peanut butter and cooked with stewing beef. The vaChihera prepared citric wines from fruits such as averrhoa carambola (matamba in Shona). They had their own unique formulations for making wines and soft drinks out of wild fruit. The drinks could vary in potency because they were left to ferment for different periods of time in the sun. The longer a brew stayed in the sun, the more potent it became. Some of the drinks were non-alcoholic, and made from a variety of seasonal fruits, including tsubvu (vitex payos) and chocolate berry finger leaf (Mutsvubvu tree in Shona). These beverages had a meaning in the life of the Rozvi. There was beer made from rapoko or millet and corn. Each of these drinks was prepared as part of the misumo (proceedings).

The purpose of a musumo (singular: musumo; plural: misumo) was to pass information to the authorities within two structures. The first structure involved the family of the deceased and the second involved authority in the states. All of these groups received special misumo, to communicate the purpose of the gathering, which they already understood. The beer honored their presence, as well as the event. The misumo for Pasipamire told state authorities and family members that the gathering would wake Pasipamire's spirit and allow it to return to his Chitungwiza home. All of the food and drinks were prepared for that purpose. There were several brews of beer, some made locally and others prepared by villagers in the surrounding communities. There were numerous beer and fruit gourds reserved for the traditional authorities. Before the different types of heifers, cows, goats, and sheep were slaughtered, the master of ceremonies, Mbuya Nehanda, led the prayer by clapping her hands together with the palms curved like two empty bowls, making her claps sound acoustically like thuds, while she said:

"See now Gombwe Chaminuka, my spiritual father
We are here to honor your medium Pasipamire
Requesting him to return to Chitungwiza
To guide the children you left behind
As you can see things have changed since Madhedhede killed you.
The knee-less white people continue to subjugate us.
We continue honor and praise you to have mercy on us."
(Traditional author unknown)

The prayer changed into an earnest petition, in which Nehanda intensified her emotions and listed all of the problems she was now facing without his assistance:

Now the Madhedhede too have no rest from the knee-
less people. We also hear that they have no rain in kwaBulawayo. We are requesting your highness to return to guide the children of Zimbabwe who miss you tremendously
(Traditional author unknown)

Perhaps Nehanda was exaggerating. She was the one missing Pasipamire's advice, protection, and comfort. This was the moment when she had to request his presence spiritually to help with this mammoth task. Indeed, the English were coming, riding on horseback.

93

The English are the real witches with white faces long hair and no real

knees. They ride animals akin to hyenas and zebra

The knee-less people continue to ride into the villages evicting us

from our land. Slavery is back in a different format

Our own birthplace is no longer ours.

This beer we now place here on the

Muhacha tree is for you my royal highest one.

The meat we have lined up here include beef goat and

mutton and Kudu. We place here too raw beef, mutton, and goat

meat for the lions that roam free to partake with us in mind.

They all participate with us to receive your royal favors

forever and ever. Amen.

This misumo allowed the feasting to begin. There were wooden plates with raw and roasted red and white meats of all types. There were dishes with sadza and vegetables. These dishes were not part of the musumo because sadza and vegetables are not food for lions. The meats were intended to attract lion spirits to lead the fight. The meat dishes were served, while music and dance ensembles played on. A characteristic of the RTR is that death is celebrated. People tend to express their bereavement by sharing food, including alcoholic beverages. Different meats were laid out to be placed on shrines near the Shavarunzi Mountains. Sooner or later, the wooden plates would be empty, a sign that the prayer had been accepted.

The wake was a way to build anticipation or hope. This ceremony was carried out to build hope for the Chakanyuka family. A successor to Zimbabwe's highest office would automatically take responsibility for Pasipamire's family, including his conjugal roles. The traditional authorities had really gathered at this rite because it offered them an opportunity to discuss politics, their own succession plans, and much more importantly, to formulate a strategy to prevent their imminent invasion by the Europeans. Mbuya Nehanda was in her early twenties around 1884. In accordance with Shona culture, Nehanda Charwe was possessed by the Gombwe spirit when she was still in her mother's womb. Nehanda was aging pretty fast, as her family and the Hwata Shumba Soko and Samanyanga communities prepared for this important occasion.

Mukwati arrived at the rite from the Matobo Hills. He lived among the Njerere people, who are more indigenous to the Matopos Hills than any other ethnic group. At the conclusion of the rite, a member of the Chakanyuka clan was appointed to oversee the family Pasipamire had left behind. It is widely believed that Mukwati was also possessed by the Chaminuka spirit at that moment. He came to the rite to prepare for the defense of the motherland.

Mbuya Nehanda, as the master of ceremonies, was more concerned with engaging the chiefs to discuss and design a defense strategy for the Mutapa states. Mbuya was expecting a clear vision, precise focus, and unyielding determination from all the chiefs. The Portuguese invaders had been kept at bay because chiefs such as Nyachuru and Mashayamombe kept commandos to protect the barter trade. They were visionaries in their own right. Many of these chieftainships had been in existence since Nyastimba (1430–1450) or were created during his reign. Chieftainships created personal bodyguards and commandos to ensure the success of their family enterprises. These chiefs were great hunters as well as statesmen. They were landlords whose rule had survived the test of time, and they could trace their genealogies back to the Mutapa kings.

Mbuya led the deliberations, which attended by hundreds of local and international dignitaries. The international community came from as far afield as present-day Angola, DRC, Namibia, Tanganyika, South Africa, and Zambia. They considered the unity of the Mutapa states as responsible for the success of Zambezi Valley enterprises, in which the Arabs, Indians, and Portuguese and later the Africans were engaged in successful barter trade. They too saw the Chaminuka wake as an opportunity to discuss business and to offer their condolences to Queen Bavea and her family. It was an opportunity to create, diffuse, and distribute the resistance to colonization. The local people knew that Mbuya could engage in a beneficial dialogue with Mwari. It was the right moment to form a united defense under the direct command of the African Triumvirate (AT). The AT had the ability to design innovative logistics and tactics to further a national strategy against British imperialism.

There was much ululating and clapping of hands each time any member of the AT spoke. This was a patriarchy-centered community that had made a great deviation from the norm when it unanimously appointed Nehanda Charwe, whom they affectionately referred to as Mbuya, to head the most powerful office in the Mutapa states. They formed clusters by ethnicity and sat around the open fires, where the meat was being prepared. It can be assumed that the sizzling alone was sufficient to attract uninvited guests, such as African dogs, jackals, and even hyenas.

The guests were greatly entertained by mbira and drummers who had come from all over the world of the Rozvi. There were choirs of women with maracas made out of gourds stuffed with monkey nuts. This improvisation created a rhythm that kept the delicate mbira music in tempo. There were tall and short drums and each gave a different beat. There were boy-dancers who wore ankle maracas known as magavhu. Each time the dancer made a move, the magavhu vibrated loudly, in time to the music. There were snuff-snorting singers dressed in black to commemorate Pasipamire's death. Others, dressed in white or black gowns, were spiritual mediums. They created melodies for songs such as "Chaminuka NdiMambo Shumba inogara yega musango". (Chaminuka is the lion king that lives in the jungle.)

The choreography was not learnt from written notes but the musicians and dancers had rehearsed it often; this was not their first performance. They had performed in numerous shows throughout the Mutapa states. The mbira players from

Seke were renowned for their Chaminuka praise ballads. The entire show was a spectacular event bringing all the paramount chiefs, regional spiritual mediums, and other traditional authorities together to celebrate the life and reign of the Chaminuka. During the performance, other people interjected with their own personal testimonies to the great things the Chaminuka had done. The song "Ndashaya wandidenha" (I could pick a fight right now) was played by a mbira band from Domboshawa, part of the Shawasha homeland. It was a moment to express anger as well as happiness, while celebrating the death of Pasipamire. The Shawasha troupe had accompanied Paramount Chief Chinhamhora and his sub-chiefs Murape and Chiweshe, the main traditional authorities of the Shawasha state. The dispute about gold mines between the Hwata and the Shawasha was resolved amicably at some stage; this was one of the cases that the Chaminuka had heard in his court, which provided an appellate function, as the final authority for all the Mutapa states. The Shawasha and Hwata were related through intermarriage. They had come to Pasipamire's wake because the Chinhamhora chieftainship derived its authority from the Chaminuka. The Shawasha totem was Soko Murehwa, the monkey, and their genealogy was connected to that of Paramount Chief Svoswe. The Zimbabweans of today are a close-knit community because of the ubiquitous Rozvi traditions. Another head of state who attended the wake was Chikwaka of the Matemai totem. He was ready to fight and had brought with him about five hundred warriors armed with rifles, as well as bows and arrows. However, this occasion was a wake for the highest priest of the Rozvi Traditional Religion and the head of the entire Rozvi kingdom; it was not necessarily the moment to discuss readiness for war. It was a commemoration of the good deeds Pasipamire was renowned for. Several heifers were slaughtered to appease the spirit of the Chaminuka, as well as those of the regional and family mediums.

Pasipamire was the head of state as well as the Gombwe of the national religion. What made this wake unique was the fact that Pasipamire did not die of illness or any other natural causes but was assassinated by Lobengula's impis early in 1883 (Ranger, 1982). It can be assumed that the Mukwati were possessed by the Chaminuka after the rites of the wake concluded. If the argument proposed by Kazembe (2011) is taken into consideration, the Gombwe spirit could have possessed both Pasipamire and Mukwati at the same time. The two Magombwe lived in different locations. Mbuya Nehanda had invited Lobengula Khumalo to the wake but he did not respond positively. It can be assumed that he was very busy entertaining BSAC agents. Paramount Chief Rewanyika of the Batonga was present with his various heads of state. Barotseland was unique among the Mutapa states because it was a huge tract of land across the Zambezi River, covering south Angola and land south of the Congo. The authorities in those states were part of the Chaminuka territory by conquest (Chivaura, 2009).

At any wake ceremony in the Rozvi community, certain procedures must be followed. The probate associated with Pasipamire's death had to be validated by his family. Thus, the Chakanyuka family, including his widow Bevua and her children, were present and led the procedures jointly with Mbuya Nehanda. Bevua wanted the spirit of Pasipamire to return to his village, while Mbuya Nehanda wanted her spiritual father to show up and provide much-needed advice about the inevitable invasion. Yes, the British were coming, there could be no mistaking that. The British East India Company had made it possible for the empire to expand to incorporate the British Raj 1757–1858. According to Robb (1981), British rule had expanded from India into the Far East, absorbing states such as Burma and Thailand. This reality caused sleepless nights among the chiefs, who learned the news from missionaries, Dutch hunters, and gold prospectors.

By the end of the celebration, Bavua was given a companion from the Chakanyuka village. The role of this guardian of Pasipamire's family was to look after the material needs of everyone who had been supported by the deceased. This person also inherited Pasipamire's assets, including cattle, goats, and sheep and took on the debts of the deceased. Pasipamire came from the Chakanyuka village, in the valley of the Hunyani and Munyati Rivers. The Chakanyuka villagers had brought a black heifer which was to be slaughtered as part of the rituals. There were many naked fires, over which the vaChihera ladies were preparing food for the many visitors and invited guests.

This wake exemplifies the essence of the RTR and its spiritualist belief system. Viewed from the Rozvi perspective, spiritualism is a cosmological reference point that explains everyday social practices. It provides conceptual assertions that leads to questions: what are the consequences of practices or behaviors? Spiritualism was embedded in everyday language through coded words. The community was able to discuss political issues in a way that did not threaten the authority of the RTR. The wake was another forum for the Rozvi to renew their covenants with the Chaminuka. Their faith was based on a belief in Mwari, the Lord of all creation, communicating through the Magombwe, including the Chaminuka, Nehanda Nyakasikana, and each family's ancestral spirits. In the late 1880s, this belief system gave the Rozvi much satisfaction and a sense of security in a world being targeted for occupation by European imperial powers. The RTR offered hope to its followers. It was an opportunity for Mbuya and the chiefs to co-construct a shared vision of freedom, unite Zimbabweans, and draw up a plan to defend their turf.

The RTR system was created by the founding fathers of the Rozvi Empire and Mutapa states. Introduced during the 14th century, it has existed up to the present day through many practices, including ancestor praise and the celebration of death. Zimbabwe's cultural perspectives are grounded in the practices and knowledge of the Rozvi precursors to today's Shona. The Rozvi tradition was a self-consciously cultural and communitarian philosophy that focused on the RTR and the state as pillars of government, shaping its practices, framework, and foundations. At the wake, Nehanda sought to discuss the colonization threat within the context of Rozvi traditional culture, searching for solutions to the European threat and the ongoing Ndebele and Nguni subjugation.

In 1660, the Munhumutapa Empire was conquered by the Rozvi, whose militia was better armed than that of the Munhumutapa. The Rozvi introduced warfare technology and were able to defeat the Portuguese in 1693 (Mudenge, 1974). They established their principality at Danamombe and began a process of codifying traditional practices and trade. In a later study, Mudenge (1988) explores the role of Rozvi artisans, ironmongers, gold, and iron ore miners and gifted traders. The Rozvi were champion goldsmiths and masons. They built their city and temples in the style of the ruins of the Great Zimbabwe. The wake was a standard practice designed to ensure the continuity and survival of the nation. The community practiced democracy in selecting a village elder. However, the group that assembled was not a village community but representatives of all the Mutapa states. The succession plan followed a defined lineage, crowded with family dynasties from the Hwata, Shumba, and Samanyanga ethnic groups, among others.

These dynasties held the undisputed right to rule in the Mutapa states. This right was challenged, first by the Nguni or Ndebele and then by the British, who were on their way to take control of all of the Mutapa states. The British South Africa Company was created to make this conquest a reality. The Company launched a campaign of psychological warfare by creating a Ndebele state within the group of Mutapa states. The Company and Ndebele launched a campaign to smear the Shona with derogatory insinuations. According to Selous (1969:22), Lobengula ordered the death of all Shona soon after his meeting with Nehanda Charwe, in which she warned him of the consequences of the Rudd Concession and Moffat Treaty in 1888. Lobengula tried to revoke these deals but it was too late.

The wake is an example of a continuing Shona custom acculturated from the Rozvi. It celebrates both the past and the future of those who have died. The past is explored to illuminate the charitable deeds of the deceased. At the end of the rite, a successor can be nominated if the life being celebrated was that of an ordinary person. In most cases, a younger brother or family elder is chosen to take care of the family left behind. However, Pasipamire Chaminuka was no ordinary person. He was the king of Zimbabwe, contrary to what Frederick Selous and his compatriots wanted to believe (Selous, 1969). They co-constructed Lobengula Khumalo as the de facto king of Zimbabwe. The strategy of Cecil Rhodes paved the way for the Rudd Concession (1884). Lobengula gathered the Dutch courage to enter into treacherous agreements with agents of Rhodes: Smith, Moffat, and Charles Rudd. The Chaminuka reigned supreme in the Kingdom of Mutapa, known as the Mutapa Empire (c. 1400–1760), the Rozvi Empire (c. 1684–1834), and the Mutapa states (c. 1834–1890) (Owomoyela, 2002). The Chaminuka was the king of the Mutapa and Rozvi empires, as well as the highest priest of the Rozvi Traditional Religion. The Mutapa Empire was made up of self-governing states that were the precursors to the Republic of Zimbabwe. Thus, the Mutapa and Rozvi traditions have been passed down from one generation to another through narratives among the Shona and records maintained by missionaries and Portuguese traders (Mudenge, 1974).

The goal of the missionaries was not just to spread religion. They were also interested in assessing and discovering the mineral wealth of Africa (Holmes, 1993). The oracles foretold the coming of the white people and the escalation of slavery. Chronicles about the Mutapa states indicate that one reason the Chaminuka Mutota requested divine intervention was because he recognized the need for a powerful Gombwe that could defend the empire from subjugation and slavery. When the first Europeans, Henry Hartley, and Frederick Selous, arrived in the country in the late 1870s, the Chaminuka made sure that they understood that he was the ultimate controller of the Mutapa States. Much later, in 1890, Nehanda actually encouraged the chiefs to allow missionaries into their regions and villages. This was another way for local people to learn about the colonizers.

Many of the missionaries were part and parcel of the imperial governments of Europe, whose goal was to pacify the Africans in preparation for annexation.

Early missionaries, such as David Livingstone, confused religion with witchcraft, perhaps deliberately, as there was no reason for him to wish to understand something he sought to replace. According to Holmes (1993), Livingstone's writings make clear that he had little understanding of African Traditional Religion (ATR). Livingstone described the traditional beliefs as a form of black magic—similar to the witchcraft once practiced in Europe, based on what his two East African friends Chuma and Susi, told him. Holmes has suggested that Livingstone tried to ask the Christian Lord to make rain, to no avail. He could not heal the sick, at least during his first visit, and his inability to carry out such tasks spread doubt among members of the Sechele tribe, which he was attempting to win for Christ. Livingstone degraded African traditions by discounting them as "savagery" (Holmes, 1993). Mbuya Nehanda had a reputation for putting food on the table. She could cure diseases and attend to most of the community's health needs, although she could not find a cure for Lobengula's illness, acquired through his relationships with the knee-less people. The term, "knee-less people" was descriptive. The local people could not see the knees or limbs of the arriving Europeans because they wore pants and long skirts, which covered theirs body from the waist down to the ankles.

By 1884, missionaries had not had the chance to create a successful mission among the Rozvi. They had been in the courts of Mzilikazi and Lobengula looking for mining concessions. The Rozvi had refused to cooperate, except for Chivaura Kadungure Mapondera, who demonstrated his authority over Zimbabwe by giving a mining concession to Frederick Selous around 1887. Selous went on to create a very successful mining operation in the Mazowe Valley (Beach, 1988). The last successful missionary was Father Gonçalo da Silveira, who was ultimately accused of witchcraft during the reign of Emperor Chaminuka Negomo Chirisamhuru (1560–

1589) (Mupepi, 2015). At this point, the empire and the rest of the region missed an opportunity to receive the Gospel, along with many new skills, such as reading and writing. They also missed numerous other opportunities and a chance to acquire the technology to make durable homes and clothes. Kazembe (2011:5) blames the Chaminuka for the failure of Christ the Savior to proceed further south of the Sahara, arguing that the Savior stopped on the Horn of Africa before returning to the Middle East.

If the people of this region had embraced Christianity in the 15th century, later accusations of witchcraft would not have been possible. Witchcraft is the practice of, and a belief in magical skills and abilities, used to bewitch others and make them ill. Illnesses inflicted in this way could lead to the deaths of those who had been cursed. Sorcery is a practice that is common in backward communities; it can be found everywhere in the world, including Africa. Sorcery is a complex concept that varies culturally and societally and is therefore difficult to define with precision. Evans-Pritchard (2010) has suggested that witchcraft often shares common ground with related concepts, such as sorcery, black magic, superstition, possession, healing, and spiritualism. It is usually seen as distinct from these when examined by sociologists and anthropologists. African Traditional Religions, such as the RTR, are much more focused on ancestral veneration and ritualistic practices, such as celebrations of major life events, such as birth, marriage, and death. It is difficult to generalize about ATRs because of the diverse range of ethnic groups that made up the Mutapa and Rozvi empires—and indeed, the entire African continent. It can be argued that Mutota Chaminuka decided during his reign to unify the RTR, beginning with languages, totemic identity systems, and the structure of the state and religion, to create one unique organization. Murenga Chaminuka was viewed as the only person capable of incorporating local knowledge and nature studies into the competences that enlisted commandos would need to defend the Mutapa Empire prior to and after the arrival of Nehanda Nyakasikana.

Bhebe (1979) has argued that the RTR was more oral than scriptural because the people who founded it were highly skilled memory keepers, who told stories within the village system instead of writing them down. The followers of ATR today have modified their practice by mixing Christian beliefs with African traditions.

The Company strategy was to do away with local culture and introduce new practices that came complete with language, religion of Christianity, and formal education in which the required religion and language were taught to a colonized people. Niehaus (2001) presents a powerful ethnographic study of witch hunting and accusation in the South African lowveld (previously the Eastern Transvaal, now Mpumalanga Province) during the 1980s. Niehus writes in a post-colonization era and sets a high benchmark for future studies on this topic in Southern Africa, mainly through the remarkable richness and polyphony of Niehaus's ethnographic work, but also through his confrontation of what can be called the politicization of witchcraft. Although witchcraft has been a staple topic in anthropology, researchers have, remained largely silent about the relevance of witchcraft in contemporary South Africa. Witchcraft certainly does present some fundamental challenges to researchers and politicians. The Company regarded Nehanda Charwe to be the instigator of witchcraft. In Bishop Knight-Bruce 1895 Diaries on Mashonaland had this to say in support of a complete psychological warfare to colonize Shonaland:

I am afraid the Mashona are a very dirty race. In this they differ entirely from the Zulus and their cognate tribes. Once I asked one of my men, who was almost a pure Zulu, what had made him ill, and he said it was because he had not washed his face that morning—"You always have a headache if you don't wash your face." But the Mashona have no such ideas. Their kraals are a model of picturesque dirtiness (1895:1)

There is no truth in what the Bishop wrote. How many Shona homes did he enter? It was the perception of the conqueror to fabricate the most absurd sentiments about the enemy. The Bishop mentions cognate ethnic groups of the Zulu which are the Ndebele and Tswana. He appears to hold the superiority of the Zulu because they had won a few battles against the Dutch as well as the British (Barthorp, 2002). It was the known idea that the Ndebele were amenable to the conquest of Shonaland to create the failed Ndebele kingdom (Keppel-Jones, 1983).

When I have arrived at a village too late to choose a clean spot, I have been startled next morning at the dirt of the place in which I have slept. At a short distance, the collection of huts is picturesque beyond words. As a rule, it is on a hill composed of big granite boulders. That is sufficiently beautiful. Sometimes the hill takes the form of a huge rounded mass of granite. Then the action of the rain, and dew, and sun seem to have no appreciable effect on it. But it is when the hill becomes disintegrated by the action of water and sunshine, and falls to pieces, leaving immense blocks [28/29] lying one on the top of the other, looking as though the Titans had been there at play, and the many-colored trees grow in the clefts, that it is most striking.

The Bishop contradicts his role as one who was sent by God to propagate the gospel. The castigation of a home that has offered one a place to sleep is being ungrateful contrary to the teachings of the Christian faith. Treating the Bible as a literature text, Jesus Christ teaching his disciples in St. Matthew 10:40 stated: "He that receiveth you, receiveth me". Genesis 18:4 and 19:3 suggest the Shona who accepted the Bishop into their homes were not savages but a people who had their own land, civilization, and religion. The last part was very scary to the Bishop because he had been hired as the first Bishop of Mashonaland and he was not doing a decent job.

Then on and under and between these rocks the Mashona build their houses, at every possible level, up and down the hill. Sometimes two huts would be put on one slab, or the huge slab with its one hut would be a playground for the naked black children. I have seen them playing about on an overhanging rock at a height which would turn an English nurse sick with fear; but no one seemed to mind, and the children did not fall (Knight-Bruce 1895).

The Company's strategy was to introduce a new religion to make a complete indoctrination of the Shona people and conquest a reality. In Koch and Koch (1984), Karl Marx asserted that religion was the opiate of the masses. He could have implied that the masses who are very often poor, go to church to worship as well as to discuss their problems with others in the same predicament. The Company included members of the clergy in the Pioneer Column whose was to pacify the masses to make annexure real.

The wake of the Chaminuka was a national celebration of Pasipamire's important work in repelling the Nguni, Ndebele, and white men. The wake is a very important ritual in the Shona Traditional Religion. The Chaminuka managed engage successful fights with the aid of a disciplined army and a united community. The medium of Nehanda Nyakasikana was a daughter of Charwe Hwata, who lived in one of Chief Chidamba's villages, on what is now Christon Bank outside Harare. She organized the Chaminuka's wake in her capacity as the highest priestess of the RTR and top-ranking officer of the Rozvi states. She was referred to as Nehanda Charwe (c.1864–1898) or Mbuya Nehanda by Zimbabweans and many in the Mutapa states. Nehanda's mission was to raise the awareness of Rozvi/Zimbabweans that their freedom was under threat from the white people, whom she described as "knee-less" because they covered their legs with long skirts and pants. It was a name derived from observation and not intended to be derogatory. The death of Pasipamire introduced the political changes that had been foretold by various oracles. Although Nehanda could not change this predicament, it was her role to help Zimbabweans appreciate the technology and wisdom of the knee-less people, as a strategy to advance their struggle for liberation.

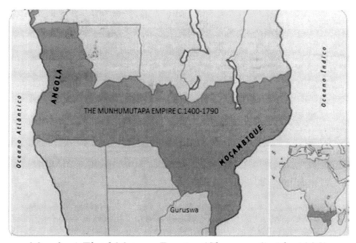

Map 3: A Fluid Mutapa Empire (Clarence-Smith, 1985).

In the late 19th century, Charwe became Nehanda Charwe, the medium of Gombwe Nehanda Nyakasikana presiding as the highest priestess in the entire Mutapa Empire (see Map 2). In the stories told by villagers in various parts of a fluid Mutapa Empire when Nehanda Charwe became of age she was automatically promoted to the highest seat in the traditional government and Rozvi Traditional Religion (RTR) organization. In this role, Mbuya Nehanda acted as the legal counsel to the Paramount Chiefs Hwata, Mangwende, Mashayamombe, Mutoko, Nematombo, Nyachuru, and Nyangombe Swosve, among many others, whose authority was granted by the Chaminuka. Her position was dualistic because the incumbent was also the highest priestess of the RTR. The RTR was constituted by practices and beliefs founded by Mwari. In Chikuse (2014):

Mwari was also known as 'Dzivaguru', 'Sororenzou', 'Nyadenga', 'Muvumbapasi', 'Musiki', 'Musikavanhu' and 'Dziva'. Associated primarily with the Rozvi, he did not speak to the people through human mediums under

107

possession but freely from all sorts of objects, e.g. children, animals and rocks.

Nehanda Nyakasikana was brought into the world as the strategist of the empire. She did not speak from a rock but found sanctuary in the shrines that are scattered in the hills and mountains in central Africa. The Chaminuka as the Emperor ruled sizeable size of Southern Africa (Clarence-Smith, 1985).The Nyakasikana Gombwe could not be differentiated from the other Chaminuka mediums. The only difference that has been persistent is that the Gombwe Nyakasikana seemed to prefer female to male mediums. One of the roles was to stop Portuguese Imperialism which brought slavery in the Zambezi Valley in fifteenth century (Mudenge, 1974)

When, like other African deities, Mwari withdrew from the people owing to their intolerable and arrogant behavior, his place was taken by the clan guardian spirits, the Mhondoro. A large aspect of the Mwari religion was this Mhondoro cult whose principal Mhondoro at Mavinga, (Southern Angola), Tokaleya Tonga and Nyika (Zambia), Zumbo and Great Zimbabwe (Zimbabwe) was Chaminuka. The Chaminuka medium apparently resided in the Eastern Enclosure of the Great Zimbabwe. Traditions say Chaminuka used to interpret the squawking of the sacred fish eagle, hungwe, on its annual visits to Great Zimbabwe.

The relation between the Mwari cult, based in the Matopo Hills, and the Rozvi power in the past is uncertain. It seems clear that the cult already existed in the Torwa state, and the Changamire Rozvi came to terms with it in some such way as the Ndebele did after them. According to traditions the Mbire worshipped Mwari at Great Zimbabwe until the place became over-populated and Mwari directed them to Matonjeni (Chikuse 2014:4).

Evidence indicated that the chiefs whose authority was bestowed upon them by the Chaminuka used to send periodic delegations to the Mabwe aDziva (The Rocks of Dziva) in the

Matopos Hills. These delegations bore gifts as tribute, and petitions for help, particularly in the matter of rain and war. Women from each clan were selected to safeguard the clan's charms and they spent a period at the shrines in the entourage of the god. These nuns were called mbonga and their other job was to instruct the marriageable girls in their wifely duties (Chikuse 2014:5).

During the First Chimurenga, Matonjeni shrines filled the political vacuum created by the defeat of Lobengula by using Mwari vanyai (messengers) networks to coordinate the anti-colonial struggle that united both the Shona and Ndebele people. Nehanda Charwe in 1883 soon after the assassination of Pasipamire journeyed to kwaBulawayo anticipating to warn Lobengula about Europeans who were up to no good. In this role Mbuya was akin a diplomat who went from village to village warning the people about the impeding colonization. She urged people to unite and to form armies or commandoes to resist colonization. At first, Nehanda had encouraged the people to get closer to learn about the knee-less people's way of life, their technology about ballistics, reading and writing. She had the forum of the chiefs who were appointed by the Chaminuka. These appointments reflected the wishes of the people and the way in which the Chaminuka had structured the empire. Democracy is not a new phenomenon in Zimbabwe; it existed during the era of the Mutapa kings and was the foundation of the elders' quorum in the chief's court. The central court (or padare in Shona) was a legal forum located in the villages. Here justice was dispensed in civil and criminal proceedings.

How did Mbuya Nehanda organize her gigantic workload in a world that was dominated by men and a society in which women did not have many rights? How was Rozvi spiritualism invoked to govern the people? These questions will be answered in the course of discussing the Rozvi Traditional Religion and the way it was intertwined with the Mutapa government. The role of Mbuya Nehanda was constantly evolving, in response to increased threats to national security. To be the medium of a Gombwe like Nehanda Nyakasikana meant many things. For example, the medium grew up differently from other children; her diet was different. Most girls who became mediums could not date or contemplate marriage, unless the Mhondoro concurred.

This study examines an occasion when the traditional authorities were invited by Mbuya Nehanda to review the assassination of Pasipamire Chaminuka. The Chaminuka's wake was an opportunity for the traditional authorities to discuss politics and the spiritual crises that had fallen on the Mutapa states. It gave them a chance to develop a strategy to defend the country from imminent attack, restructure the RTR, and nominate an acting Chaminuka. The wake was an opportunity to restructure the RTR and the Mutapa states. It was a moment to look squarely and collectively at the imminent British invasion.

When Pasipamire was murdered, the assailants mutilated his body and removed his organs, which they kept as lucky charms. There was no other explanation for such savage behavior. His body was the worst sight the Shona villagers had ever seen. Normally, the Nguni and Ndebele were the cattle rustlers and kidnappers; they often left behind elderly people, either dead or dying of their injuries. It can be argued that the Chaminuka was a very divine person who had successful dialogue with Mwari. Ranger (1999) has alluded to a voice that came from the rocks in the Matobo, among the Njerere people. Mukwati is argued to have come from the Matopos Hills to participate in the defense of the Mutapa states after 1883. Some say that Mukwati was possessed by many other Magombwe, including that of Murenga Chaminuka (Mupepi, 2015). The Matobo was at the heart of many aspects of Rozvi spiritualism. It was home to Umkulu Mlimo, the principal counsel to Chief Mzilikazi Khumalo, as well as the commander of the Ndebele warriors (Selous, 1967).

The African Triumvirate included Gumboreshumba Kagubi, who was believed to be a medium for more than three ancestral spirits including that of the Chaminuka Second

Emperor. Mukwati was the mastermind of the trio. He came from the Njerere community in the Matobo Hills and was also possessed by two ancestral spirits, including the Gombwe First Chaminuka. At the wake, the Gombwe Mukwati could not speak to the invited heads of the Mutapa states because Mbuya Nehanda was the master of ceremonies. Nehanda inherited a legacy of authority that permeated all aspects of the traditional leadership. The most difficult aspect of this legacy was the inseparable bond between the Rozvi Religion and the state. The problematic aspect of this organization was the fact that foreigners had to deal with the religious aspects of the Mutapa states when all they wanted were mining concessions. During the period when Mbuya Nehanda was practicing her trade, there was no difference between the government and religion of the state; they were one organization. In later years, Mbuya Nehanda found herself in a business relationship with the Native Commissioner, Henry Pollard, exchanging gold for self-loading Martini-Henry rifles (Mupepi, 2015). The government was part of the national religion and Nehanda chaired the proceedings in her capacity as its highest priestess, as well as a minister without portfolio.

The wake procedures were held in the village of Chief Chidamba, located to the west of present-day Harare in the Christon Bank area. There were no written minutes but the invited guests held the deliberations in their memories and retold the story in villages far and wide.

Mbuya Nehanda was one of the greatest counsels who ever belonged to the traditional authorities. These chiefs derived their authority from the Chaminuka, beginning with Nyatsimba Mutota (1430–1450). The late Pasipamire Chaminuka (c.1770–1883) had delegated much power and authority to Chingayira Nyamanhindi Makoni and Chivaura Kadungure Mapondera. In the re-construction of the Great Indaba held in November 1884, the Rudd Concession had already been concluded. In the court of Chief Chidamba, there were five other chiefs, including Goredema, Gwindi Hwata the 8th, Negomo, Makoni, Makope, Mashayamombe, Mapondera, Nyachuru, and Chingowo. They met at the

Pagomba on the Mazowe River. It was a natural depression encircled by the Shavarunzi Mountains and the Mazowe River, which emerged from the pond, fed by streams and springs, and flowed through the saddle and wind-gap overlooking the Mazowe Valley. The Pagomba is now part of the Mazowe Dam.

The invasion of Zimbabwe in 1890 was real and most of the traditional leadership where not aware of the Rudd Concession and Moffat Treaties. The year was 1884 and the agenda included the assassination of Pasipamire Chaminuka the year before and the proceedings of the Berlin Conference, which were on-going. Other issues included the continued Ndebele subjugation and the imminent invasion by the knee-less people. The Magombwe referred to as the African Triumvirate (AT) in Mupepi (2015) were Nehanda Charwe, Gumboreshumba Kagubi, and Mukwati Chaminuka. Nehanda Charwe's totem was that of the Hwata (the African secretary bird); Mukwati and Kagubi are assumed to have belonged to the totem of the Samanyanga (Nzou). Totemism is viewed as a Shona tradition designed to identify ethnicity by requiring each group to associate itself with one particular animal or bird. It implies that each ethnic group should apply the principles of totemism as a model for society. Totemism is associated with animistic religions, in which animals are nature spirits that interact with particular ethnic kinship groups and serve as their emblem (Levi-Strauss, 1958).

Honoring these traditions, there were various pots of purpose-brewed beer for the members of each totem, as required by the RTR. There were several pots for Pasipamire, referred to as misumo. These brews were accompanied by the slaughtering of the largest bull ever to appease the Gombwe spirit of the Chaminuka. Taking the lead in these unique proceedings was Gumboreshumba Kagubi, in his capacity as the Second Chaminuka, and Murenga, the husband of Nyanda, mother to Nehanda Nyakasikana. Basically, Kagubi was asking his spiritual father Mutota to return to the Rozvi, Hwata, Mazezuru, Manyika, and Karanga. All of these smaller and larger ethnic groups were acculturated into the

Rozvi traditions and qualified to receive Magombwe spirits into their families. Thus, Kagubi in person was performing the ceremony known as kurova guva or "awakening the dead" to ask his spiritual father, Mutota, to return to help his children, who were on the verge of losing everything they owned. Lobengula had continued his wheeling and dealing with the enemy, ignoring the advice of Mbuya Nehanda and Umkulu Mlimo, the best oracles around.

Appeasing the spirit of the Chaminuka was a long and complex process. It took two weeks to organize and carry out the ceremony. The animal sacrifices had to be made one animal at a time. Whoever was making the contribution had to follow strict procedures; the meat had to be prepared over a naked fire and distributed along with pots of beer. The vaChihera women (all Hwata females are referred to as vaChihera) and Mbuya Nehanda served this food. Some of the beer was sweet; for those who did not drink alcoholic beverages, there was maburo, a drink made of corn and millet but not allowed to ferment. Many believed that these customs were introduced by the Chaminuka family, as it journeyed from Tanganyika to the lands beyond the Limpopo and Orange rivers. The second beer pot was referred to as the "chingoto". Its purpose was and is to ask the Chaminuka spirit for enough rain to ensure food security. This ritual celebrated the future. It raised the hopes of the agrarian community and encouraged its hunters and traders. This rite was followed by the slaughter of yet another bull, as a Hwata family offering or chema to the Chaminuka. Numerous pots of sweet beer were distributed to each chief. The vaChihera women helped to prepare and distribute the food. After all the rites had been carried out satisfactorily, the gathering waited to hear what Mbuya Nehanda, Mukwati, and Kagubi had to say about the succession to the Chaminuka throne. Together, Mbuya Nehanda, Mukwati, and Kagubi made up the African Triumvirate, a title bestowed upon them by the traditional authorities, for their role in bringing the people together and leading the insurrection.

The AT was at the top of the government hierarchy, as well as the RTR. The late Pasipamire Chaminuka was the king. The other officials responsible for dealing with urgent national security issues were Magombwe Mutsahuni Shumba and Goredema Hwata Mufakose. As Pasipamire Chaminuka had been murdered by Lobengula Khumalo's impis, there was a question of revenge. The principle of forgiveness in both Shona and Ndebele customs is very remote; forgiveness is associated with cowardice. An injured party will ask his brothers to help him seek revenge. It was therefore easy to start a tribal conflict by enlisting supporters to back both sides of an argument. Trial by battle was a common law practice in Europe during the Dark Ages; it was still used in Africa on the eve of colonization in 1885.

Although the oracles had predicted the murder of Pasipamire, nobody wanted to face the hard fact that he had actually been assassinated by the Ndebele because acknowledgment meant war. According to the oracles, Pasipamire's death was a planned event that would have been fulfilled in one way or another. The same predicament confronted Mbuya Nehanda, Gumboreshumba Kagubi, and Mukwati Chaminuka, the members of the African Triumvirate (AT). These facts did not bother the AT, who knew that their time was limited and that it was part of Mwari's grand scheme for them to die defending their country. Mbuya Nehanda was the youngest of the three, barely twenty. The responsibilities and authority she carried made her look much older. She never had a relationship with a man and eventually died a spinster. The members of the AT lived dedicated lives, looking forward to dying on the gallows because this had been foretold by numerous oracles. Their deaths would symbolize the ultimate freedom of Zimbabwe. The European settlers were needed, to introduce Western civilization and technology. However, the "civilization" or evolution of Zimbabwe came at a great price. The barter deals had benefited the Portuguese, for the most part. They had built Lisbon and other cities with the profits they made from Mutapa gold and ivory. The Mutapa built Zvongombe City out of straw and dagga and it did not last. The stonemasons of Great Zimbabwe and Mapungubwe appear to have vanished into oblivion (Mupepi, 2015).

The wake gave the Magombwe an opportunity to develop a strategy to defend the country. However, the death of Pasipamire had an impact on the dynamics through which the traditional authorities maintained status hierarchies. There were two aspects that relied on different principles. Under Pasipamire, the AT had met three times a year to review the trade, religion, and governance of the Mutapa states. This aspect of the Rozvi government had to continue and it relied on performance expectations. The second aspect was that established hierarchical structures had to be maintained, with or without a new Chaminuka. The chieftains and Magombwe had the structural responsibility for ensuring continuity. Each of them had been honored to have been part of the king's inner cabinet. The AT knew that Mukwati would be the next Chaminuka. Little was known about Mukwati, except that he was a capable diviner, healer, rainmaker, and chief's counsel, and better qualified for the role than lower status actors. Mukwati was not well acquainted with the chiefs on the plateau because he lived in the Matobo Hills, far away from the main Rozvi community. Other diviners, traditional healers, and Mhondoro mediums associated him with the voices in the Matobo Hills (Ranger, 1999). The chiefs and other dignitaries felt highly honored to be present at this historical occasion and to meet in person the African Triumvirate. Pasipamire was buried in his capital city, Chitungwiza, in a grave carved out of a rock from which a river began to flow that very moment and still does to this day.

The wake is an occasion held at least one year after a Shona community elder has been buried. It is a ritual celebrated with feasting and beer drinking. It is an important occasion, still practiced by Zimbabweans today. The leader of the wake can be the spiritual medium possessed by the Mhondoro of the village. It does not have to be a Gombwe. In this case, the Gombwe Goredema chaired the proceedings celebrating Pasipamire, on grounds that the medium was

Pasipamire's nephew. Mbuya Nehanda remained the master of ceremonies. The wake gives the community a chance to celebrate a leader's life and to ask Musikavanhu or Mwari to allow the spirit of the deceased to return to the village to take care of the family left behind. It is also a chance to discuss other matters relating to the future and politics; national security issues dominated the discussion among the dignitaries.

For the AT, it was a moment to raise the hopes of the people, who had looked to the Chaminuka for prosperity and progress. It was also an occasion to design and implement a strategy to fend off the intruders. There is a Shona proverb, which says that the police station cannot be closed because a policeman has died. Other officers can be transferred or recruited to fill the vacancy. The AT felt that work had to continue. It was responsible for steering the resistance and planning the defense of a great nation. They represented Great Zimbabwe in the sense that the founding fathers, the Murenga and Mutota, were typical imperialists. They were responsible for annexing many ethnic groups, including the Machawa, Majindwi, Masena, Mavenda, Machikunda, and Mavemba. All who lived in the Upper, Middle, and Lower Zambezi Valley became members of the Rozvi.

The AT had a much more difficult task at hand. It had to create, diffuse, and distribute a call to war. The Pasipamire wake proved to be the best forum for doing this. Nehanda Charwe had never experienced war. However, the Gombwe referred to as Mbuya Nehanda had amassed a wealth of experience, beginning at the end of the 14th century in fights with the Portuguese. Most people could not tell whether it was the Gombwe spirit speaking or making decisions or Nehanda Charwe. However, the demise of Pasipamire left the defense of the nation to the AT forum, guided by Mbuya Nehanda. He had led the vanguard against Ndebele and Nguni intrusions into the interior. The Ndebele changed their strategy to cattle rustling and kidnaping women and children. They wanted to conquer the Shonaland; the two kings Mzilikazi and

Lobengula ended their reigns disappointed. They were the last of the Matabele and Nguni.

Mbuya Nehanda was very positive about the future, despite knowing that she herself faced a cruel death. She believed that all Mutapa subjects had to help defend the motherland. Her main worry was the lack of appropriate fighting technology. To compensate, the AT developed a positive psychology based on the RTR. Nehanda told communities and villagers that Mwari would turn the knee-less people's bullets into water. She knew this would not really happen, but the story enabled the AT to recruit thousands of warriors. However, there was no way to solve the problem of inadequate technology and firepower. The colonists were armed to the teeth with machine guns and self-loading rifles, and had plenty of ammunition and know-how. The AT chaired the proceedings and Mbuya Nehanda was the main spokesperson. After the wake, Nehanda moved on to the next item on the agenda, which was the imminent invasion of the knee-less people; she raised the possibility of forming alliances with the Nguni and Ndebele.

Lobengula ignored Mlimo and Nehanda's advice, signing unauthorized treaties that implicated the rest of the country. At the wake, the national leaders gathered to examine the threats posed by the invasion of the knee-less people and to find a way to revoke Lobengula's illegal deals. The continued Nguni and Ndebele raids had disrupted productivity in the country and the knee-less people had been studying the relationships between the Ndebele and the Shona for almost a decade. Chiefs such as Dambukashamba, Mapondera, Mashonganyika, Nyachuru, and Nyangombe had created paramilitary organizations to buttress their business interests. At the wake, everyone agreed to divert resources to support the resistance. For the first time, the nation had a rudimentary military with a positive attitude, rather than weapons to fight with effectively. Figure 2 shows the structure of the matrix organization of which the Chaminuka was the head of state. His death left the matrix structure disconnected, unable to carry out its functions.

Mbuya Nehanda provided a detailed analysis of the predictions of the oracles. She explained that Zimbabweans would experience hunger, disease, and poverty when their land was taken away to create commercial farms and urban and mining settlements. It was inevitable that the knee-less people would seize the Penhalonga, Chishawasha, Mazowe, and Wedza gold mines. Nehanda was concerned about everything she could see happening in less than five years. The Zimbabwean people were a deeply divided community, in terms of languages and resources, which were unevenly distributed. Murenga Chaminuka, her spiritual father, had united the Rozvi by making the government inseparable from the people's religion. Furthermore, he introduced the totem system of identification, which enabled ethnic groups to differentiate themselves. This made it possible for the Rozvi to understand who they were as a people. It also allowed the Rozvi to seek marriage partners outside their own totem systems, protected from intermarriages with people who could have shared the same DNA. Here we proceed to the discussion led by Mbuya Nehanda:

Mbuya Nehanda welcoming the participants (reconstructed from Solomon Mutswairo (1983) Chaminuka Prophet of Zimbabwe):

(Clapping her hands and slightly bending her knees as a gesture of respect and welcome. She greeted each chief by name and totem as they arrived. The order was not by seniority but affiliation to the Chaminuka). "I want to start by thanking all of the great chiefs of Zimbabwe who are here today to honor King Pasipamire Chaminuka. I salute you all, starting with Paramount Chief Chihuri Simboti Shumba, our son-in-law, followed by Chivaura Mapondera Nematombo, my cousin, and Mhandu Makope Shumba Nechinanga, my uncle and Mhofu Musiyanwa Mashayamombe and lastly my own fathers, Chief Charwe Hwata and Paramount Chief Gwindi Hwata Shayachimwe. We are here to discuss how we can defend ourselves against the Ndebele and white men's invasion. Basically, we are fighting two wars on one front. Last year we lost Pasipamire Chaminuka to Lobengula's warriors, despite him having agreed not to attack us in a truce made in 1860 by Nherera Gwindi. The purpose of this meeting is to see if we can raise and equip an army to fight a war that is fast approaching. I would like to ask you, starting with Paramount Gwindi, how do you propose to defend our turf, Hwata?"

Chief Gwindi Hwata: "Thank you Vachihera." (All Hwata or Mufakose women, married or not, were/are referred to as Vachihera.) "I can give you 1,000 young men to fight the scourge of these white men but you would need to train them to use guns and gunpowder. This is a sophisticated fight. The knee-less are armed with zvigwagwaga (machine guns) and all we have are spears and assegais and a few zvifefe (English made musket rifles). Those soldiers are marksmen and well trained. We need first to source comparable arms and then train our commandos. Chivaura has brought a hundred of his commandos and they have been supplying all the game meat we have roasted here each day since we started the Chaminuka wake last week. I will make a similar commitment if we can know at the end of our discussion how we are going to pay for these arms and most importantly how we propose getting to South Africa to source the armory. How can we disguise ourselves lest we meet other white men who are friendly to the knee-less English?"

Nehanda: "Thank you, I will make a mental note of that. How about you Nyachuru?"

Chihuri Nyachuru:

Nyachuru was related to Mutapa emperor, and his ancestors were Mutsahuni, Negomo Chirisamhuru (1560–1589) and Gatsi Rusere (1589–1623) (Stewart, 1989). Oral history suggested that Mutsahuni's brothers were Mutoko, Nerwande, Tangwena, and Chinenguwo. Nyachuru was a great grandson of Mutsahuni, who had settled in the Mazowe Valley before the Hwata and Rozvi Empire in 1680 (Mupepi, 2015). It was his turn to speak:

"Thank you Ambhuya (mother-in-law). You are my sister-in-law as well as Ambhuya on the other hand" (Chihuri's first wife was born a Hwata, presumably from Hwayerera Village or thereabouts. However, Chihuri Nyachuru liked to show off his prowess in all he did.) He continued: "I can make a commitment of 1,000 fully armed men. But they will need to be trained, this is not a conventional fight. It is a hide-and-seek fight preferably in the mountains and over the hills. There is a route to Beira via Dande that can be used to get there. The Portuguese can do business with us if we can get to their trading stations without being spotted by the BSAC police. The police are like hyenas following everyone, including those who go hunting to raise food for their families. The Portuguese seem to have gotten a raw deal from the English and I'm positive they will be more than willing to help us. But we would need wagonloads of ivory and gold. I have half each of those loads. We were blessed this past six months. We harvested almost fifty tons of ivory and another 20 tons of corn and sufficient gold-dust to sink a Portuguese caravel."

Chingayira: "Ah, I can contribute the same quantities as those pledged by Nyachuru. If Nyachuru's wagons can pass through my place at Masekesa, we can make a convoy into Beira. I know a Portuguese by the name of Machado who will be able to make the most in our favor. It means Nyachuru's wagons must pass through Masekesa and I will take the lead to Beira via Tete."

Chihuri Nyachuru: "Thank you Nyati, you are great."

Chingayira: "You are welcome, Shumba."

Nehanda: (Emphasizing the Mukwasha (son-in-law) relationship to warrant greater commitment from Shumba). "Thank you Mukwasha, I do appreciate that very much. I would like to go to you, Nematombo Chivaura Mapondera."

Mapondera:

Mapondera was a great orator and fighter, who was able to use rifles, as well as spears and bows and arrows. He was related to Rozvi kings, such as Negomo Chirisamhuru (1560–

1589). He could speak for hours and was very committed to contributing to this struggle, which he was already fighting, alongside two allies from Lower Zambezi Valley, Gumbeze, and Dambukashamba (Beach, 1984).

"I'm ready even now to fight the white men who come here to exploit my people. They have been capturing my people and taking them for slavery and those innocent villagers never returned. The Portuguese had been longing to run this country since the late 14th century. My ancestors have refused to allow that to happen. I will join Shumba with two similar wagon-loads. I will have at least 5,000 trained commandos. I want to give this knee-less lunatic who thinks he is Mwari's gift to Africa hell. I will not give up my Rozvi heritage for some deteriorating white man. When we dismiss here I will be getting my commandos all ready and will assign my wagons to join up with those coming from Chihuri across the Mwenje River."

Gombwe Goredema interjecting:

"It is very true we have kept the Portuguese at bay, outside both the Mutapa and Rozvi Empire. But we lost Mavinga when they accessed the north-western part of the country and Chief Bunde was overcome by a garrison invasion. We want to stop all of that now. I see a great fight coming soon. I will be there fighting side by side with our gallant freedom fighters."

Gombwe Changamire Mutsahuni:

"Great Chiefs, I do not see a clear win," continued Changamire Mutsahuni. He was the Gombwe of the Shumba dynasty in the Mazowe area, with his headquarters located where the Mazowe Dam is today. "There can be a victory only if the Ndebele can agree to fight with us and not against us. Umkulu Mlimo is attempting to convince Lobengula to join forces with us but Rhodes is full of tricks. But Lobenguala declined advice from the Prophet Mlimo and the commander of the most treacherous Ndebele regiment, the Umbembesi.

Mzlikazi, Lobengula's father, was advised successfully by Umlimo, who came from the Njerere community in the Matopos Hills. Lobengula failed to take heed of the wisdom offered by Mlimo and Nehanda Charwe. He has built a dream upon false promises. He believes that Rhodes will make those dreams come true. Rumor has it that he promised Lobengula a speedboat, which he says he needs to patrol the Zambezi River policing the Shona. This is the joke of the century. He reckons Rhodes will give him that speedboat to cruise on the Zambezi River. The sad part of this is that he will commit suicide eventually. At this juncture, Mbuya was prophesizing events that would occur in 1894. The present looked great for Lobengula but the future was really grim for the nation of the Ndebele."

Selous (1967) has argued that the Umlimo underestimated the firepower of the BSAC. Although Lobengula was given the same Maxim machine guns, he did not have a continuous supply of ammunition to engage the enemy. The armorer of the BSAC had indicated that he had at least 300 Maxim guns, 1.5 million rounds of ammunition, and more than 500 Martini-Henry rifles.

As for Lobengula, Gombwe Mutsahuni went on, "the BSAC will give him the machine guns and automatic rifles and all the weaponry to engage in a war but he will lose because not all the impis can use fighting technology such as the Maxim guns, and Winchester and Martini-Henry rifles. Furthermore, Lobengula will require ammo which can only be sourced from the Afrikaners at Enkeldoorn and in South Africa.

But, as we are now discussing this, I'm ready to give the war command under Chisikana Nyanda about one zvurugumi rakapetwa kagumi of gold (1,000 nuggets of gold) for the war effort."

Mutsahuni was wealthy in many respects. He was an entrepreneur who traded with the Portuguese Arabs and Indians.

Nehanda: "That's why they call you a champion, Mutsahuni. We appreciate what you do for our community. I know our forefather, the Chaminuka, and others are watching over us and will give us able sons to defend our turf."

As she was talking, other Shona chiefs arrived. These were Chingayira Nyamanhindi Makoni, Nhohwe, Mutoko, Mangwende, Charumbira, Chinenguwo Shumba, Mbare Shumba, Swosve and the Princes Nyangombe Swosve and Madzivanyika Swosve, Dokora Mavhirivi, Mutasa, Mutambara, Tangwena, and Zimunya. All came from the east and eastern highlands, the central plateau, the Zambezi Valley, and south of Mutsahuni's Pagomba. They had all been invited to the great indaba or meeting.

All broke out into a chant with the following lyrics:

"Chokwadi tirikutambura variMuchitwi
Zwambwa zvefodya tauya nazvo vakuriwe
Chokwadi tirikutambura vakare vepasi
Pwere dzese dziripano variMuchitwi umo
Ho ho ho chokwadi tirikutambura nenzara

Hurwere hwawanda whatisingazive
Hwawa taparutsa zvikari zvenyu zviripo
Hwawa whemasahwira enyu uripo
Chokwadi tirikutambura vakare vepasi
Ho ho ho chokwadi tirikutambura varimuchitwi umo"

The last time there was such a meeting was when the Ndebele and Nguni attacks were escalating in the early 1840s. None of the current chiefs had attended that early gathering. There was no Ndebele representation. Lobengula had been on a cloud, dreaming of the conquest of the century, which was the envy of his cousins across the Limpopo River, the Zulu. After the chant, Nehanda, as the master of ceremony, continued.

Nehanda: "I welcome you all my lords, please take a pew on the logs and make yourselves comfortable. I apologize that we have to make do with whatever we can find outdoors to make seats. The vahera are preparing roast beef and corn on the cob, which will be ready in an hour or so. We have a maburo drink (made of millet that is not allowed to ferment) and we will pass that around for you to quench your thirst. Unfortunately, we will have nothing alcoholic until these deliberations are over. We concluded the wake rituals for the Chaminuka yesterday and all went well. For only an hour or so, we have been discussing the need to raise the resources necessary to fight the knee-less people. The reason we called you together is that we need the support of all Zimbabweans to fight the Ndebele, Nguni, and now the white men. There is a need for us to bring our resources together to form a national vanguard. It is a year now since the Ndebele murdered Pasipamire and, under that pretext, declared that they had conquered Great Zimbabwe in its entirety. The white men (knee-less people) and the Ndebele and Nguni are all armed to the teeth with automatic rifles and none of us have any comparable weapons to resist this invasion. If I may say, when you walked in, Gombwe Mutsahuni had just pledged a thousand commandos whom he was going to equip as soon as possible. He is working with Gumboreshumba Kagubi to make arrangements to send a wagonload of gold to Piet Enkeldoorn at his farm near Chivhu to purchase automatic rifles and ammunition. Another wagonload will be dispatched to Beira via Masekesa and Chingayira Makoni will source that consignment from his trading partners, who go by the names of Guveya and Machado. As you know, the Boers and English do not see eye-to-eye. Therefore, we believe our plan will succeed."

Mangwende: "We thank vaNyachuru for that great offer. I will supply at least a thousand cattle to be slaughtered and the meat will be dried and kept by the villagers, who will be responsible for the logistics. We have never been challenged like this in our states. The Portuguese attempted to control our business in the sixteenth century and failed due to the strategy developed by the Gombwe Nyamhike."

Chief Magwende realized that the Gombwe in his court, referred to as Nyamita, had repeated Nehanda Charwe. It dawned on him that, in the RTR, a spirit could possess two or three individuals in different places at the same time. He had travelled with the Gombwe Nyamita from Dombotombo, where his kraal was. In Gelfund (1959), Nyamita and Vanyanezuva were the Magombwe representing the Murehwa region. In the Seke Villages, Vanyakasikana was the Gombwe Nehanda Nyakasikana. In Hwedza, the Chaminuka Gombwe was Dzivaidema, while in the Madziwa and Dande regions, Magombwe Dzivaguru and Nehoreka were the highest angels. Their responsibilities included rain-making, healing the sick, and warning the community of any imminent disaster. A fore-warned community was a fore-armed community.

Nehanda: "Thank you vaMangwende. We appreciate your commitment to Great Zimbabwe."

Chingayira Makoni: "I would like to thank you all, Madzishe, for everything you do for our great country. I am here today, accompanied by my great counselors Sakureba and Nyarutswa, all the way from Dendzo in the foothills of the Nyanga Mountains. I say that we in Dendzo have seen this threat before when the Portuguese were trying to colonize the entire group of Mutapa states."

According to Newitt (1995), the Portuguese did business with the Mutapa kings from the fifteenth century onwards. Makoni's grandfather was a ruler (a Chaminuka or a Chikanga). He was engaged in the goldmarket places or fairs as they were known in that part of the world. They were established in the Eastern highlands at Masekesa, Machipanda, Tete, and Beira by the Portuguese and Dutch traders

The rest of the delegation interjected to praise a king known affectionately among the people by his totem, Nyati, a buffalo. They praised this Eastern Highland king by clapping their hands loudly. It is a custom in the Shona speaking community to show appreciation by clapping hands. It is a custom that has survived to the present day. Clapping is often used to praise the ancestor spirits and to show respect. The Shona fraternity had gathered to re-create itself, in preparation for the great task that lay ahead. Shona society had merged with the VaMaungwe, VaBudya, and many others, to create a culturally strong Zimbabwean citizenry. This time it was going to be tested. The Magombwe already knew what the outcome would be: losing the land to the knee-less white people. According to the oracles of Pasipamire Chaminuka, it was going to take a hundred years for Zimbabweans to regain self-rule. The oracle also stated that thousands of Zimbabweans would perish in the Armageddon.

The deliberations came to an end after nearly ten days. At exactly the same time, Cecil Rhodes and the European nations were planning their conquest of Africa. The invasion continued unabated until 1885, as planned. Lobengula had signed the treacherous Charles Rudd Treaty of 1884, which he did not understand any of the implications of. This issue had been discussed at length at Chaminuka's wake.

Reports from the Berlin conference offered a different outlook on Africa, complete with new boundaries. The colonists were putting into action their ambitions to colonize Africa. Zambia and Zimbabwe were named Southern and Northern Rhodesia. Paramount Chief Lewanika had sought Queen Victoria's protection, which led to the internal region within Zambia becoming known as the British Barotseland Protectorate of Central Africa (1900–1964). The list of British protected territories included Bechuanaland Protetorate (1884–1966), Basutholand (1884–1966), the East Africa Protectorate (1895–1920), the Gambia Protectorate (1894–1965), the Kenya Protectorate (1920–1963), the Northern Nigeria Protectorate (1900–1914), Northern Rhodesia (1924–1964), the Northern Territories of the Gold Coast (1902–1957), the Nyasaland Protectorate (1893–1964), the Sierra Leone Protectorate (1896–1961), the Southern Nigeria Protectorate (1902–1968), the Uganda Protectorate (1894–1962), the Walvis Bay Protectorate (1878–1884) and the Sultanate of Zanzibar Protectorate (1890–1963).

A protectorate was a territory that was not formally annexed but in which, by treaty, grant, or other lawful means, the Crown had ultimate power and jurisdiction. Some British colonies, such as Zimbabwe, were ruled by the BSAC through the royal charter granted to it by Queen Victoria in 1889. Others were ruled by local rulers who were supervised behind the scenes by British advisors in Whitehall.

No Mutapa state rulers or empires within the fluid Munhumutapa states wanted to be colonized apart from King Lewanika of the Barotseland, King Khama of Bechuanaland, and King Karonga of Maravi, who agreed to the creation of the Nyasaland Protectorate (1892–1964). The BSAC began to administer the newly acquired territory on January 1, 1892.

In Nyasaland, the traditional chiefs felt protected from the Nguni raiders crossing the lower Sabi, Limpopo, Zambezi, and Shire rivers to steal cattle, and kidnap children and women. However, the chiefs lost much of their communal land soon after the BSAC had taken over (Pike, 1969). The Reverend John Chilembwe argued that British legislation favored the colonist and advocated for people to uprise against the colonial state of Nyasaland. Chilembwe organized the equivalent of the Chimurenga, known in the Chewa Language as the Chimukwembe, to fight British imperialism in Nyasaland. The Chimukwembe used hit-and-run tactics to attack the sparsely settled European farmers in the Mlanje and Shire Valley regions (Joon-Hai Lee, 2005). The Malawi Barotseland and Bechuanaland protectorates varied in how they were administered but all recognized traditional authorities through the lens of the Native Commissioner. After the death of the Chaminuka, these traditional authorities never had another such opportunity to meet and discuss the way forward.

The way back home

The chiefs began the trek back to their territories to start procuring the items they had volunteered to provide. Chiefs Nyachuru, Hwayerera, Chiriseri, Masembura, Hwata, and the others did not live far from Pagomba. Others, such as Mutambara and Tangwena, had far to go. Their territories, including Makope, Mapondera, Dokora, Mutoko, and others, overlapped with the proposed Portuguese East Africa colony.

The defense issue had been discussed fully and each chief and authority had been assigned specific jobs to do. Mapondera Dambukashamba, Mashayamombe Nyachuru, and Nyangombwe were already fighting the Portuguese Company in the Zambezi Valley and receiving technical assistance from Afrikaners who disliked the Dutch royal family because they had been let down by their own King William 1 (1772–1843) of the Netherlands, resulting in the loss of Kaap Stud. They were let down in 1843 when the Boer Republic of Natal (1838–1843) was annexed by Great Britain, during the reign of the same king.

On the way home, Chihuri Nyachuru was thinking about how he was going to train and arm the soldiers he had pledged. He realized that it would not be a cheap exercise. One rifle was worth 5lb of gold dust at that time. Gunpowder was sold in ounces and pounds, like gold. Nyachuru had a gold mine near the Masviswa Hills. He had not signed any treaties with foreigners. He mined the gold and usually made three trips each month to trade with the Portuguese at Dande or trekked further downstream of the Zambezi at Zumbo on the confluence of the Mazowe and Zambezi rivers. He was thinking about how his next consignment could be used to acquire the much-needed arsenal to destroy the settlers. This meant that he had to be there in person to ensure the best deals.

Paramount Chief Hwata Gwindi remained behind, checking with his sons and elders to establish the strength of the Hwata, in terms of manpower and weaponry. His gold mines included Shamva, Mazowe, and Chishawasha (now the Arcturus Mine). His army was similar to most in the region; it had a limited capacity, based on bows and arrows, spears, assegais, and a few musket rifles (which were manufactured in England; the Portuguese were merely middlemen). Troops of archers operated in thickets on the hills and mountains, where machine guns were not effective. It dawned on some of the chiefs that the conflict was going to be a walkover for the colonists. However, no single chief was willing to surrender before the battle had even started. The colonists had superior firepower; they were a paramilitary organization either attached to the British Army or the British South Africa Company. Clearly, possessing the right technology at the right time would be decisive for the British colonists.

The period of 1885–1889 was one of triumph for the British colonists. The British South Africa Company was founded on the strength of the Royal Charter signed by Queen Victoria in 1889. Cecil Rhodes and Alfred Beit floated their company, the British South Africa Company (BSAC) on the London and Johannesburg stock exchanges. The company received recognition akin to that of the British East India Company. Its first directors included the Duke of Abercorn, Rhodes himself, and the South African financier, Alfred Beit. Rhodes hoped that the BSAC would promote colonization and economic development across much of southern Africa, through a network of subsidiaries, affiliations, and agents. According to Galbraith (1974), Rhodes focused on the area south of the Zambezi, in Zimbabwe and the coastal areas to its east, from which he believed the Portuguese could be removed by payment or force, as well as the Transvaal, which he hoped would return to British control.

The First Chimurenga failed in the sense that the British prevailed, but it was a huge success for the descendants of the Rozvi, who were able to build on the past to re-engage and win.

Chapter 3 provides an overview of how the Pioneer Column journeyed from Bechuanaland British Protectorate to Zimbabwe, and how the missionaries got to work before they even settled down.

Chapter Three
The Pioneer Column

The party at the Pagomba dispersed with less fanfare than they had arrived with. When the dignitaries arrived, there had been greetings and ululations led by Mbuya Nehanda and the VaChihera women. Each arriving chief and his entourage were greeted by totem. Mbuya Nehanda was told which welcome protocols to follow by the scouts, who met the visitors and led them to the Pagomba venue. The meeting went well, and it seemed as if the Chaminuka had only recently passed away.

Then the Pioneer Column arrived, a crack commando group disguised as gold prospectors, elephant hunters, and missionaries. They all looked as if they had no limbs: they were the knee-less white people the oracles had warned about (see diagram 3 and 7)

Diagram 7: Frank Johnson leads the Pioneers for a fistful of dollars (Zimbabwe National Archives, 2014)

The chiefs and other dignitaries had returned to their homes. Mbuya Nehanda and her lieutenants had gone up to the hideout in the Shavarunzi caves. The question was: how could communities defend themselves against British aggression? News travelled far and wide via a network of villages, and cowgirls and cowboys who met in the pastures between communities and villages. The local spiritual mediums, chiefs, and elders were part of a network that extended to Mbuya Nehanda through the RTR. Nyachuru and Mapondera had returned to Masviswa Ndire and the Nyota Hills, some 15 miles northwards. They were still discussing the Chaminuka wake. The topic that filled their minds was the imminent invasion by the knee-less people from Europe (see diagram 2). None of the chiefs had been outside the Mutapa states. The only white people they had seen were Frederick Selous, Henry Hartley, Thomas Baines, elephant hunters, and a few Portuguese, who entered the plateau by way of the

Musengezi and Mazowe rivers by sailing upstream on the Zambezi River. These were traders who were based at Dande, Mamvuradonha, Masekesa, and Tete. There were numerous Portuguese traders, including viceroys stationed at Beira as representatives of the Portuguese trading companies and government. In diagram 8, the Pioneer Column is illustrated crossing the Runde River heading towards Fort Victoria (now Masvingo).

Diagram 8: Negotiating the Runde River heading for Fort Victoria

European perceptions of Zimbabweans varied. They were influenced by what their friends, the Matabele, told them about the Rozvi, who became the Shona community of today. The Shona evolved out of the Rozvi, who were previously a cluster of smaller ethnic groups that lived on the plateau, in the middle and lower Zambezi, and in the Sabi and Limpopo river valleys, including the Pungwe and Gonarezhou basins. These communities were deeply divided before the reign of Emperor Nyatsimba Mutota (1430–1450). He began a unification process through which the Rozvi Traditional Religion (RTR) became the fabric and foundation for all the ethnic groups. Many communities from all over southern central Africa were re-constituted to become the Rozvi. When the Pioneer Column arrived, they were following in the sixteenth century footsteps of Father Goncalo da Silveira (1526–1561) who had experiences leading to his martyrdom February 15, 1561.

Following in the footsteps

Father (Fr) Goncalo da Silveira, the Society's first martyr on the African continent, was born in Almeria, near Lisbon, Portugal. He was the tenth child of the Count of Sortelha and was brought up for a position in the royal court. He studied at Coimbra and was at the university when Fr Simon Rodrigues and his Jesuit companions came to establish a college at Coimbra and through his acquaintance with the Jesuits, he entered the Society in 1543, been newly converted by Portuguese traders. Fr Silveira, another priest and a brother arrived in Mozambique in February 1560 and worked their way to Otongue where Gamba lived two months later. After minimal instruction, Gamba and his court and 500 others were converted and Father Silveira was so encouraged that he had dreams of converting southern and central Africa and the easiest way to do so was to convert southern Africa's most powerful king—King Munhumutapa—whose capital was 100 miles north of the Zambezi River in Zimbabwe.

Fr Silveira prepared hard for his new mission and had walked hundreds of miles to reach his destination. Before he left he baptized 50 neophytes, heard the confessions of the Portuguese whom he had summoned and entrusted his Mass equipment to them, keeping only a crucifix for himself.

Father Goncelo da Silveira

With the help of Antonio Caiado as intermediary, a Portuguese who was much trusted by the Munhumutapa. Fr Silveira finally arrived at the king's village on December 26, 1560. There he met Chirisamhuru Negomo, the young local chief who was newly made "the golden king" because gold had been discovered in his territory. Chirisamhuru was uncivilized and uncultured and within 3 weeks Chirisamhuru and his people were non-believers of the Teachings of Christ because no one had taught them about Christianity. Fr Silveira taught everyone in the king's court and baptized 300 individuals. The story is told about how the Arabs who had been courting the king were so jealousy of the success of Christianity and framed Fr Silveira as a spy and sorcerer. When the king heard this, he took the story's accuracy prima facie and ordered Fr Silveira's death.

The Arabs were afraid that they were going to lose the king's lucrative trade. That night just before he retired, he told Caiado he was ready to die for doing the right thing. He knew that the Muslim had poisoned the king's mind. But he had forgiven the king and his mother who were all young who had been deceived by the Arabs. Caiado then instructed 2 of his servants to remain with Fr Silveira throughout the night while he prepared to bury Fr Silveira. Today there is a thriving Silveira Mission outside Harare.

Zimbabwe's First Martyr Bernard Mizeki

The story of the First Martyr Bernard Mizeki is told through the First Bishop of Mashonaland George Wyndham Knight-Bruce who arrived as part of the Pioneer Column missionary contingent in 1890, Zvobgo (2009), Reynolds (2011), and Noll & Nystrom (2011), and others.

In Noll and Nystrom (2011) Bernard Mizeki was converted into Christianity through the work of Cowley Father's mission and studying the bible in the night school organized by German missionary Baroness Paula Dorothea von Blomberg in South Africa. He and five others were some of the first converts, baptized in St. Philip's Mission, Sir Lowry Road, on 7 March 1886. Shortly thereafter, the 25-year-old Bernard started work at St. Columba's Hostel, which was run by the missionaries for African men. After working for a while was sent to Zonnebloem College to train as a catechist. When he qualified in January 1891 Bernard left South Africa to accompany the new missionary Bishop of Mashonaland, George Wyndham Knight-Bruce, as a lay catechist and medical worker among the Shona people in Southern Rhodesia (Noll and Nystrom, 2011).

Zvobgo (2011) suggested that Mizeki was initially well received by the people under Chiefs Mangwende and Nhohwe. He settled in the kraal of Mungate Mangwende. Bernard built his home there, and gained a reputation as a teacher. He took children who wanted to learn into his home to teach them the gospel, as well as traveled around the countryside, and to the bishop's residence in Umtali to help with translations and preparing mass and baptisms. In Zvobgo (2009), Mizeki was at loggerhead with the ATR or Shona Traditional Religion on matters about polygamous marriages and rituals that encouraged men to drink beer. Drunkenness was a social problem and Mizeki preached about the evils of alcohol and marrying multiple wives.

Diagram 8: Catechist Bernard Mizeki Spreading the Gospel in Chief Mangwende villages

In March 1896, Mizeki married Mutwa who was baptized as Lily who was an orphaned granddaughter of the Mangwende and a Christian convert. African Anglican priest Rev. Hezekiah Mtobi, recently arrived from Grahamstown, South Africa led the ceremony (Noll and Nystrom (2011). Mizeki was thus admitted into the Mangwende kinship network, which some resented.

With the Mangwende's permission, Mizeki moved his growing community (several families, as well as young boys he was entrusted to teach), about two miles at Dombotombo. They resettled across the river in a fertile area with a spring, but also near a sacred grove which was believed to be inhabited by spirits of the tribe's ancestral lions. These were shrines protected by Magombwe Nyamita and Nyanezuva who were of the same ranks with Nehanda Charwe in the RTR (Gelfund, 1959). Rather than make offerings to such spirits, Mizeki made the sign of the cross in the air, and carved crosses on some of the trees, and later felled some trees while preparing a field to plant wheat (Noll and Nystrom, 2011). Mizeki made enemies with the adherences of the RTR such as Chiefs Mangwende and Nhohwe who were neighbors. Both had attended the Chaminuka wake because their chiefdoms were granted by the Chaminuka. The things that offended these traditional authorities which Mizeki taught were polygamous marriages, snorting snuff tobacco, and beer drinking.

On the night of 18 June 1896, Mizeki was dragged from his home and stabbed with a short spear. The arrowhead of the spear could have been stained with a poison as was the practice in those days. However, Mutwa his wife, found him still alive and went for help. She and others reported seeing a great white light all over that place, and a loud noise "like many wings of great birds". Bernard's body had disappeared by their return. Muchemwa, a son of the Mangwende and an ally of the Magombwe, was later found responsible for Bernard's murder as well as the destruction of the mission settlement there.

Bernard Mizeki's work among the Shona bore fruit, beyond the posthumous daughter Mutwa bore. After long years of mission work in Mashonaland, the first Shona convert to be baptized was one of the young men whom Mizeki had taught: John Kapuya. John was baptized only a month after Mizeki's death, on 18 July 1896. In 1899, a white Anglican priest returned to the area, and re-established the mission, as well as a school. Today, Bernard Mizeki College stands close to where he lived, and the Mangwende's kraal, above the village, is crowned with a large cross to commemorate Mizeki (Zvobgo, 2009).

In the 1930s, a chapel was built on the site of Mizeki's martyrdom, and consecrated in a great ceremony in June 1938. On the fiftieth anniversary of his death in 1946, an even larger celebration was held, attended by Mutwa and their daughter, and included a proclamation issued by the Governor of Southern Rhodesia Sir Campbell Tait (1886–1946).

Mizeki is honored with a feast day on the liturgical calendar of the Episcopal Church (USA) on 18 June

(Reynolds, 2007). His martyrdom is a commemoration in the Common Worship of the Church of England. The Anglican Church of Southern Africa commemorates Mizeki in its Calendar of commemorations and other special days on the 18th day of June each year (Robert, 2011). The Anglican Church of Canada has a Memorial for Mizeki on this date (Reynolds, 2007).

In 1973, a church serving mostly Xhosa migrant workers, was dedicated to Bernard Mizeki in Paarl, South Africa. At the same time the Bernard Mizeki Guild was established for Anglican laymen who sought a more intense, African-style worship life including all-night prayer vigils, healing, and sharing of dreams (Ranger, 1987).

Composed largely of Xhosa-speaking migrant workers, Bernard Mizeki Guilds spread across South Africa. Guild members wear purple waistcoats, a special badge. Anglican migrant workers could identify with Bernard Mizeki as a fellow migrant who sacrificed himself for Christ. Members of the guild aspire to make the annual pilgrimage to the Mizeki festival in Zimbabwe (Ranger, 1987).

The First Bishop of Mashonaland G. W. H. Knight-Bruce

Knight-Bruce established the Anglican Church in Zimbabwe starting with Chief Mutasa community in the Eastern Highlands. He founded St. Augustine, St. Faith, and St. David's mission schools for boys and girls. In Marondera the Bernard Mizeki College was founded long after the teacher Knight-Bruce and student Mizeki had both passed on. In Hwedza district Bishop Knight-Bruce was invited into the home of Paramount Chief Madzivanyika and converted his son Chief Goto. The first chapel was built at Goto's village or kraal and was subsequently followed by Mount St. Anne's Mission. Frederick Selous whilst collecting cartographic information had enlisted the services of Paramount Chief Madzivanyika's son, Prince Chipiro as a guide (Selous, 1969). Knight-Bruce's mission into Zimbabwe started in 1888. In 1892 he wrote the following in his diary:

When I read the proof-sheets of the extracts of my Journal for 1891, I felt that the scanty allusions to the spiritual aspect of the work might be misunderstood; but as the Journal consists mainly of notes written at camp fires or during the intervals of travelling, little appears except what was necessary to recall the events of the day. There was little time to record conversations with chiefs and people, interesting though they were. I consider that our Heavenly Father's intention that the Gospel should be preached to the Mashona has been so plainly shown by His leadings during the late years, and that His blessing on the work, when begun, has been so continuous, that any intermittent allusions to either would rather obscure the great end to which day after day material work was tending.

Some of the chiefs he spoke to in 1890s were Chipuriro where he opened as mission station, he named St. Phillips and in much later years Nymhondoro Secondary School was established in Lower Zambezi Valley. Some of the revelations of those wishes had been shown in the priceless work of Fr Goncalo da Silveira and Catechist Mizeki. Bishop Knight-Bruce left to seek medical treatment in England where he died from Malaria fever in 1896. The Anglican Church has grown from strength to strength in a country where change happens all the time.

The Salvation Army Enterprise Wagon

The story of the Salvation Army Pioneers is drawn from Nyandoro (1993), Schmidt (1992), Selous (1899) [1969], and Alderson (1896) [2017], among many others. The Salvation Army was there in 1890 at the beginning of a country later named Southern Rhodesia. As Cecil Rhodes's plans to expand the British Empire grew, the Salvation Army also expanded its operations into Northern Rhodesia (Zambia) and Nyasaland (Malawi). The Salvation Army's special wagon named the *Enterprise* drawn by a span of 18 heifers, was a project that took time to build and was only ready in March 1891. The first officers to arrive in Zimbabwe on the wagon where Captain and Mrs. Pascoe Captain David Crook a former seaman who sought Christ towards the end of his many sea voyages, Edward Cass who came from Zululand Natal, Captain Bob Scott, Edgar Mahon, and Theodore Searle. Kimberly and Port Elizabeth were the venues selected for sending off this adventure whose goal was to win Africans for Jesus Christ. The journey debuted April 6, 1891 from Kimberly, Transvaal, South Africa.

Figure 3: Doing the most good, all the time

Mishack Nyandoro writing in his book entitled: A Flame of Sacred Love: The Salvation Army in Zimbabwe 1890–1991 (1993), recognized that the London Missionary Society which had sent Robert Moffat in 1859 had been operating around kwaBulawayo for a while. The Gospel was not new among the locals despite their liking of rustling cattle and kidnapping women and children from the Shona communities (Selous, 1969). Nyandoro listed the first Church organization (dates of arrival in brackets) in the country as the Jesuits (1560) followed by the Anglicans and Catholics (1890) American Board of Commissioners for Foreign Missions

140

(1893), Seventh Day Adventists (1895), American Methodist Episcopal (United Methodist) (1896), Brethren in Christ (1897) and South African General Mission (1897).

The Salvation Army (Army) is positively associated in establishing the first Christian community in Zimbabwe. The Army arrived in Salisbury then, November 18, 1891 on their ox-drawn wagon named *Enterprise.* Some of the party members were sick with fever and had not eaten a decent meal since they left Kimberly in March. Cecil Rhodes met the new arrivals and gave them a farm which they named Pearson Farm. Rhodes also instructed the Company to allocate the Salvation Army a business stand on Montague Avenue. Work to build a chapel started immediately following the Anglicans and Catholics who had put up their first chapels on the corners of Union and Second Streets and Fourth Street and Herbert Chitepo Avenue. The Montague property was ready to build on it had been serviced by the public works department of the Company. In the following year, the Army began work on the Pearson Farm. The people who had lived in the area and had been moved to or were being moved to the newly created African Reserves at Chiweshe, Chipuriro, Madziwa, Masembura, Chiriseri, Domboshawa, Chikwaka and many others within a radius of a hundred miles from the Salisbury Post Office then.

The work of the Army was very interesting to the Africans but the problem of language stopped the work from taking off the ground until a young boy by the name of Zebedia Munjaranji was converted to be a Salvation Army soldier. Munjaranji came from Karoi and was gifted at learning the English Language very fast. The Army took him and sent him to Howard Institute. Students nicknamed him *Muturikiri Mukuru* implying Senior Translator. Munjaranji was born in Masembura village under Chief Chiriseri of the Hwata dynasty. He left home to find work at the newly created Salvation Army Pearson Farm. He was one of the first students of Major Leonard Kirby and Major Kunzvi-Nyandoro (whose father was working with Mbuya Nehanda in the resistance). The two officers and forty students moved from Pearson Farm to Paramount Chief Nyachuru who had recently relocated from where the Mazowe Dam is today to land between Mwenje and Save Rivers. Here the Salvation Army had been allocated 100 acres to build a mission station consisting of a primary school, teachers' training college, vocational school for nurses, and hospital. Munjaranji translated the hymn books and bible from English to Shona Languages. He also translated English texts into the Shona Language to make lessons more understood. He had an excellent comprehension of Nyanja, Ndebele, and Chichewa Languages enabling the Army to open the Chikankata Mission in Northern Rhodesia.

During the pioneer days, the work of the Army was very difficult to conduct if one was an African. In the communities surrounding Howard Institute, Pearson Farm, Bradley Institute, and Usher Institute, adherents of the traditional practices expected African students to uphold the ATR. At the same time the Churches expected students from their school systems to embrace the teachings of Christ and spread the Gospel among members of their communities. During that time, the Hwata and Shumba communities attended all-night ancestor veneration at Shavarunzi, Ndire, and Masviswa hills under the directions of Masvikiro Gutsa and Ganyire. To resist the existence of the ancestral spirits and the powers invested in the Svikiro or Medium could result in serious misfortune. The Army was also strategic in its recruitment, it recruited students from parents who were staunchest believers of the Shona Traditional Religion such as:

Major Misheck Nyandoro (Nyandoro-Kunzwi)
Major Ben Mohambe
Major David Muchenje
Major Chitsvatsva (Nyachuru)
Major Chisuvi (Nyachuru)
Major Syrus Kunaka Soko (Nyangombe Svoswe)
Brigadier Nathan Mushaninga
Brigadier Mbeva
Major Joseph Nhari (Nyachuru Corp)

Major Paul Shumba Nyachuru
(Granduncle to writer)
Major Ben Gwindi (Paramount Chief Gwindi Hwata (a relation to Nehanda)
Captain Lazarus Rusere Mudyiwa Nyachuru
Major Chinyemba Shava (Mufakose, a relation to Nehanda)
Major Elijah and Mrs. Gertrude Nyangombe Soko Mutswairo (Grandparents to writer)
Major and Mrs. Kunzwi-Shava Dutiro (Gombwe Dutiro)

Some of the first soldiers drawn from the first corps in Harare other places were:

Mrs. Mabel Solomon (Mbare Citadel)
Mr. Bob Garande (Makope Village)
Corp Sargent Major William Yafele (Chinyika, Goromonzi)
Guyson Kuruneri (Bandleader Chinyika, Goromonzi)
Shadreck Mbirimi (Corp Sargent Major Mbare Citadel)
Jotham Chidavayenzi (Envoy, Nyachuru)
Major Wilson Gore (Chiweshe)
Major Shadreck Guyo (Chiweshe)
Major Washington Njiri (Mhondoro)
Major Josiah Muchapondwa (Chiweshe)
Major Christopher Mashayamombwe (Mhondoro)
Major Robias Zinyama (Seke)
Brigadier Mazhindu (Mt. Darwin)
Brigadier Newton Marongedza

There were many converts to the Salvation Army which has remained the Church of choice in Mashonaland Central, Mashonaland East, and Mashonaland West.

The death of Captain Edward Cass

Captain Cass and others were killed by members of the resistance who could have had a hideout in the Shavarunzi Mountains on June 16, 1896. Africans in the entire Mazowe

Valley had been organized by the African Triumvirate comprised of Nehanda Charwe, Gumboreshumba Kagubi, and Mukwati Chaminuka. Many chiefs had sent members of their families to fight to liberate Zimbabwe. The following were some of the princes and princesses:

Nyangombe (Madzivanyika)
Tapfuma (Nyachuru)
Mashayamombe (Mashayamombe)
Muchemwa Mangwende
Chingayira Nyamanhindi Makoni (Makoni)
Chikwaka (Goromonzi Chikwaka)
Nyandoro (Nyandoro-Kunzvi)
Chipuriro (Chinenguwo)
Kadungure Chivaura Mapondera
Gumbeze (Chief Dokora)
Dambukashamba (A Mozambican chiefdom)
Gwindi (Gwindi Hwata)
Mandu (Makope)
And many others.

Captain Cass and his wife Ida were still at the Mazowe Pearson Farm when the chimurenga had erupted. Difficulties and unforeseen hardships had beset all the white community in the Mazowe Valley. Cass was associated with the white farmers in the area. He brought them food when the war had escalated. He made one fatal error to take his wife to the Mazowe mine where other white farmers had taken refuge. He was killed before he reached the mine on June 17, 1896 (Nyandoro, 1993).

Pioneering free enterprise

Europeans arrived in the heartland of the Hwata community on September 12, 1890, shocking the local people, who had never seen a white person before. Mbuya Nehanda was a 26-year-old woman, unmarried, and the highest priestess among the Hwata. Spiritually she was answerable to Pasipamire Chaminuka in two respects. First, he was the head of the Rozvi Traditional Religion founded by Nyatsimba Mutota, his great-grandfather, and secondly, he was the spiritual father of Nehanda Nyakasikana, who was the child of a relationship between half-siblings Murenga and Nyanda.

At each station they stopped, one or two individuals opened trading stores and that was the beginning of a cash economy. Thomas Meikles and others such as Susman Brothers and Wulfsohn (Macmillan, 2017) built retail outlets and distribution centers in Southern and Northern Rhodesia. Those businesses were successful for a long time and were instrumental to creating sustainable economies 1890–1980.

In any growing population, sufficient food and nutrition are needed for human beings to develop and realize their potential. Europeans coming to Africa wanted land to raise their own families, far from persecution in Europe. They were desperate to develop their own dreams. Their superior technology made colonization easy. There were unlimited choices available to most Europeans seeking fame and fortune. Australia, the Americas, and Africa were all favorite places to relocate. The expansion of the British Empire made many aspirations possible. This growth also spread Gospel and made "civilization" a reality for Zimbabwe. Many British subjects chose southern Africa; they had the option of settling in Lesotho, Northern and Southern Rhodesia, Nyasaland, South Africa, Swaziland, Botswana, or Malawi. These destinations had a lot to offer, good weather, virgin land, and the chance of discovering a gold or diamond mine. In those years, the name Nehanda Nyakasikana was familiar to those who settled in Northern or Southern Rhodesia (Mupepi, 2015). Her name, along with that of Chaminuka, were and still are praised in fluid Mutapa states.

According to Newitt (1995), the Portuguese claimed an affiliation to the Eastern part of the Mutapa States, through a history that went back to the Captaincy of Sofala (1501–1569), the Captaincy of Mozambique and Sofala (1570–1676), the Captaincy-General of Mozambique and the Rivers of Sofala (1676–1836), and the Province of Mozambique

(1836–1926). Later, after the Scramble for Africa (Mupepi, 2015), the Colony of Mozambique (1926–1951) was established to maintain the Province of Mozambique established in 1836. Newitt (1995) has suggested that the Portuguese claimed certain parts of Africa after the Voyages of Discovery. Portuguese trading settlements and later colonies were formed along the coast from 1498, when Vasco da Gama first reached the Mozambican coast. According to Newitt (1995), Prince Lourenco Marques explored the area that is now Maputo in 1544. He settled permanently in present-day Mozambique, where he spent most of his life; his example was followed by other Portuguese explorers, sailors, and traders.

According to de Galbraith (1970), the Prince founded a capitalist state in what later became Delagoa Bay. The area received military support from Portugal, through Prince Lorenzo Marques. After the Berlin Conference in 1885, the colony became Portuguese East Africa. The city and port of Lorenzo Marques was well positioned to attract European settlers, particularly from Portugal. In the 19th century, the colony developed along the same lines as Southern Rhodesia and was organized and governed by chartered companies including the Companhia de Mocambique and the Companhia do Nyassa, in which the British held more than 40% of the controlling equity (Galbraith, 1970). Three companies, the BSAC and the two corporations of Mozambique, developed the colonies of Mozambique and Southern Rhodesia back to back, cooperating in all aspects of security, economic development, and governance. The state of Mozambique was founded by Portuguese sailors, traders, and administrators, including Prince Lorenzo Marques, who was married to a local African woman. Frederick Selous of Southern Rhodesia was in a similar predicament—with three African wives, he was one of the first polygamous Europeans in Southern Rhodesia (Mandiringana and Stapleton, 1989). It would have been normal for these two colonies or others in Africa to advance a discourse of multiculturalism but their development reflected the hegemony of the European colonists in all aspects of economic and political life.

Developing British Imperialism

James C. Bender (2004) provides a detailed account of the Battle of Texel, the final naval battle of the First Anglo-Dutch War. The confrontation took place on July 31, 1653 between the fleets of the Commonwealth of England and the United Provinces; the English declared victory. After their victory at the Battle of the Gabbard in June 1653, the English fleet of 120 ships under General George Monck blockaded the Dutch coast, capturing many merchant vessels. The Dutch economy began to collapse immediately: mass unemployment and even starvation set in.

Scammel (1989) has argued that the Second Anglo-Dutch War was precipitated in 1664, when the English forces moved to capture New Netherland. Under the Treaty of Breda (1667), New Netherland was ceded to England in exchange for the English settlements in Suriname, which had been conquered by Dutch forces earlier that year. It can be argued that the Dutch were competing for world leadership during that time. For example, in Scammel (1989), the Dutch would again take New Netherland in 1673, during the Third Anglo-Dutch War, it was returned to England the following year, thereby ending the Dutch Empire in continental North America. They left behind a large Dutch community under English rule that persisted with its language, church, and customs beyond the 18th century

In Southern Africa, the Dutch founded the Dutch Cape of Good Hope as a refueling station of the Dutch East India Company in 1652. The Dutch and English formed trading companies that eventually pushed the Spanish and Portuguese merchants out of business. The British East India Company operating out of Zanzibar and Mombasa soon dominated trade between the Far East and Europe. According to Beck (2000), the Cape Colony became a governorate of the Dutch East India Company in 1652, and the outcome of the Battle of Muizenberg (1795) brought about British occupancy. The colony returned to the Dutch at the Peace of Amiens (1802), but the British re-occupied the colony with the Battle of Blaauwberg, after the start of the Napoleonic Wars.

From England to Rhodesia

In Southern and Northern Rhodesia and Nyasaland, the settlers became Rhodesians. The indigenous community had no choice; its members too became British subjects. Together, they embarked on a grand economic development plan (Van Vuuren, 2017). There was no fairness in the way the prosperity was shared. Rhodesians adopted separate economic development from South Africa. Cecil Rhodes is remembered in history as the architect of apartheid in South Africa. During his premiership, the Hut Tax of 1892 and the Native Act were debated in the South African Parliament and made into law. In Rhodesia and Nyasaland, Rhodes implemented the Land Apportionment Ordinances approved by the board of directors of the BSAC in 1890 (University of Michigan, 2014).

Diagram 7: Thomas Meikles building a consumer economy

Warwick (2004) has suggested that the end of the colony was subsequently affirmed in the Anglo-Dutch Treaty of 1814. With the arrival in Port Elizabeth of the 1820 settlers, the British began to settle the eastern border of the colony. Warwick has argued that the English settlers triggered the Mfecane (1815–1845) by beginning to introduce the first rudimentary rights for the Cape's Black African population. In 1833, they abolished slavery. The Dutch farmers resented the abolition of slavery and resisted this social change, as well as the imposition of English language and culture. The Dutch felt forced to move into the interior, creating inertia among the Ndebele and Nguni ethnic groups, which had to trek even further across the Limpopo River into Zimbabwe.

The period of 1885–1889 allowed the European settlers to develop political paradigms and theories of knowledge that paved the way for the exclusive administrations in South Africa, Southern and Northern Rhodesia, and Nyasaland. These administrations protected their own interests, as well as those of their national governments in England, France, and Portugal. The 1885 Berlin Conference on the Scramble for Africa served the interests of the superpowers Belgium, Great Britain, France, Germany, and Portugal. They all created corporations such as the British South Africa Company (BSAC) and the British East India Company (BEIC)— enterprises that developed the infrastructure, rules, and regulations of eastern and southern Africa. Both the BSAC and BEIC were created by royal charters, which empowered the directors of those companies to create mining and agricultural enterprises as a way of introducing a consumer or cash economy that would ultimately shape the civilization of southern and eastern Africa in what is now Angola, the Democratic Republic of the Congo, Kenya, the Sudan, Malawi, Tanganyika, Zambia, and Zimbabwe.

In South Africa, a different civilization sprung up, following the break between Afrikaners and the Dutch Monarchs. The Dutch settlers broke away from the Netherlands because its monarch could not sustain a military presence in Southern Africa to protect them (Boxer, 1969). In 1651, the English parliament passed the first Navigation Act, which excluded Dutch shipping from the lucrative trade between England and its Caribbean colonies, and led directly to the outbreak of hostilities between the two countries the following year. This was the first of three Anglo-Dutch Wars that lasted on and off for two decades. Boxer has argued that the conflict eroded Dutch naval power; the English took advantage of this situation. By the 19th century, Britain had become a superior naval power and British aggression continued into South Africa. For example, the First Boer War (1880–1881), in which the English attacked the Republic of the Orange Free State (1854–1902) and the Boer Republic of the Transvaal (1856–1877 and 1881–1902), and later carried out the Jameson Raid (1895–1896) organized by Cecil

Rhodes and the colonists, are examples of continued British aggression.

According to Ross and Anderson (1999), the southern part of the African continent was dominated in the 19th century by a set of epic struggles to create within it a single unified state. Ross and Anderson have argued that British expansion into southern Africa was fueled by three prime factors: first, the desire to control the trade routes to India that passed around the Cape; second, the discovery in 1868 of huge mineral deposits of diamonds around Kimberley on the joint borders of the Boer Republic of the Transvaal or South African Republic (called the Transvaal by the British), the Orange Free State, and the Cape Colony, and thereafter in 1886 in the Transvaal during a gold rush; and third the race against other European colonial powers, as part of a general colonial expansion in Africa.

Chambon (1999) cites Michel Foucault's concept of "episteme", arguing that the conditions of discourse change over time, from one period's episteme to another. Foucault demonstrates parallels in the development of many fields, such as linguistics and economics. Thus, the Dutch, frustrated by a lack of support from the motherland, developed a strategy for survival. Their first act was to create a new language unique to their situation, Afrikaans. They then developed a new style of governance that ensured their success. Other European settlers supported it because it benefited any person of a European race. The system was known as apartheid. Chambon has argued that Michel Foucault's ideas apply to the European settlements in Southern Africa. The British administrators put the Dutch system forward as a new economic approach, using it to develop separate economic development practices that were then applied throughout all of the British colonies in Africa. For example, the Hut Tax (1894) and the Master and Servants Ordinance (1841) illustrate the way in which the English and Dutch co-constructed South Africa, Northern Rhodesia, Southern Rhodesia, and Nyasaland (Durkheim, 2011). In 1908, political tension between the English and Dutch led to the National Convention. Its role was to settle the terms and constitution of a governmental, legislative, and economic Union. These proposals were transmitted to the British government in London which duly prepared a Bill to give effect to these wishes (Clark and Worger, 2011).

The economic and political developments in South Africa impacted similar efforts north of the Limpopo, as far afield as East Africa. The Bill was passed by the UK Parliament on September 20, 1909, when King Edward VII proclaimed that the Union of South Africa would be established on May 31, 1910 (Clark and Worger, 2011). This legislation brought into being the South African state as it is known today, served as the South African constitution for over fifty years, during which time the Statute of Westminster greatly increased South Africa's independence from Britain (Mabin, 1983). Although South Africa became a republic in 1961 and left the British Commonwealth because it would not give up segregation, the structure of the 1909 Act continued to live on in its replacement, the Republic of South Africa Constitution Act. Britain turned a blind eye to segregation in South Africa as well as in Rhodesia because it sympathized with the White minorities in an environment in which the Blacks were achieving self-rule in all countries north of the Zambezi River. The last remnants of the 1909 Act finally disappeared in 1983, when the apartheid-era government enacted a new constitution, the Constitution of the Republic of South Africa Act (110 of 1983) (Mabin, 1983).

In 1888–1889, the Rudd Concession and Moffat Treaties were signed and delivered, regardless of whether or not Lobengula understood what he was doing. The Rudd Concession was a written concession from King Lobengula of the Matabele granting exclusive mining rights in Zimbabwe and other adjoining territories to Charles Rudd, James Rochfort Maguire, and Francis Thompson, three agents acting on behalf of the South Africa-based politician and businessman, Cecil Rhodes, on October 30, 1888 (Mupepi, 2015). The concession was viewed as illegal for three reasons. The first is that Lobengula Khumalo was not the king of

Zimbabwe. The second is that neither party had the authority to enter into agreements that could bind Zimbabwe. The third is that Lobengula did not rule any land apart from kwaBulawayo. He had abdicated his rightful kingdom in Zululand as a result of the Mfecane (1815–1845) and other issues pertaining to the succession to the Zulu crown. According to Keppel-Jones (1983), Lobengula tried to seek an injunction to stop the agreement from being implemented, but his efforts failed. The Rudd Concession provided Queen Victoria with a foundation to grant a royal charter to Rhodes's British South Africa Company in October 1889. The Pioneer Column was created specifically to physically occupy Zimbabwe in 1890. It punctured a cultural equilibrium that had existed from time immemorial and marked the beginning of white settlement, administration, and development of the country that eventually became Rhodesia, named after Rhodes, in 1895 (Keppel-Jones, 1983).

Mbuya Nehanda journeyed to kwaBulawayo to meet with Lobengula and offer him advice on how to rebuff the BSAC agents who crowded his courtyard. Lobengula did not take her advice. He tried to pay for her legal counsel by giving Mbuya Nehanda three heifers. As Parsons (1993) reports, Mbuya Nehanda refused to accept the payment on the basis that Lobengula had not taken her advice. Lobengula had granted Sir John Swinburne the right to search for gold and other minerals on a tract of land in the extreme southwest of Matabeleland, along the Tati River and between the Shashi and Namaqualand rivers in about 1870, in what became known as the Tati Concession. However, it was not until around 1890 that any significant mining in the area commenced.

Lobengula had been tolerant of the white hunters who came to Matabeleland; he even went so far as to punish members of his tribe who threatened the whites (Parsons, 1993). The Matabele chief was wary of negotiating with outsiders but was locked into an ongoing argument with Charles Rudd, F. R Thompson, and Rochfort Maguire from 1884 until 1888 (Meredith, 2007). During these negotiations,

Lobengula turned down the advice of Mbuya Nehanda and gave his agreement to Cecil Rhodes through Dr. Leander Starr Jameson, who had once treated Lobengula for gout. Lobengula probably felt that he was returning a favor when he granted the Rudd Concession through Dr. Jameson. In Selous 1969, the Rudd Concession 1884 was created to give the BSAC exclusive rights to mining. As part of this agreement, and at the insistence of the British, neither the Boers nor the Portuguese would be permitted to settle or gain concessions in Matabeleland. Meredith (2007) has noted that Lobengula's court was inundated with Europeans prospectors seeking for permission to enter and look for mineral wealth in Zimbabwe. Nehanda Charwe warned Lobengula about getting involved in matters concerning Zimbabwe because it was not his land. This advice was not accepted. In Selous (1969) it is alleged that Lobengula disappeared in 1894 regretting his actions in 1888.

Lobengula sent two emissaries to the British queen but these envoys wasted time and could not travel right away and had to wait for several weeks until a ship sailing to England was available (New York, 1893). Selous discusses how Lobengula's emissaries missed the ship sailing from Cape Town to England which could have got them in London on time to meet with Queen Victoria. It appeared that they were delayed by Alfred Beit's associates in Cape Town buying the necessary clothing they needed for the journey. In the meanwhile, the Rudd Concession was signed by Lobengula on October 30, 1888 and in addition to mining rights it gave the Company the right to settle and create farms and a cash economy. It was too late to rescind the agreement (Keppel-Jones, 1983).

The implementation of the strategy developed at Pagomba happened in differing scales and sizes, as each chief trained soldier to confront the settlers. Mapondera did not waste any time; he already had an operational army numbering some five thousand strong young soldiers between the ages of 16 and 30. They were stealthy and understood the African savanna as well as the hills on the plateau. They had been operational since Mapondera took over the family trading business from his father Gorejena around 1860, when he was in his late teens.

The story of Chingayira Nyamanhindi Makoni is drawn from Mupepi (2010), Mudzigwa, (2007), Ranger (1988), and Steere (1973), among many other sources. Makoni too had a powerful army inherited from his father, Chief Makoni. The family had been trading with the Portuguese since their arrival in the 14th century. According to Chidziva (2014), the VaShawasha and VaMaungwe authorities, including the Chinamora and Makoni, engaged with Portuguese emissaries such as Guveya and Machado, developing militiamen who could support their businesses if disputes broke out in the barter trade. Makoni managed the militia with his brothers and cousins. They were renowned for sabotaging the BSCA supply chain from Beira into Harare. The whites had underrated Chief Makoni's army, considering it a bunch of barbaric Africans who did not understand rifles or gunpowder and could use spears and knobkerries at best. As a result of this underestimation, the surveyors attempting to map the country were all killed.

According to Mupepi (2010), Chief Makoni was not alone in his struggle for freedom. He had numerous supporters; Mbuya Nehanda was very supportive of the three Makoni chiefs, of whom Chingayira was the most senior. The Chimurenga was not conventional warfare, but a guerrilla fight launched by the current ruling government, rather than freedom fighters. The Chimurenga was a philosophy rooted in the strategy developed by Emperor Murenga, the Second Chaminuka and father to the medium of Gombwekadziguru, Nehanda Nyakasikana (c. 1450–1480). The epistemology for defending a growing empire was based on ambush, surprise attacks, the use of lethal arrowheads, the knowledge of local indigenous systems, and the unity of villagers within the larger Rozvi community. Murenga was the second medium of the Chaminuka. Stories that have survived from the 14th century indicate that he studied nature and conducted experiments to test the strength of various venoms and lactic acids from trees and shrubs, before determining a lethal dose for archers and the military to use on arrowheads. All the Magombwe had the power to change weather patterns, particularly in time of war. During the Shangani and Mazowe patrols, a clear blue sky could be covered in a fog that not even the Londoners had experienced before (Mupepi, 2015). The ontology of a Chimurenga combines psychological as well as physical warfare. Murenga may have believed that a human being performs at his best when he his life and the lives of those he cares for are at stake. Many chieftainships created by the Chaminuka were awards for chivalry. The irony is that hunters and fighters had the same competencies, while certain chiefs, such as Nyachuru, excelled at both. They could cull elephants and collect the ivory for business. They could defend their business interests when the need arose, and the interests of the Chaminuka in the same manner.

During the First Chimurenga, many freedom fighters were trained at home under the guidance of those chiefs who had regular militia. In the VaMaungwe community in the eastern highlands, Kamba from the village of Makoni helped to sponsor the war. According to Headrick (1988), chiefs and hunters such as Kamba traded with the Portuguese from Tete and Beira in the future Mozambique. Technology was transferred when the hunters were taught to use rifles, dynamite, or gunpowder. Kamba secured guns and ammunition and even asked Guveya, his main principal supplier, to train the Makoni militia in a technology transfer deal. Headrick argued that the traders could advance their own interests and did not owe a duty of care to the colonists, who only wanted possess the land and its mineral wealth. The traders could focus on meeting their sales targets and return to Europe to bring more goods for sale. According to Berkel (2015), oral traditions in Portuguese East Africa have been combined with trade records during the height of the barter trade era to make historical sense of the Mutapa Empire. For example, narratives from Makoni villages indicate that Kamba named his sixth son "Guveya". Both names, Kamba and Guveya, exist in the trade records, suggesting that the stories held in the memories of Rusape villagers were relatively accurate. Another story is that Chingayira killed 12 white settlers on his own. This incident appears in the records of the district native commissioner during that time (Chief Native Commissioner, 1902). Chingayira did not allow the settlers to create commercial farms in Makoni when he was still alive. The Company felt that the only suitable punishment for Makoni was decapitation. Whites used dynamite to force him out of the cave. Ndapfunya and Chipunza were Chingayira's relatives, probably younger brothers, with a vested interest in the Makoni paramount chieftainship. Local people helped the whites identify Chingaira. In every resistance movement, there are those who sell out others out for various reasons. Without the assistance of collaborators, the white soldiers would have failed to identify him.

According to Mudzigwa (2007), the story of Chingaira has travelled far and wide around the world. A story that originated in the Makoni village tells how, when Chingaira's cave was dynamited, his younger brother Muchira was the first fighter to come out, followed by his brother-in-law Gwena. Eventually Chingaira had no choice but to surrender. He was immediately arrested. They took the valiant Chingaira to the court at Tsorodziwa, where they shot and beheaded him. Commander Watts, the leader of the BSAC police, ordered his soldiers to behead the chief (Mudzingwa, 2007). He then took the head as a trophy to show Cecil John Rhodes. Together they sailed back to Britain on the same ship. Chingaira's head became a treasured trophy, amusing visitors in a museum, which still refuses to part with it. The graves of the white colonists at Rusape Cemetery testify to Chief Chingayira's military prowess (Mudzingwa, 2007).

According to Steere (1973), the BSAC was in conflict with the local population for a couple of reasons. The first was that the local people were not included in the schemata and modus operandi of the BSAC. The second was that the BSAC did not consult with the legal rulers of Zimbabwe. It continued to base its authority on the Rudd Concession, despite its flaws. Father Shearly Cripps was in conflict with the British South

Africa Company over land distribution and he sided with the local people, irritating the BSAC. Cripps observed the mistreatment of Africans by the BSAC. The Shona gave him the name "Mupande", or man who walked with a great step. The Company made Father Shearly Cripps a prohibited immigrant for 12 months because he criticized the way the BSAC treated traditional chiefs, such as Chingaira. He returned to England but later came back to the region, where he wrote a book entitled, *Africa for Africans* (1927). Arthur Cripps lived for some time in Manyene Communal Lands, about 120 km south of Harare and 20 km north of Chivhu. One part of Manyene is known by the name he gave it when he established his mission there, Maronda Mashanu (The Five Wounds). Father Cripps was buried in the chancel of the church (now a ruin) at Maronda Mashanu.

The discourse on Mapondera has been drawn from many scholars including Mupepi (2015), Hove (2011), Ranger (1988), and Isaacman (1977). Paramount Chief Chivaura Kadungure Mapondera was born around 1810 and died in 1904, when he was probably in his nineties. Isaacman (1977) focuses on Mapondera and his two deputies, Dambukashamba and Gumbeze. The Company considered these three traditional authorities dangerous. Isaacman (1977) has argued that the three commanded support and respect in the villages of Northern Zimbabwe and eastern Mozambique. The villagers felt a sense of solidarity with the freedom fighters because the colonists had robbed them of their land. Zimbabwe and Mozambique, in the latter stages of the 19th century, were not separate countries, but part of the Mutapa states (Cahoon, 2015). When the Scramble for Africa concluded in 1885, the European superpowers agreed not to interfere with each other's colonization plans but to support each other against rebellions. Thus, the two companies, the BSAC and the BSAC of Mozambique, stood side by side in fighting Mapondera, Dambukashamba, and Gumbeze in the Zambezi Valley and on the plateau. According to Beach (1988), Mapondera sought revenge when his brother was killed by a European trader and the villagers joined to support their chief. He increased his commandos to over five thousand, all fully armed, with comparable rifles and artillery. Isaacman redefines the concept of social banditry to explain how the Chimurenga was conducted and how it impacted colonization and influenced the creation of the modern states of Southern Africa.

Chief Mapondera helped to lead the Shona people of Southern Africa, particularly in the Mutapa States, against British colonial forces, soon after the assassination of Pasipamire Chaminuka in 1883. Hove (2011) has interrogated the diverse images of the combat participants in the struggle for Zimbabwean independence and recognized that the Chimurenga took almost a century to make freedom a reality. The numerical inversion in the dates ironically mirrors the radical transformation in the perceptions of the hero Mapondera who acted along with Dambukashamba, Nyachuru, and Chipuriro and many others, to progress the resistance. At that time in moment, Zimbabwe was constituted by numerous independent states that had not experienced an invasion since the Rozvi in 1694 and none had those memories except in folklore Hove has examined the three genealogies, concluding that the First Chimurenga combatants were inspired to do what they did—in , Mapondera+9, Dambukashamba and Gumbeze.

According to Beach (1988), Stewart (1989) and Hove (2011), Mapondera was unique as a freedom fighter. He spent his personal wealth on building an army. He collaborated on the plateau and along the eastern coastline and Zambezi Valley with various ethnic groups to defend the African turf. His campaign took off long before the African Triumvirate met in 1884. He did not waste any time tolerating the deals Lobengula Khumalo was attempting to make with the colonists. As Beach (1988) points out, Mapondera asserted his authority in many ways. For example, he entered into a business deal with Frederick Selous over the Mazowe Mine. In this partnership, he anticipated living amicably with his new neighbors, but the murder of his brother damaged race relations.

Mapondera was a descendant of the Rozvi dynasty of Zimbabwe and he married Chimoyo, who was a sister of Gwangwadza and the daughter of Chiumbe of the Nehoreka Chaminuka dynasty. Mapondera felt that he and the Rozvi had an obligation to fight because they and their descendants would lose everything if they let the colonists get their way. Thus, his rebellion was the first, even before the Ndebele uprising in 1893. By the end of 1884, the news of the Rudd Concession had spread throughout Shonaland.

Mapondera was an outstanding commander and politician, as well as a businessman. To him, the British colonists seemed more cunning than the Portuguese. For example, the British colonists moved into the interior soon after the Pioneer Column arrived in September 1890. The Portuguese started to scramble after they saw how serious the British were. Coelho (2006) has developed a theory of political chicanery based on the argument that the Portuguese were settled in the interior of Southern Africa and the Dande (Mount Darwin) and Guruve (Centenary) areas before the British. Many treaties had been signed and sealed between Portuguese traders, such as Makoni, Guveya, Mutasa, and Machado (Beach, 1994).

After the murder of his brother, Mapondera proclaimed that the BSAC would never rule his country while he was still alive. In the view of Beach (1988), Mapondera might have won if he had kept the battle only in Northern Zimbabwe. He led a successful rebellion in the Guruve, Mazowe, and Mount Darwin areas of Shonaland Central. Although his initial force was under 100 men, the numbers increased after the Pagomba meeting in 1884. He turned himself in in 1903 and died in jail in 1904 after a hunger strike.

Hove makes the case that, when the Rozvi Empire was folding, the children of Dhewa Basvi moved northwards from Bikita into parts of Manicaland, the Midlands, and Masvingo, and all over the Shonaland. They included Chiduku, Tandi, Ruzane, Samuriwo, and Nyamweda.

Isaacman (1977) has provided an analytical framework to help scholars to differentiate between types of individuals whom various authorities have indiscriminately lumped together and labelled terrorists. This was a people who had been greatly offended; the fighters were trying to recover their chattels, freedom, and land. By analyzing the specific context in which the assumed transgressions occurred, as well as the strategy and goals of the purported criminal, sharp distinctions between freedom fighters and unscrupulous company officials become readily apparent. These distinctions, in turn, if used in a discriminating and critical manner, provide an important vantage point from which to examine, and in some cases, re-examine, a variety of Zimbabwean reactions to annexation. The second distinguishing feature of the Chimurenga concept is its apparent universality. Bayo (2004) has suggested that numerous examples exist from disparate localities such as Algeria and Kenya to support the contention that the fight for freedom was a national issue and not merely the responsibility of the traditional authorities. The need to be free occurs in all types of human societies, including those in Zimbabwe. Bayo (2004) has argued that the tribal and kinship organization was used to create the synergy to defend the country.

The Chimurenga was not reported fairly in the Western media. There were distortions as to the nature and boundaries of the Mutapa states. These would have been explained to Rhodes, had he cared to discuss them with the landlords, rather than focusing on Lobengula, who was gullible and did not rule Zimbabwe. He was an aspirant ruler who got his own people killed in an attempt to make a dream come true.

Chapter Four
Daylight Intrusion

The occupation of Zimbabwe was a planned event. It was carried out with military precision. Every step and detail was immaculately examined and presented to Cecil Rhodes before the Pioneer Column rolled out of Macloutsie in the Bechuanaland British Protectorate and entered Zimbabwe under a very doubtful agreement (Mupepi, 2015). In Britain, the colonial office wanted to be informed of the progress made by its pioneer settlers from day one until the end. The reality is that they entered Zimbabwe illegally, under a dubious agreement between themselves and Lobengula Khumalo. Lobengula and his tribe, the Ndebele, engaged in a series of business negotiations with the agents of Cecil John Rhodes. These agreements were misrepresentations, a fact that Lobengula only realized when it was too late. Rhodes knew what he was doing and had numerous globally positioned advisors. The Company set up shop at a place it named Mount Hampden in the heart of the Hwata territory and proclaimed British rule. Immediately, it banned all barter trade with the Portuguese, Arabs, and Indians (Mupepi, 2015). The British government under the administration of Lord Salisbury passed an ultimatum in 1890 to remove Portuguese traders from the Zambezi Valley immediately (Livermore, 1992). It dispatched its naval force to the confluence of the Shire and Zambezi Rivers to block any entrance into the Shire or Zambezi valleys and to destroy any resistance. According to Livermore (1992), the Portuguese raised concerns because they had been in the Zambezi Valley since the late 14th century. The British argued that they had effectively colonized the territories north of the Limpopo and Zambezi Rivers through the Pioneer Column occupation, opposing claims made by Portugal that the land they had discovered belonged to Portuguese colonies. Livermore has argued that the British government empowered Cecil Rhodes and Alfred Beit and the British South Africa Company to be the chargés d'affaires in Northern and Southern Rhodesia and Nyasaland. British rule was implemented when the Union Jack was raised at Mt. Hampden in September 1890.

Tindall (1967) has suggested that the colonists in these new-found lands took many risks in developing an infrastructure and building sustainable businesses. However, no consideration was given to the Africans' rights to the land they owned or its natural resources. The AT, at that moment, was still canvassing for national support. In some places, such as the eastern, northern, and southern states, the resistance had been embraced. Mazarire (2000) has pointed out that chiefs in the southern states, under Chibi, Mazorodze, and Nyajena, sabotaged the railroad and telegraph network. In the eastern highlands, the transportation system was paralyzed on the treacherous Mvumba Mountain passes, as ox-drawn wagons carrying up to twenty or more tons of much-needed supplies were ambushed by commandoes sent by the traditional authorities (Mazarire, 2006). This resistance was of particular interest to the AT and Mbuya Nehanda. She continued to lead the campaign, while studying the situation very closely. According to Mazarire (2006), it was widely thought among the colonists that the Shona would not rise against the settlers; they tended to describe the Shona as "docile". Mazarire has shown that the strategy adopted by the AT involved building a consciousness and growing an awareness of what had befallen the Mutapa lands. Martin (1981) accepts that the success of the Chimurenga was based on the logistical support provided by villagers, who sustained the freedom fighters. All of the freedom fighters were volunteers, supplied with the resources the traditional authorities promised them at the wake of the Pasipamire in 1884.

Martin has shown that the united colonists expanded trade between Britain and the new-found lands of Southern Rhodesia, Northern Rhodesia, and Nyasaland. With the assistance of the BSAC and the money markets in Johannesburg, London, and New York, the colonists created the prazos or commercial farms and large agricultural estates, where they successfully raised tea, coffee, cotton, and corn, as well as tobacco. All of the labor was forced labor. The colony became a consumer market, where goods and services were exchanged for cash, letters of credit, and bills of exchange or negotiable instruments issued in Johannesburg, London, or New York. Thomas Meikles became a transporter, as well as a successful retailer and distributor ferrying goods to and from the Port of Beira in Portuguese East Africa or Durban, South Africa (see Figure 1). Business, along with the commercial farms and urban and mining settlements created sustainable jobs, something the country had not experienced before. This progress resulted from European settlement and it benefited the colonists, at the expense of the Africans.

In the British Empire and later the Commonwealth, bills of exchange were easily accepted because the commercial banks quoted on the London Stock Exchange established branches in the colonies too. Other oligopolies, such as those organized by Cecil Rhodes in the Johannesburg Rand and Kimberly Reef, created their own banking system that could meet the needs of the miners instantly, rather than waiting for head offices in London to approve credit lines. The colonists created inclusive business opportunities for themselves. It was a time when land had been demarcated to improve the economic situation of the settlers at the expense of the Africans. At this stage, poverty and disease set in among people who had previously been living off the land, the now-banned barter trade, and growing beef and dairy industries that had all been taken over.

However, the Hwata and other ethnic groups living on the plateau had adopted some of the technology from Europe to increase corn and dairy farming production. They far surpassed their Iron Age predecessors. However, they kept being evicted from the fertile valleys of Angwa, Gwaai, Hunyani, Limpopo, Mazowe, Mupfure, Musengezi, Mzingwane, Odzi, Pungwe, Runde, Sabi, Sanyati, Save, Shashe, and Thuli. They were eventually relocated to areas between commercial farms and mining settlements that were barren and poorly watered. These areas became known as the African Tribal Trust Lands (ATTLs).

The commercial farms and mining settlements preoccupied the colonists. They started building an infrastructure to advance a consumer economy. This approach did not work and the BSAC resorted to the use of forced labor or chibharo. Panayi (2005) describes the labor camps as simplified detention facilities, in which the inmates were forced to engage in penal labor. Labor camps have much in common with slavery and prisons. Conditions at labor camps varied widely, depending on the operators. The so-called native commissioners who worked for the Company from 1890 onwards, specialized in forcing Africans to work for nothing (Galvao's Report, 1961).

The ideology of capitalism includes trade, industry, and a means of production, where a laborer receives a wage, capital earns interest, and the capitalist takes a calculated risk to make a profit and at times experiences losses (Therborn, 1980). The colonists built a capitalist economy but did not pay wages under the chibharo system or pay rent on the land they took from Africans. The current discussions of the resettlement plans in Zimbabwe do not consider the psychological damage done to Africans in 1890–1980. Political scientists and historians do not discuss compensation to Africans, arguing instead about payments made to the colonists for land improvement, as if the colonists had been contracted by the local chiefs to do that.

The biggest challenge the colonial administrators faced was the need to build an infrastructure to advance the economies of the colony and make profits in the long run. In the short term, labor was needed to develop a base from which businesses could operate. According to Nzula and Potekhin (1979), the colonists had no choice but to collaborate with the traditional chiefs to secure forced labor. It may have been a simple case of quid pro quo, where the chief cooperated with the colonial administrators to re-assert and secure his old status as a recognized chief. The Company empowered chiefs who towed the lines of their colonial masters, even to the extent of evicting families who refused to cooperate.

According to Mhute (2001), there are some photographs of the men and women who were forced to develop the infrastructure in colonial Southern Rhodesia. Alongside its uses in societal representation in the European context, photography was also annexed to the colonial definition and categorization of the "other", namely the non-European races in Africa and other parts of the world. Mhute has pointed out that Africans were not allowed to see their own images, captured through photography by the colonial powers, because they were intended for a European readership. The image of savages portrayed by missionaries such as Livingstone became realistic with the aid of pictures that were taken out of context (Holmes, 1993).

The Hwata community practiced pastoralism, as well as livestock management. They learned from their trading partners about dairy farming and horseback riding. When the British came, they embarked on a separatist policy in which Africans became third-class citizens. Their religion and government were focused on Rozvi traditions and customs; they had no definite plans for national defense. For people in the Mazowe Valley, it was too remote to imagine a group of knee-less people arriving to take over their green valleys. They had repelled the Portuguese and felt that they could do the same with the English. The Hwata Paramount chieftainship was the highest authority in terms of religion and government. It refused to be associated with forced labor, which was ethically wrong in its own traditional laws. According to the Chief Native Commissioner (1902), the native commissioners were expected to collect the hut tax on behalf of the BSAC. Those who failed to pay were forced to pay in kind, by providing forced labor.

Alternatively, the BSAC collected cattle in lieu of the hut tax. Cattle were an important indicator of wealth and a source of milk and beef. They were also useful as beasts of burden, bridal wealth commodities, and objects of sacrifice to propitiate ancestors. The hides and skins were useful in making clothes, including footwear and trunks for both men and women. Ropes and other items were made out of leather.

Mbuya Nehanda was not the only woman who had held a very influential position among her people. There was also a similar leadership in Southern Angola among the Mbande ethnic group. Princess Nzinga Mbande. In Tvedtem (1997), Princess Nzinga organized a successful revolt against Portuguese settlement in sixteenth century successfully. Nzinga continued her struggle against the Portuguese. Now in her 60s she still personally led troops in battle. She also orchestrated guerilla attacks on the Portuguese which would continue long after her death and inspire the ultimately successful 20th Century armed resistance against the Portuguese that resulted in independent Angola in 1975 (Tvedten, 1997). One of the goals of Nehanda Charwe was to eliminate colonialism with all its evils of forced labor abuse of Africans and slavery.

In Hine (2011), the African Diaspora during 1898, at the age of 23, Mary McLeod organized the resistance against the subjugation of the African American people. She opened a high school, hospital, and the Daytona Normal and Industrial Institute for Negro Girls. McLeod saw the need to fight for equality by way of education and the provision of healthcare among her people. The popularity of Daytona Normal led to its merging with the Methodist-run Cookman Institute for Men in Jacksonville in 1923, thus becoming the Bethune-Cookman College. Bethune served as the merged college's first president from 1923 to 1942 and again from 1946 to 1947. She was, at the time, one of the few female college presidents in the nation.

While establishing crucial educational institutions, Bethune also in 1917 began decades of leadership among women's groups when she was elected President of the

Florida Federation of Colored Women. McLeod was elected President of the National Association of Colored Women (NACW) in 1924, which was founded by St. Pierre-Ruffin in 1896 (Hine, 2011).

Prior to Nehanda Charwe, Tete Minge (1820–1837) held the office of Paramount Chief Hwata on an acting basis. Minge was appointed as Hwata II. During that moment in time, the Hwata family had many other female priesthood holders who were usually the choice of many Magombwe as well as royal Mhondoro. The Europeans arrived in the heartland of the Hwata community on 12 September 1890, instantly culturally shocking the local people who had not seen a white person before. Nehanda Charwe was a 26-year-old lass, unspoken for and the highest priesthood holder among the Hwata. Spiritually she was accountable for her leadership role in the Rozvi Traditional Religion to Pasipamire Chaminuka in two respects. First, he was the head of the Rozvi Traditional Religion founded by Nyatsimba Mutota, his great grand ancestor and secondly, he was the spiritual father of Nehanda Nyakasikana having been conceived out of an unpopular relationship between Murenga and Nyanda, half-related siblings Mupepi, 2015).

In any expanding population, appropriate food and nutrition will be necessary to make human beings healthy. Europeans wanted land which they knew was up for grabs in Africa. They had superior technology to make colonization a walkover. There were unlimited choices available to most Europeans seeking fame and fortune. There was Australia, the Americas, or Africa as favorite relocation places. Those British subjects who chose southern Africa had the option of settling in Northern and Southern Rhodesia, Nyasaland, South Africa, or Botswana. These destinations had a lot to offer such as mild weather, virgin land, and, chances of striking a gold or diamond mine. In those years the name Nehanda Nyakasikana rang a bell to those who settled in Northern or Southern Rhodesia (Knight-Bruce, 1895).

The British government agreed that Rhodes's company, the British South Africa Company (BSAC), would administer the territory stretching from the Limpopo to Lake Tanganyika as a protectorate under charter (Parsons, 1993). Queen Victoria signed the charter in 1889. Rhodes used this document in 1890 to justify sending the Pioneer Column, a group of white settlers protected by well-armed British South Africa Police (BSAP) and guided by the big game hunter Frederick Selous, through Matabeleland and into Shona territory to establish Fort Salisbury (now Harare). During the same year, Rhodes was elected as the Prime Minister of the British Cape Colony (Keppel-Jones, 1983).

Events in South Africa continued to impact decision making in Northern and Southern Rhodesia and Nyasaland. According to O'Malley and Mandela (2008), the Cape Colony had a franchise system that was open to men of all races, dating back to its early constitution in 1853 and the achievement of "Responsible Government" in 1872. Under this system, the right to vote was based on a franchise of £25 worth of property, regardless of race. The BSAC offered no such rights to the Africans throughout its rule. During the ensuing decade, increasing numbers of the Cape's Black African citizens became politically active. O'Malley and Mandela have claimed that, by the 1880s, the Cape's Prime Minister, Cecil Rhodes, was disturbed by the prospect that white politicians could eventually be sidelined in many Cape constituencies where non-white voters formed a majority. In Keppel-Jones discussed that as more and more African citizens exercised their right to vote under the law as it existed, their vote looked to soon be decisive. In the Transvaal and the Orange Free State colonies, Africans had no vote, and in Natal nearly all Africans were effectively excluded from the franchise. Rhodes was unhappy that in many Cape Constituencies, Africans could be decisive if more of them exercised this right to vote under the law as it existed. In a speech in Parliament in June 1887, in which the franchise question was debated, Rhodes made clear his view: The native is to be treated as a child and denied the franchise Crais, 2001). We must adopt a system of despotism, such as works in India, in our relations with the barbarism of South Africa

(Magubane 1996: 108). Therefore, the Cape Franchise and Ballot Act of 1892 eventually raised the franchise qualifications from £25 to £75 to the disadvantage of Africans, colored people, and poor whites (Simons and Simons 1969: 50).

The Matabele Uprising started in 1893, when Lobengula finally realized that his actions had lost the land, including the ground on which he had built his kwaBulawayo. Information about how the Matabele fought has been drawn from many sources, including Makazhe (2003), (2007a) and (2007b), Cary (1998), Ferguson (2004), and Ranger (2010). The First Matabele War was fought between 1893 and 1894 because Lobengula failed to take advice from the missionaries and some of the Magombwe, including Mbuya Nehanda, Umkulu Mlimo, and Mukwati Chaminuka. There were others who saw the mistake the Matabele king was making but could not do anything because Lobengula did not take advice from people outside his inner circle. Mlimo advised the king to follow his father's path by consulting the priests of the Ndebele Traditional Religion, of which he was one. He argued that King Mzilikazi had consulted with the Mlimo on all decisions related to war. However, Lobengula was like a little boy who had been promised new toys. In the end, he began to see sense after seeing how destructive European firepower was. According to Makazhe (2003), the chiefs in the south-east of the country and Mashonaland did not go to the aid of the Ndebele. They had realigned themselves to support the AT. The result was that the Ndebele were terribly defeated but managed to destroy Major Allan Wilson and his troops across the Shangaan River. According to O'Reilly (1970), Allan Wilson and his men were outnumbered and all perished. Lobengula had 80,000 spearmen and 20,000 riflemen, armed with nine-pound Martini-Henrys, which were modern weapons at that time. However, poor training meant that these were not used effectively. He had been warned by Mbuya Nehanda in her last visit to kwaBulawayo in 1884 and 1887. The British South Africa Company had no more than 750 troops in the British South Africa Company Police, with an undetermined number of possible colonial volunteers and an additional 700 Tswana (Bechuana) allies. Cecil Rhodes, who was Prime Minister of the Cape Colony and Leander Starr Jameson, the Administrator of Mashonaland also tried to avoid war to prevent a loss of confidence in the future of the territory. Matters came to a head when Lobengula approved a raid to forcibly extract tribute from a Mashona chief in the district of Fort Victoria, which inevitably led to a clash with the BSAC.

In 1894, the BSAC issued Land Ordinances to demarcate the land. These instruments were heavily contested inside and outside the country. The demarcation emulated the Franchise Act of 1892 and the Hut Tax (1894) was passed in South Africa by the Cecil Rhodes administration. In South Africa, Cecil Rhodes was concerned that many Africans were qualifying to vote because the law allowed those who could raise twenty-five pounds to vote, under the terms of the Franchise Act of 1892. In Southern Rhodesia, the BSAC adapted the Hut Tax as a way to develop the infrastructure. This was met with much resistance by the African Triumvirate, who had been advised not to participate in the Matabele Uprising of 1893 (Mupepi, 2015).

Annexation strategy

The Pioneer Column was a strategy designed to enable the British South Africa Company, owned by Cecil Rhodes and Alfred Beit, to occupy Zimbabwe. Advertisements had been published far and wide to recruit men and women of European stock who could ride a horse and shoot straight (Johnson, 2009). Rhodes was very anxious to secure the gold and other precious resources his agents had discovered in Zimbabwe. Gold mines such as Chishawasha, Mazowe, Penhalonga, Shamva, and Wedza were mines-in-progress. Hwange coal was used in the smelting plants and foundries of western and central Zimbabwe. There was no need to drag coal from Hwange to the Penhalonga mines, as the dry Mopani trees generated enough heat to smelt the ore.

Rhodes was willing to pay anything to get into the heart of Zimbabwe. Lobengula Khumalo, the son of Mzilikazi, was used as a decoy so that Rhodes could get his way. The disappearance of Lobengula in 1894 was probably a case of pride going before a fall. The Matabele chief was persuaded that the white men were telling the truth because they pampered him with gifts, including assignations with some of Rhodes' lady friends. This led to his downfall (Parsons, 1993). Using an agreement obtained fraudulently, the Rudd Concession was secured in 1888. Rhodes then asked Queen Victoria to issue a Royal Charter to his company, the British South Africa Company. It was approved in 1889, giving the BSAC the power to occupy Zimbabwe. The Pioneer Column was billed as a rescue commando unit that would rescue the Shona from the intrepid Ndebele (Schmidt 1992). This too was a misrepresentation to the Queen. There was no attempt to rescue the Shona. These were the facts that Mbuya Nehanda attempted to tell Lobengula. The irony is that Umkulu Mlimo agreed with Mbuya Nehanda and Mukwati. They understood each other, within the context of Rozvi and Zulu spiritualism. They all revered their ancestors and Mlimo had buried King Mzilikazi in the Matobo Hills, where he and Mukwati lived. Lobengula refused to listen to Mbuya Nehanda because he believed that the Shona were jealous of his relationship with Murungu (white man) Rhodes. He also thought Mlimo was too old to continue advising him, after having served his father Mzilikazi in Natal, Transvaal, and then Zimbabwe (Ranger, 1979).

Charles Rudd was instrumental in securing Lobengula's signature for Rhodes's British South Africa Company (allegedly on behalf of Queen Victoria, though without any official knowledge or authority). He then sought and obtained a charter from the British government that allowed Rhodes to act, in a limited way, with the government's consent. The next step was to occupy the territory.

The Battle of Mazowe

According to Gann (1965), the timing for the Mazowe attack in June 1896 assumed that Company troops were preoccupied with the Jameson Raid (1895–1896). In that onslaught, many colonists perished, including members of the clergy, such as Captain Edward Cass of the Salvation Army. The Salvation Army had been allocated a farm, which they called Pearson Farm, some 18 miles north of Salisbury, and a stand in Salisbury Township on Montague Avenue. The militia under the command of Paramount Chief Mashayamombe began the attacks, using hit-and-run tactics and targeting settlers in isolated places, such as Centenary or Chipuriro. Mashayamombe was concerned about the welfare of his people, who had been evicted illegally from the Mhondoro area to make way for commercial farms and European settlements, such as Hartley and Gatooma. Records maintained by White (1989) indicate that Paramount Chiripanyanga, the grandson of Shayachimwe Mukombami Hwata, worked closely with Mashayamombe, Gutsa, Mbuya Nehanda, Kagubi Murenga, and Mukwati, among many others, to launch an effective attack on the colonists. Figure 3 shows Hwata Chiripanyanga becoming the Mambo (King) of the Hwata people in 1892. Generations of Hwata Mambos and their subjects had bought guns from Portuguese traders in exchange for gold from the Mazowe and Chishawasha mines. The guns were used for hunting and protecting themselves against Ndebele invasions. When the news of the Mashayamombe rebellion reached Mazoe, Mambo Hwata summoned all his subjects and asked them to bring their guns (zvifefe). Mambo Hwata then asked the family spirit medium, Mbuya Nehanda, to consult the oracles and ascertain what course of action they should follow. Mbuya Nehanda assured the Hwata people that they were fighting for a just cause and that the spirits of their forefathers (masvikiro), would protect them, in the same way that they had led them from Buhera through the proverbial *Mutunhu usina mago* (the path without hornets) to many conquests.

The strategy

Mbuya Nehanda urged her people to seek work from the colonists as a strategy for learning about the habits of the enemy. Some joined the British South Africa Police force as policemen and others were employed on farms as farm-hands. Other community members worked in farmers' homesteads as cooks, nannies, and gardeners. Many of these employees later defected to join the militias of Paramount Chiefs Chikwaka, Chinengundu, Nyandoro-Kunzvi, and Mashonganyika, among others. A militia with only 50 men could find itself with hundreds of men, all ready to die for their country. In 1896, Kadungure Mapondera, Chioko Dambukashamba, and Gumbeze were already fighting the BSAC in the north of the country, on the border with Mozambique and in the rest of the Zambezi Valley. One of the deserters was a policeman by the name of Mhasvi of the Nyandoro clan of Harava. As commander of the army, he taught Hwata men to shoot with guns (Madzivanzira, 2017).

Mambo Hwata gave orders to cut the telephone lines and provided his men with fake letters to deliver to all the British families in the area. Their instructions were to kill whoever came to collect the letters. This news reached British families in the area and they sought refuge at the Mazowe Mine (Rusare, 2015). An initial army of 20 villagers attacked a British convoy of 6 men (Faull, Cass, Dickenson, Pascoe, Fairbairn and Stoddart), who had left Mazowe Mine, driving a donkey cart towards Salisbury. Their wives were left behind at Mazowe Mine. The villagers killed Cass, followed by Dickenson. Shortly afterwards, the Hwata soldiers attempted to ambush the remaining four British men by pretending to be friendly. The four became suspicious of their knobkerries, and started to open fire. In Rhodesian Heritage (2010) the story of the Mazowe Patrol is detailed to provide readers with what transpired:

The donkey cart was hastily turned around, with Pascoe and Faull scrambling in front, and Fairbairn and Stoddart following behind. After travelling a hundred yards, the Hwata shot at Faull and his body slumped to the ground. Fairbairn returned fire and killed a Hwata youth. There was an exchange of fire between the Hwata villagers and the remaining two British men, who fled to the mine after Fairbairn's gun jammed.

Rusare (2015) derived an ontology of the Mazowe Battle from Ranger (1967), who had access to the records of the British South Africa Company for 1890–1923. Ranger's chronicles of the First Chimurenga discuss the military strategist, Chief Chinengundu Mashayamombe, who took directives from the African Triumvirate (AT), made up of Mbuya Nehanda, Gumboreshumba Kagubi, and Mukwati Chaminuka. The Rhodesian army suffered several military defeats at the hands of Chief Mashayamombe. The settlers admitted that Chief Chinengundu Mashayamombe was an effective commander of the freedom fighters. Observers noted that, although the battle raged for three days, the British South Africa Company police could not dislodge Mashayamombe. Rusare (2015) has argued that the most significant clash was at Mashayamombe, where the colonists could not defeat Chinengundu and suffered more casualties than the local people.

Sibanda and Moyana (1992) have suggested that, during this fighting, Native Commissioner Henry Pollard was captured and executed. This is just an assumption because his body was never found. Many stories suggest that when the war broke out on June 17, 1896, Henry Pollard was visiting his family at Mt. Darwin. No one knows whether he made it back to Mazowe. The Mazowe Valley was home to carnivorous animals, such as lions and hyenas. Pollard did not grow up in Zimbabwe and could have underestimated the time and also the strength of a pack of African dogs.

In the Rhodesian Heritage (2010), it is mentioned that the Native Commissioner of Salisbury who was in-charge of the police department dispatched another patrol of 13 men to assist Dan Judson at Mazowe Mine. They left at 10.30 p.m., under the command of Captain Nesbitt. Their departure could have been observed by Africans, who sent their traditional fire messages from hilltops to warn others of approaching danger.

Captain Nesbitt's party endured gun attacks from the Hwata people; one man and his horse were injured. They arrived at the mine at dawn on June 20, 1896, three days later. The Rhodesian Heritage suggested that a party of 30 men and 3 women departed from Mazowe for Salisbury at midday on June 20, 1896 with a wagon of 6 horses and 12 men on foot. The Africans including those from the Africans commenced attack from both sides of the road after just half a mile but with no injury. The gun attack intensified when the party reached Chomukoreka near Vesuvius Mine, before Chidamba's Village To the rescued party, every tree or rock appeared to hide an African man who appeared invisible because of the tall grass. At that spot, Troopers McGeer and Jacobs were shot dead, together with the horses belonging to Captain Nesbitt and Trooper Edmonds. The Rhodesian Heritage suggested that Pascoe could have decided to sit on the roof of the wagon to look out for the enemy, and he survived dodging arrows and bullets. Bullets continued to hail down on the sides of the wagon, which was protected by metal sheets. There were about 50 Africans in pursuit with a wide variety of guns which included Lee-Metfords, Martini-Henrys, and muzzleloaders into which they crammed nails and stones (Rhodesian Heritage 2010). The grass swarmed with freedom fighters and Trooper Van Staden died after his head was blown off and Ogilvie and Burton were wounded. Another bullet ripped through the face of Burton and he fell into the wagon to be tended by the women. Hendrikz, who had split from the main party, received a bullet which passed through both cheeks, taking with it a piece of his tongue and jawbone (BSAC 2017). When the men reached the Tateguru River, they failed to quench their raging thirst as the firing never let up. When the party reached open land, just before Gwebu River, the Hwata people pulled back after they received information that reinforcements with a Maxim gun (chigwagwagwa) were to be sent from Salisbury (Rhodesian Heritage, 2010). This plan had, however, not been followed through and Nesbitt's party was able to proceed to Salisbury. The Africans celebrated their success in driving white British people from their land, temporarily. Captain Randolph Nesbitt Crosby received the Victoria Cross from the Queen of Great Britain (The BSAP, 2017)

British revenge

The triumph of the local people was short-lived. The BSAC reorganized and returned to Mazowe with many soldiers to re-establish control. The Mazowe battle did not just include the Hwata people, it included all the African communities within a radius of at least 200 miles because Chipuriro and Mavhirivhi who participated in the fight were situated more than 200 miles in the Zambezi Valley. The Company established a base at Fort Mazowe from where they squalled the locals to tell them who the ringleaders of the rebellion were. Beach (1989) suggested that Mapondera, Gumbeze, Dambukashamba, and their commandos had fled into neighboring Mozambique. They found many homes deserted. Some villagers had fled north to what became Chiweshe Tribal Trust Lands, while others went and hid in the Shavarunzi, Nyota, Chinhoyi, and Masviswa caves. In Manicaland the Eastern Highlands became a place where the freedom fighters under the direction of Chingayira Makoni could operate from and hide successfully. In Lowveld Chiefs Chjbi, Ndanga and Nyajena, among others went on a rampage to sabotage the telegraph and rail roads (Mazarire, 2000).Those in nearby Shavarunzi caves were smoked out with dynamite which destroyed part of the shrine. These damages can be viewed from the dormitories of Mazowe High School on the southern saddle of the Shavarunzi Mountains. British soldiers went from village to village where they shot and killed any male that appeared on site, burnt several huts of the villagers, and stole cattle and grain. In Beach (1989), the purge went on for three months and to save the colonists. In order to serve their people Mambo Hwata, Nehanda Charwe, Mhasvi Hwata, Gutsa Hwata, and others, came out from hiding and surrendered to the police. The African Triumvirate was missing the mastermind who was Mukwati Chaminuka. He was never found up to this day. In Mupepi

(2015), there was no evidence found for their participation in the rebellion which killed many British people. Selous (1969) suggested that as many as 500 settlers had been killed in the 1894 war and another sizeable number exceeding 300 were missing. However, the freedom fighters under the leadership of Mukwaiti Chaminuka, Gumboreshumba Kagubi, and Nehanda Charwe, were tried for the murder of the Mazowe Native Commissioner, Henry Pollard and sentenced to death. What can be surprising is that the royal charter did not specify limitation of what the Company appointed judges could be. But death sentences were limited to the Privy Council throughout the British Empire then, Crais (2001) propounds that historians have tended to analyze the success or failure of a colony by the interventions imposed to maintain law and order. The confusion among the African Triumvirate was the fact that Lobengula was not a ruler of Zimbabwe. His father Mzilikazi Khumalo was granted land in a treaty signed or with the concurrence of Emperor Pasipamire Chaminuka. The British wanted to avoid recognizing Chaminuka because he had told them outright that he was not going to let his people subjugated by the colonists (Selous, 1969). It was apparent then that Frederick Selous and Thomas Bain sought to create Lobengula as the bona fide ruler of Zimbabwe to enable conquest to happen. All the derogatoriness in which the Bishop of Mashonaland joined to get funding for his tenure were part of a public relations to psychologically attack the Shona community. Labelling Mbuya Nehanda as a witch were planned state formation and cross-cultural encounters which fueled the raison d'être in all the two struggles: First Chimurenga (1883–1904) and Second Chimurenga (1966–1980). The first Chimurenga continued till 1904 when its gallant fighter Kadungure Chivaura Mapondera died in a Salisbury prison of hunger strike. He had turned himself in 1902 to stop the Company harassing his family and villagers (Mupepi, 2015).

However, during the trails, Mhasvi Hwata was surprisingly pardoned for exemplary behavior after his arrest. Gutsa was hanged together with Nehanda Kagubi,

Nyangombe Swosve and many others. Among those from Mashayamombe were his sons, and members of his commando group. Others escaped jail and went to join Mapondera who at that time in 1898, was still fighting the Company, this time in Dande or Zambezi Valley. The people from Nyachuru village were removed from the Mazowe Valley (where the dam was constructed) and relocated to what became Chiweshe Tribal Trust Lands to honor the Native Policeman Mutenhesanwa who had fabricated the evidence to incriminate Nehanda, Kagubi and others of the murder of Native Commissioner Henry Pollard (Mupepi, 2015).

As a consequence of this defeat Hwata, Nyachuru, Mapondera, and others lost their chieftainship. They lost their lands, stretching from the outskirts of Harare to Mazowe and Mvurwi. Nyachuru was relegated to the Masviswa Hills sandwiched between the Ndire shrine and the Salvation Army Mission named as Howard. Their subjects were placed under the rule of other chiefs such as Negomo and Makope and the newly created Chiweshe chieftaincy.

Although a large part of Mazowe Valley is named after Chiweshe, these are, in fact, lands of the Tavara Negomo, Nyachuru Mutsahuni and Makope dynasties, descendants of Munhumutapa (Mupepi, 2015).In A small section of the Hwata family founded a dynasty at Dande in Guruve under a new Mambo Hwata Chitsinde in the Zambezi valley in 1959, but the majority of descendants of Hwata remain scattered in the Chikwaka Chiweshe Madziva Masembura Mhondoro and Domboshawa communal lands. Some have moved away to find new homes elsewhere in Zvimba, Hurungwe, Chinamhora, Mrewa, Goromonzi and Guruve. A number of Mufakose families related to Nehanda, Goredema and Zumba have been making claims to be returned to the land of their ancestors since 1980. The aim of the state has been to resettle all Zimbabweans, not necessarily on their former land, but to make all those who were displaced and disadvantaged by colonialism, comfortable in ways considered reasonable by the people themselves.

Chapter Five
Nehanda's Arrest and Trial

Introduction

The stories about Mbuya Nehanda are many; as one moves from one village to another in Zimbabwe, one hears different versions of the same tales. The same can be said about the literature on Nehanda Nyakasikana, Nehanda Charwe, and the First Chimurenga. It is a mammoth task to develop a body of knowledge that incorporates the different perspectives that exist on the subject. A few carefully selected studies have therefore been analyzed alongside narratives from some present-day villages in the communal lands to understand the events leading up to the arrest, trial, and conviction of Nehanda Charwe (c. 1864–1898). The trial of Nehanda was politically sensitive at home and abroad. The Company had not declared a dividend since its inception in 1890. In a recent report, the University of Michigan (2014) has compiled accounts of the activities of the BSAC, showing how its key officers, Cecil Rhodes, Alfred Beit, and Charles Rudd, were reprimanded by the House of Commons for their involvement in the 1896 rebellion and the trials of those accused of leading the revolt. The House of Commons, led by the Marquess of Salisbury, ruled *ulra vires* the decision to sentence Nehanda Charwe and others because it was not within the parameters set by the Royal Charter of 1889 (Ferguson, 2004).

The decision to execute Nehanda, Kagubi and others was *ultra vires* in relation to the power granted to the BSAC by the Royal Charter of 1889. The goal of the board of directors was to move quickly to a point where the entire operation could start to make some money. Many scholars, including Ranger (1967), Beach (1998), and Charumbira (2008) have documented the arrest and trial of Nehanda Charwe and I will not be repeating their findings here. However, I would like to draw insights from the stories in popular African novels, such as *Mutswairo* (1956, 1983, 1994) and *Chakaipa* (1959), which include reconstructed accounts drawn from the memories of those who were present during the First Chimurenga. These stories have been passed down from one generation to the next, recalling the African Triumvirate and the key actor, Nehanda Charwe, whom they affectionately refer to as Mbuya Nehanda. When a fictitious story is told many times, particularly from one generation to the next, it becomes part of the local reality. Nehanda's stories have become a reality among the Shona and Ndebele, the two main contestants to the Zimbabwean space (Thompson, 2006).

How it could have started

The aim of the colonial administration was to physically remove the Africans from their rightful land and property and literally dump them in what turned out to be reservation camps (Mutswairo, 1956). There were many who saw Cecil Rhodes as an ambitious figure in late Victorian imperialism, and others who, while acknowledging the grandeur and nobility of his aims, deplored the unscrupulousness of his methods (Keppel-Jones, 1983). Nehanda diffused the message of freedom, which became a sensation overnight among the villagers. Colonization had made the local people poor and homeless. The indigenous folk started to view the colonists as evil because they were forcing them away from their land. The message ignited a sense of hope which motivated the entire African population to support the revolution. Colonization had made the local people poor by depriving them of right to farm their land as they wished. It also enabled the traditional leaders, such as chiefs, to organize and support the Chimurenga. Negative perceptions about the colonists were exacerbated when the entire country's cattle herd had to be put down because of an infection of rinderpest disease. According to Tambi, Maina, Mukhebi, and Randolph (1999), rinderpest disease is believed to have originated in Asia, spreading through the transport of cattle. Other cattle epizootics are noted in ancient times. In around 3000 BC, a cattle plague reached Egypt. Rinderpest later spread throughout the remainder of Africa, following European colonization. According to Tambi et al., this was the first time the disease had manifested in southern Africa at a time when the local people had no knowledge of the disease. When the settlers decided to put down all the infected cattle, the local people suspected foul play.

The leadership of the African Triumvirate (AT) had to be resourceful, using its position in the Rozvi Traditional Religion (RTR) to gain support. They were the highest order of priests in the structure of the RTR, but they did not have the technology to carry out their plans. Their positions in society generated the staunchest support throughout the country. As a close-knit Shona society, they had each other but not the ballistics to make defense realistic.

The AT saw Rhodes and his Company as usurpers of Zimbabwe's wealth. In the British Medical Journal (1953), Rhodes and the Pioneer Column are described as very brave men and women of British stock who braved the Dark Continent to create the British Colony of Rhodesia. The Pioneer Column included a medical contingent, however deficient its knowledge and equipment would seem by modern standards. The medical team carried quinine and anesthetics and applied the principles of asepsis. The British Medical Journal argued that the experience of the Pioneer Column should be marveled at, as a relentless struggle against savagery, disease, and climate. On the other hand, one wonders which participants were the savages: the intruders or the indigenous villagers. The Pioneer Column treated local people as if they had no rights to their own land (Keppel-Jones, 1983).

Galbraith (1970) has argued that the Africans should never have been labelled "savages", when, in actual fact, the colonists led by Rhodes were illegally occupying Zimbabwe.

The impression of savagery arose as a result of the aggressive behavior of the Pioneer Column, which invaded a foreign land without authorization. Galbraith has argued that the behavior of Rhodes and Beit in the Jameson Raid on the Transvaal included schemes to get rich quickly at the expense of innocent lives and was far more savage than the behavior of the innocent Shona communities. Nehanda and others believed that the Column was making a short business trip and would soon return to wherever it had come from. The British South Africa Police (BSAP) was created in 1889 by the Royal Charter which authorized the formation of a police force. It absorbed elements of the British Bechuanaland Police which had the responsibilities to protect and police Mashonaland. At that time Bechuanaland included present-day Zimbabwe; the present boundaries were created because of the Scramble for Africa 1884–5 (Onslow and Berry, 2010). The BSAP came to loggerheads with the African Triumvirate, supported by militant chiefs and villagers, who wanted their freedom. The BSAP was created to support the annexation of Zimbabwe as a British colony.

The African Reserves, as they became to be known, were barren, rugged and poorly drained soils that often received less rainfall than the original homes of the Africans. The Company aimed to confine Africans to these reservation camps, which were located conveniently between commercial farms and mining and industrial locations. Mutswairo (1956:23) echoed the sentiments of the Africans in a prose poem entitled "Nehanda Nyakasikana". One verse reads as follows:

Nehanda Nyakasikana, how long will the children of the soil continue to suffer and eat the maggots from their wounds while the usurpers continued to plunder Zimbabwe's wealth? (Mutswairo, 1956).

Nehanda, Kaguvi, and Mukwati organized the first resistance to colonial settlement. This confrontation led to unprecedented guerrilla warfare. The Company's police department (the BSAP) was organized by the Principal Native Commissioner of Mashonaland. The BSAP's motto reflected what it stood for: *"Pro rege, pro patria, pro lege—For King, For Country, For Law"* (Gibbs and Phillips, 2000). The BSAP was made up of full-time policemen and women who were pseudo-commandoes. They were backed by the British Army and colonial reserves. In 1896, Native Commissioner Henry Pollard disappeared and was presumed dead, while conducting his normal duties in the Mashonaland District of Mazowe, headquartered at Mount Hampden (Gibbs and Phillips, 2000). There were numerous clashes throughout the country but the Mazowe Patrol, leading to the death of Captain Edward Cass of the Salvation Army and others, the demise of Major Allan Wilson, and the Shangaan River Patrol all constituted attacks against Nehanda Charwe, Gumboreshumba Kagubi, and Mukwati Chaminuka (Selous, 1969).

Importance of household dynamics

It can be assumed that the RTR played a critical role in shaping broader social structures, relationships, and women's lives. The structure of women's subordination in the Shona community, in both the domestic and social spheres, was negotiated, disputed, and transformed over time. The accusations levelled at Nehanda Charwe were baffling to the native commissioners, who expected to find a man leading the uprising. In Zimbabwe at that time, a spirit medium of either gender was highly respected. This respect was a part of the religion that all Zimbabweans subscribed to.

Elizabeth Schmidt, in her book *Peasant Traders and Wives: Shona women in the History of Zimbabwe 1870–1939* first published in 1992, has suggested that the household was a territory of struggle that manifested in disputes over the allocation of labor control, female reproduction, and the distribution of resources. Nehanda was on trial, accused of the murder of Native Commissioner Henry Pollard, within a system of government in which ideological practices were reinforced by Victorian perceptions and women were oppressed. According to Schmidt (1992), African women were not allowed to own land; their only assets were a few cows left over from their bridal price or roora (in Shona). Women did not count in the genealogy of the family. Their role in a family was to raise children on behalf of their husbands. This perception was shared by the English during the Victorian era. Bucker (2005) has argued that women were belonging to the domestic sphere. The Shona also required women to provide their husbands with a clean home, put food on the table, and raise children (Mazarire, 2000). Thus, women were viewed as conduits of a relationship rather than being partners to it. Bucker has argued that marriage abrogated a woman's right to consent sexual intercourse with her husband giving him ownership over her body. The mutual matrimonial consent sanctified by RTR priests, such as Mukwati Chaminuka or priestesses such as Nehanda Charwe, became a contract once the lobola or roora was paid to her father, to give herself to her husband as he desired (Schmidt, 1992). Nehanda was accused of the most heinous crime, yet she was possessed by an ancestral spirit that recognized God's ability to create or take life. According to Bourdillon (1982), the ancestral spirits worked on an agency between the ultimate superior power known among the Shona people as Mwari or God, and the African people to create life as well as take it away. Nehanda was dedicated as a wife to the Gombwe Nehanda Nyakasikana.

The role of Nehanda was to preside over the Rozvi as their highest priestess, defend the empire from slavery and unscrupulous traders, and safeguard her chastity, which was closely related to abundant rain and the ability to treat diseases. If a severe drought occurred, it was believed to be the result of the Gombwe's wrath at the violation of chastity. If there was disease outbreak, the Magobwe were expected to find a cure and treating those suffering from it. The oracles of the Chaminuka foretold that all of the mediums of the Chaminuka, including Nehanda Nyakasikana, faced violent deaths (Kasembe, 2011).

Nehanda Charwe was put on trial, accused of the murder of Henry Pollard. If convicted, she faced death on the gallows even though she was possessed by a spirit of the Chaminuka (Mupepi, 2015).

Hut taxation and chibharo (forced labor)

The Pioneer Column had to start somewhere in building a cash economy. They introduced hut taxation as a way to raise funds to build their infrastructure. Forced labor (chibharo in Shona) was introduced to make use of local people in the construction of this infrastructure. Voluntary contributions from the local people were limited to the women who prepared food for men working to construct roads and bridges. The Pioneer Column did not waste time but set out to develop an infrastructure from scratch. They needed to advance the process of colonization to make their dreams to come true. Rhodes wanted British imperialism to reach from Cape Town to Cairo within a short period of time. He hoped to fulfill his own ambition to make as much money as possible as the colonies expanded. There were no roads or bridges to make trade or commerce a reality. Rhodes's health was failing him when he left England as a young boy; the doctors had lost all hope unless he moved to warmer climates, such as those found on the eastern coast of South Africa (Ferguson, 1999).

According to Gann and Duignan (1969), in 1892, the BSAC was under pressure to make the Rhodesian settlement work. Rhodes had been made the premier of the British Cape Colony in 1890. Some of the laws assimilated into Rhodesia were taken verbatim from the South African legislature in Cape Town. For example, the Hut Tax and the Native Reserve Act (Floyd, 1962) were both adapted for use in the Southern and Northern Rhodesia and Nyasaland strategic plans. The land-grabbing colonists and their imposition of forced labor and hut taxation caused the Royal Mhondoro mediums, Nehanda, Mukwati, Kaguvi, and many others, to challenge the BSAC. In their minds, the BSAC had no right to force anyone to work, either for a wage or for nothing at all. It had no right to impose a tax on Africans. Taxation and other laws were introduced fully after the so-called conquest. The following traditional song describes how the BSAC forced Africans to work as slaves:

Iyahe Madhunduru ndirerere mwana
Iyahe Madhunduru ndirerere mwana

The English is as follows:
Iyahe or iyaho (part of an untranslatable lyric, which has to be pronounced phonetically) Trenches or Water-drain (Mind my baby while I work on the trench ...) (Traditional author unknown)
This single verse would continue in harmonious crescendos and staccatos alternating with humming in crescendo-decrescendo all day long. The song represented the evils of slavery and forced labor. Individual families were forced to work in lieu of the hut tax or simply as forced labor. The headman would point out villagers who had not paid their hut tax or simply pick and choose people to send to labor camps. Chosen families, including toddlers, would all go together to the manual labor camp.

As the singers labored, using trenching picks and shovels to make contour ridges on European farms, or building roads and bridges, they had to compose songs as a way to motivate themselves and find the energy to continue working. There was also a song composed for the headman who decided which families to send to forced labor camps:

Iwe Sabhuku nyatsa kunwa doro
Iwe Sabhuku nyatsa kunwa doro

This song was performed in the same manner as the water-drain song (Traditional, author unknown). However, the Sabhuku song was composed for the headman (Sabhuku) who had the authority to decide which families should go to labor camps and which should be excused. Villagers often invited the headman to their family celebrations, where they treated him to lots of food and beer. Families that could not afford lavish entertainment to corrupt the headman faced certain disadvantages. These songs accompanied Jiti jive choreography, which became popular in the latter half of the 20th century, when Chimurenga music was popularized in English. The following Sabhuku lyrics can be translated as follows:

You Sabhuku you better drink that beer well (with variations below)
You Sabhuku you must know what you are doing
You Sabhuku you must now look after my baby (while I toil in the trenches)
You Sabhuku were caught in your birthday suit drunk as a newt (Traditional author unknown)

The songs were created to motivate laborers to find strength to toil all day long. In the villages, there were no celebrations during the war. However, village communities are gregarious and very traditional, so there were occasional drinking sessions here and there. Villages such as Nyamweda, Mashayamombe, and Chidamba were in close proximity to each other—not more than 100 miles apart. The distance was exacerbated by wild animals and undeveloped roads. Cowboys and cowgirls often met in the pastures, herding cattle, goats, and sheep. The pastures were a convenient venue, where gossip, current affairs, and other news could be created and distributed. For example, people in the Mazowe Valley were expecting the arrival of the Pioneer Column long before they arrived at Mt. Hampden. Chingayira Nyamanhindi Makoni knew that land in the Eastern Highlands was being surveyed and pegged to make room for the railroad long before Company surveyors set foot on his land (Ranger, 1982b).

Reputation of the spiritual mediums

According to Gelfund (1959), the royal Mhondoro of Nehanda Nyakasikana possessed the daughter of Nehanda Charwe around 1864. Charwe became the most important female medium, whose mission was to organize the freedom of Zimbabweans. Nehanda Nyakasikana's spirit communicated with the First Chaminuka Sororenzou, father to Murenga. It was Murenga who committed incest with his half-sister Nyanda and gave birth to a baby girl who was then possessed by the Gombwe, Nehanda Nyakasikana. The reputations of Nehanda Nyakasikana and her father, Murenga Chaminuka depended on the defense of the Munhumutapa Kingdom. They were born to rule Zimbabwe. In 1883, Pasipamire Chaminuka was murdered by the Ndebele. According to Ranger (1982a), mediums were under pressure, as adherents of the African Traditional Religion could challenge the reputation of any medium who was not steadfast in the fight for freedom. The AT was committed to forcing the settlers to return to their homelands in Europe (Bourdillon, 1979). This was not going to happen. The new land had everything a Briton of that time could ever want...sunshine all year round, the fertile red alluvial soils of the savanna grasslands, and well drained hills and valleys to make their dreams come true. The colonists rationalized their conquest in many ways. They argued that the Lord had sent them to spread the Gospel and defend the Shona from the Ndebele (Welsh, 2009).

During the latter half of the nineteenth century, three groups among the Shona were distinguishable as those with a low social position. These were slaves (or nhapwa in Shona), women, and children. These groups were less well-off because they could not access material resources. Chavhunduka (1980) has argued that women and children were vulnerable to the raw fact of negotiability. If a man did not have cattle with which to pay a fine, to exchange for food in time of famine or to pay to a patron he could offer a female dependent instead. According to Beach (1999), as Gumboreshumba Kagubi faced the gallows for his role in the murder of Native Commissioner Pollard, he asked if he could pay for the crime by offering his children and wives in lieu of the death sentence. This request was rejected.

In a family that was desperate, a girl child who could not be exchanged for food was a burden or another mouth to feed. The Charwe family was not desperate. It belonged to the affluent Hwata chieftaincy, whose wealth was derived from dairy farming, the administration of the Rozvi traditional authority, and gold mining. They were far removed from poverty. For example, when Nehanda Charwe provided legal counsel to Lobengula prior to 1884, she was paid in cattle— around ten cows per consultation (Beach, 1977).

Nehanda: myths and reality

According to Bourdillon (1982), the role and influence of the spirit mediums Nehanda Nyakasikana, Gumboreshumba, Kaguvi, and Mukwati Chaminuka cannot be understated. During the early 1890s, there was a robust belief in the African Traditional Religion until missionaries attempted to degrade it to promote the Christian faith. The African Triumvirate, made up of Nehanda Charwe, Gumboreshumba, Kaguvi, and Mukwati Chaminuka was believed to speak with the voice of Mwari. Kazembe (2011) notes that Murenga Chaminuka and his father, the First Chaminuka Sororenzou Chaminuka, are said to have prevented Christian doctrine from coming to the Munhumutapa Empire. However, as time went on, Emperor Chisamhuri Negomo Mupunzaguta (1560– 1589) accepted Father Gonçalo da Silveira into his court, baptizing him as Dom Sebastiao in 1561 (Nicolaides, 2011). Thus, Christianity was not totally new in the Mutapa states at the time of the arrival of the Pioneer Column. There were no clergy to follow up or missionaries to water the seeds that Father da Silveira had sown. According to Gelfund (1959), the Rozvi Traditional Religion was led by those three maGombwe (plural), who were a step away from Chaminuka and a step away from God. Murenga, and Nyanda were the only known children of the emperor by different mothers. The Gombwe or Royal Mhondoro known as Nehanda Nyakasikana came to possess the child born out of the incest committed by Murenga and Nyanda. This chapter follows the Spirit of Nehanda Nyakasikana as it possessed Nehanda

Charwe up to the point when she was convicted and sentenced to death in 1898.

Advisory capacity

On September 12, 1890, white settlers of British extraction, led by hunter Frederick Selous, hoisted the British flag in the territory of Hwata, in present-day Harare, Zimbabwe. Nehanda Charwe was a Hwata by totem (a secretary bird in Shona). The Hwata bird had a habit of feeding on insects in the African savanna grasslands. It represented the identity of the Rozvi descendants who conquered Zimbabwe under the leadership of Changamire Dombo (1684–1866). Isichei (1997) notes that Dombo adopted the title of Changamire instead of Chaminuka. His son, Dombo II, changed the title to Mambo, meaning "the ruler". The Pioneer Column claimed the land as a British discovery in the name of Queen Victoria and named the country Southern Rhodesia. According to the Anglican Church map of missionary activities in 1888, there was an expansive area in Mazowe called Nehanda (Welsh, 2009). At that time, Nehanda was a powerful spirit medium, responsible for advising on spiritual matters and preserving Zimbabwean culture and identity among all the chiefs in Zimbabwe. According to Parsons (1993), Lobengula Khumalo acknowledged and respected Nehanda as a powerful spiritual medium among the Shona people. He preferred Nehanda's oracles to those of Mlimo, a Ndebele Gombwe. Mlimo had counselled Lobengula's father Mzilikazi, who had been visited by many European people who were agents for Rhodes, including Thomas Baines, Selous, and Bill Hartley, all of them hunters and mineral prospectors. Mlimo had been there too when Charles Rudd and Robert Moffat were negotiating for the Rudd Concession (Poland, Hammond-Tooke, and Voigt, 2003).

By the time he was in his 40s, Lobengula had ambitions to take over all of Zimbabwe to create the Matabele state his father, Chief Mzilikazi Khumalo, had failed to create (Poland, Hammond-Tooke, and Voigt 2003). Lobengula was aware of the greater firepower provided by European guns; this is how he became trapped in Charles Rudd's scheme. He was promised, among many other things, machine guns, automatic rifles, and a speedboat to use on errands in his new dominion on the Zambezi River (Parsons, 1993).

A tale from Negomo Nyota Village

This story is about Negomo Village on Nyota Mountain in the Mazowe Valley and Mutswairo's (1956) first novel, written in the Shona language. Nehanda had the right to sit in the administrative courts of all the chiefs in Zimbabwe as an advisor. She was a high priestess of the Rozvi Traditional Religion. The chiefs held their positions because her spiritual father, Chaminuka. One of the trials she presided over was a case brought to Chief Makope by a plaintiff who was the son-in-law of the Chief. The plaintiff claimed that, when he married the Chief's daughter he was not allocated part of the Chief's land to preside over as a sub-chief. The facts of the case included the plaintiff having married the Chief's daughter with his second wife. In terms of African traditions, a man could marry anyone's daughter, provided the in-laws agreed to the marriage and the would-be son-in-law was able to raise the lobola required. However, there were other conditions that applied if a man wanted to marry a princess. His background was important. Questions that needed to be answered were: was he of royal background? Was he rich? Was he a great hunter who could sustain the expectations of a princess? Thus, the plaintiff who presented himself in Makope's Court found himself being cross-examined by Nehanda Charwe, as the Gombwe of Nehanda Nyakasikana. The plaintiff claimed that he had been mistreated and compared himself to another individual, who had married the eldest daughter of Chief Makope's first wife. In Mutswairo's *Feso* (1956) Nehanda reviewed the case and advised the Chief that the plaintiff was merely a commoner who could not sustain the lifestyle of a princess. In addition, he could not compare himself to Negomo, who was already a chief in his own right. In an attempt to clutch at straws, the plaintiff also quoted Chief Nyachuru, who had married Chief Chingowo's daughter. In that marriage, Chief Chingowo had given the newly married couple thousands of acres of red, alluvial, arable soils in the pockets of Mutorashanga, up to the source of the Mwenje River, as an addition to the Nyachuru estate. Chief Chingowo was said to have given the newlywed couple additional land because he could afford it and wanted to be closer to his grandchildren. Thus, the case was dismissed.

In the history of the British Empire, no human creation has had a greater positive impact on the rapid growth of the settlers' fortunes than the British South Africa Company. The debate continues unabated, with some arguing that the British East India Company (BEIC), founded by John Watts and George White, had a greater impact on civilization than the BSAC. For example, Andrews (1985) has suggested that the BEIC promoted the British Empire in the Far East as well as Africa from the early 1500s onwards. The BEIC was instrumental in developing trade for the British Empire. Its performance can be measured in relation to the wealth and trade pacts it established in every part of the world it did business in. Other scholars, such as Rotberg (1988) have provided an insight into the work of Cecil Rhodes, explaining how he created a Company that created sustainable jobs in British South Africa. While performance of these two corporations cannot be compared realistically, Rhodes and his partners were under scrutiny for their involvement in the Jameson Raid of 1895–1896. Rotberg (1988) maintains that the goal of expanding the Empire was in sync with the colonists' schemes to get rich. The colonists were driven by ambitions to better themselves; as such, the local people were victims of circumstances. The capitalist system was unquestionably the greatest system for promoting innovation and social cooperation ever introduced into the Mutapa states. The system gave colonists the opportunity to earn a sustainable living by creating value for themselves. For example, farmers produced food, which was consumed by the miners, who in turn produced gold or iron ore, which were used in many industries and households. From 1890 to 1980, business and capitalism transformed the former Mutapa states into the breadbasket of Africa, south of the Sahara. This enormous development mainly benefited the colonists. The Africans were employed and earned skimpy wages that barely met their consumption needs in a country transformed from a barter trading system to a cash economy, based on free enterprise. The First Chimurenga was designed to resist capitalism. The Zimbabweans saw capitalism as an evil system that had destroyed the fabric of their society. In addition, the settlers did not value lobola and abused African women whenever they chose to (Mandiringana and Stapleton 1998).

On the trail of Nehanda, Judge Vincent considered the circumstances of the accused before making his judgment. He dismissed the case at first because the witnesses were not consistent. However, ultimately, Judge Vincent had to make decisions that would help the BSAC advance its goal of creating a market-driven economy.

Mupepi (2014) suggests that members of the Pioneer Column could have read David Hume's works (1752) on the capitalist market economy, decision-making, and investment. They also could have read Adam Smith's book, *The Wealth of Nations,* first published in 1776. By the time the colonists left for the new world in Southern Africa in 1820 (the Port Elizabeth Settlers) and certainly by the time of the Pioneer Column in 1890, the book was already a text in most high schools and colleges in Great Britain. By reflecting upon the economics at the beginning of the Industrial Revolution, the Wealth of Nations touches upon such broad topics as the division of labor, productivity, and free markets. Mupepi (2014) views capitalism as an economic system and ideology based on private ownership of the means of production and their operation for profit. The African Triumvirate was disrupting free enterprise by supporting revolution. The settlers appreciated Adam Smith's ideas about imposing a division of labor to advance production. The AT was socialistic in outlook. Nehanda believed that the settlers' capitalism was the work of an evil spirit. Nehanda and all the traditional authorities felt that nothing the BSAC did was fair. It was shocking to Nehanda to realize that people she had welcomed were now weighing the evidence to facilitate her prosecution. The AT felt that there could be no equality under the BSAC. The organization and the development of the Chimurenga could have started from this viewpoint.

A Princess at the helm of the struggle

In his Canterbury diaries, Bishop Knight-Bruce (1895) makes it clear that the colonists were aware of Nehanda's power and influence. As the British Empire expanded, British colonists, colonial administrators, and ordained ministers used established church doctrines and practices to form overseas branches of the Church of England. As new nations developed and became sovereign states, many of their churches became organizationally separate, while remaining linked to the Church of England through the Anglican Communion. Bishop Knight-Bruce was appointed the First Bishop of Mashonaland on the recommendation of the BSAC in 1894. Knight-Bruce was accompanied by the lay catechist and, ultimately, martyr, Bernard Mizeki, (c. 1861–1896), who, under Knight-Bruce and his successor Bishop Gaul, would carry out missionary work amongst the Shona people. Mizeki was one of the first Africans to be killed on the order of Chiefs Mangwende and Magombwe Vanyamita, Dzivaidema, Vanechipande, Vanyanezuva, and Nyarutswa, among others, who collaborated with the African Triumvirate. Knight-Bruce and Paramount Chief Swosve opened the first Anglican school and chapel in the village of his son, Chief Goto, during the rebellion in 1894. The situation was attributed to poor communications. It took a month to move from Wedza to Harare on foot. The journey was made more difficult by the lack of roads and the dangers posed by wild animals, such as lions and hyenas, among many other carnivores.

Nehanda Kagubi and Mukwati had travelled throughout the country to warn people about the uprising against the knee-less people. Kagubi covered the Eastern highlands of present-day Manicaland, while Mukwati went to KwaBulawayo, Matopos, and the Midlands to share information about the Chimurenga. Nehanda covered the center of the country, canvassing for support. In the Mhondoro area, Nehanda and Mukwati were received well, since that was Pasipamire's home.

The prosecution questioned Nehanda about her role in the uprising. She replied that she had a responsibility to teach her people what was right and what was wrong. Her people had been evicted for no reason—how could it be wrong for her to discuss this issue with her elders?

The prosecutor was not very interested in other witnesses until the police informant mentioned that Nehanda had worked with Kaguvi and Mukwati. The other freedom fighters, who had escaped from jail or were still at large, included Nyandoro Kunzvi and Kadungure Chivaura. Mukwati had the qualities of the Chaminuka; he was never captured. The Chimurenga had fighters who worked independently of the AT and others who worked for chiefs, including Makoni and Mangwende.

The judge viewed Nehanda as their leader because police informants confirmed that she was possessed by a spirit responsible for defending the Mutapa Kingdom. To make her prosecution easier, the judge described her as the officer commanding the resistance. Her efforts had sparked a vision of freedom throughout the country. According to Vambe (1972), the traditional authorities were seen as priests working to create an awareness of the evils of colonialism. They were responsible for distributing information about the colonists, including who they were, where they came from, and what their business was. Vambe (1972) has suggested that that this work was carried out via a network of spiritual mediums in the courts of chiefs throughout Zimbabwe. The Magombwe were the owners of Zimbabwe and the chiefs were merely agents, representing the civic wishes of their people. The Magombwe were responsible for food security and health. Some of them had the power to fight and defend the rights of their people. In the Mazowe Valley, there were numerous

Magombwe, including Ganyire Shumba, Goredema Hwata, Nehanda Charwe, and Kagubi Samanyanga.

Chiefs such as Dokora, Mutoko, Negomo or Nyachuru, and many others were part of the freedom movement alliance. The alliance turned to guerrilla tactics when the odds of losing became greater. The AT wanted the people to understand the evils of colonialism so that they could contribute effectively to the struggle. Mudenge (1988) has pointed out that Portuguese trade began during the 14th century and continued into the 20th century, only to be stopped (at the instigation of Cecil Rhodes) by the 1890 British ultimatum issued to Portugal (Coelho, 2006). This trade enabled the chiefs, whose main trading partners were the Arabs, Indians, and Portuguese, to acquire rifles and other weapons to protect their businesses in the Zambezi and Mazowe Valleys.

Defending the remnants of a magnificent empire

Pikirayi (2011) has argued that palaces such as the Mapunungwe Ruins in Northern Mpumalanga in South Africa the Khami Ruins in Botswana, Mavinga Town in Southern Angola, the Lozi in Shona, Ndau ethnic groups in Mozambique and Zambia, and the Rozvi descendants in Namibia and South Africa illustrate the extent of the Munhumutapa Empire. It was a robust kingdom that came with its own technology and was built by conquering smaller ethnic groups. Pikirayi has attributed the decline of the Munhumutapa Empire to persistent Nguni raids. The Changamire dynasty, based in Zimbabwe, was successful at maintaining trade with the Portuguese in the Zambezi Valley. It also prevented the Portuguese from advancing across the plateau during the 18th century. This dynasty was subdued by Nguni raids during the 1830s. The Mutapa state controlled the fertile and auriferous northern plateau margins near Mt. Fura, as indicated by the stonewalled Dzimbabwe at Zvongombe, Ngome, Chomagora, and Ruanga, and non-stonewalled centers such as Baranda and Mavinga (Pikirayi, 2011).

Mudenge (2011) notes that the empire survived for five centuries, from about 1400 until the last chief died at the turn of the 20th century. For Nehanda, Kaguvi, and Mukwati it was imperative to defend what was left of the empire. Although it happened before their time, the AT felt the loss of the Zambezi plateau to the Portuguese during the 17th century, and wanted to prevent future losses. Mudenge (2011) has argued that, in the 19th century, the Portuguese Prazo system defeated the Mutapa and claimed the Tete and Masekesa areas for Portugal. The British Ultimatum in 1890 forced the Portuguese to leave the area that became Northern Rhodesia, Southern Rhodesia, and Nyasaland. According to Newitt (1995), the African resistance was organized after the death of Changamire in 1883. Portuguese traders who needed permits had to rely on trading partners, such as Chiefs Makoni and Negomo, to sanction their activities in the country. It was widely believed that the AT began to organize the Chimurenga in 1883, after Pasipamire Chaminuka had died.

A leadership blunder

The villagers in Chidamba, Negomo, and elsewhere in the Mazowe Valley were very disappointed when the bullets of the colonists' Maxim guns did not turn into water, resulting in the death of many freedom fighters. On the other hand, the AT felt that it had to coerce people to fight and defend their turf. As the settlers began to enter Zimbabwe, they brought with them guns, bibles, and horses, which were all new to the country. Many chiefs came to Nehanda for counsel. Her advice was at first conciliatory; she reassured them that the visitors were only traders who would soon return to wherever they had come from. This was not the case; the situation caused a lot of anxiety among local people who had not been told who their new neighbors were. The anxiety increased when local people were forced to leave their fertile lands for areas where rainfall was scant. The soils in the Chiweshe Tribal Trust Lands were sandy and could not raise enough food for a family. The rainfall was sporadic compared to that in the Mazowe Valley, which has red alluvial soils and reliable rainfall.

Colonialism brought forced labor, hut taxes, the theft of cattle, and illegal occupation. In 1896, Nehanda began to call for unity with the Ndebele. She then progressed to physical confrontation with the colonists. She spoke as the great oracle spirit and Princess of Munhumutapa, calling on the Shona to rise up and drive the European settlers out. She promised that the power of the great land spirit Mwari would turn bullets to water. This did not happen; instead thousands of Zimbabweans fell under the fast bullets of the settlers' Maxim machine guns. Gelfund (1959:36) has said that being possessed meant that a person, the medium, could have two or more spirits. Several spirits could possess one person, who would still retain his or her individual personality. The individual personality would lead a normal life, for example, by getting married and raising a family. Thus, Nehanda Charwe, speaking as herself, could have made the statement that Mwari would turn bullets into water. She could not explain the settlers' weapons for many reasons. First, it was impossible to swallow the bitter pill of colonization; leaders had to say impossible things to avoid stoking resentment. Poisoned arrows and single-fed muskets had worked well prior to 1890, but they were no match for the machine guns and self-loading Martini-Henry rifles that every colonist possessed.

How the villagers rebelled

After the Mazowe attacks and other incidents, in which both sides lost lives, in particular, the villagers, the African Triumvirate went into hiding. The villagers had never seen so many dead bodies caused by a single weapon, the Maxim machine gun. There were drastic food shortages in the villages. It was almost six years after the villagers had been driven off their fertile land and none had been following the rituals to grow food because of the disruption. There was a drought followed by the rinderpest, an unknown disease that attacked cattle. All this created dissent among the Africans, who blamed Nehanda, Kaguvi, and Mukwati. They were supposed to explain the causes of the drought, cattle sickness, and children's hunger. This situation made it easier for Christian missionaries to spread the Gospel and introduce the Christian doctrine of Loving Thy Neighbor and the Forgiveness of Sins. Many who listened were impressed and decided to convert to Christianity (Mutswairo and Chiwome et al. 1996).

Insinuations about Nehanda and her religion

In typical colonial racist style, the stories written about Nehanda by Rhodesian colonialists, in many journals and diaries, refer to her as a "tribal witch" (Selous, 1967). However, the colonists accepted and acknowledged her power and understood how she had inspired Zimbabweans to fight Company rule. Nehanda united all Africans to fight British imperialism, which attacked and demeaned everything African to pave the way for capitalism and Christianity (Welsh 2009). Africans did not publicly denounce any foreign culture; it was discourteous to do so. The African Traditional Religion had sustained Africans for centuries. According to McFarlane (2007), it is an exaggeration to argue that the British were desperate to find an excuse to start a war in order to justify the conquest of Zimbabwe. It was obvious that the British would win; unlike the Zulus, the Shona had no formidable battle techniques. In Northern Rhodesia, when mineral rights were being divided up between the BSAC and the in-coming Zambian government, it was suggested that the predecessor to the BSAC Roan Consolidated Copper Mines compensate the Zambian government for the appropriation of profits from the time of inception to 1964, an amount totaling four million pounds (Limpitlaw, 2011). In 1899, Rhodes and his partner Beit were reprimanded and fined by the House of Commons for their role in the First Chimurenga and irregularities relating to mineral concessions and treaties. Both Rhodes and Beit attempted to resign over the Jameson Raid. The Northern Rhodesia report alleged that Rhodes and Beit were responsible for creating the tribalism that divided the Shona ethnic groups and the Ndebele. During the First Chimurenga (1883–1904), both Rhodes and Beit had to resign as members of the board. The massacre of Major Allan Wilson and his party were among the charges leveled against Rhodes and his Company.

Mutswairo has emphasized the importance of spirit mediums in framing a discourse of resistance in Zimbabwean history, as reflected in the prose of Nehanda Nyakasikana. The African Triumvirate (AT) created, diffused, and distributed knowledge about British colonization—clearly blaming the knee-less settlers and other colonists for all of the country's problems (Ranger, 1980). In particular, they accused the BSAC of having brought the locusts and rinderpest disease that attacked the crops and killed the cattle. During that time, an African's wealth could be measured by the size of his or her herd of cattle. According to Bouchard (2013) the country was rife with myths, suspicions, and contested realities. The colonists were suspected of having brought the disease that reduced the African wealth and caused the Chimurenga to intensify. African traditional beliefs were inseparable from the myths that made Nehanda and others into legends.

Creating an awareness of the resistance

The prosecutor wanted to find Nehanda guilty of collaborating with chiefs and other mediums to start the revolution. Nehanda's main concern was to create awareness that the country had been annexed by European settlers and to reassure her people that a united African force was needed for decolonization to happen. The prosecutor could not find evidence to convict Nehanda because the awareness campaign was spread too widely, with many leaders beyond the African Triumvirate echoing her call for freedom, until it reached all corners of the country.

Accusations

Nehanda was accused of influencing the First Chimurenga, which began in 1883. The Company was deliberately myopic. In the BSAC Report (1898), the secretary of the board of directors mentioned that, in 1898, the BSAC was finding it difficult to pay a dividend to its investors, who were getting tired of waiting. The Company made Nehanda a scapegoat for all the troubles the colony was facing. Nehanda was the catalyst that triggered mass resistance to the colonization of Zimbabwe. Eager to meet shareholder deadlines, the BSAC hoped to downplay the importance of the people's revolution. Much of the literature suggests that Cecil Rhodes was mainly concerned with the Ndebele, rather than the Shona (Selous, 1899: 1–9). At home in Europe, Rhodes wanted BSAC shareholders to believe that he, as the managing director, had everything under control. Although the BSAC had superior firepower, the Africans were fighting for all their earthly possessions and the future of their children. Nehanda was accused of treason and the murder of Native Commissioner Henry Pollard; both charges carried a death sentence.

Avoiding arrest

The Triumvirate avoided arrest because they were constantly on the move. They never stayed in one place for more than a day. They had to spread the war cry and cover as many villages as possible. Mukwati and Mloyi diffused the resistance in the Matabeleland area. Nehanda was eventually captured at the end of 1897 and brought to trial in 1898 for her part in the killing of Native Commissioner Henry Hawkins Pollard. Pollard had created great resentment among the Hwata by thrashing Chief Chiweshe for failing to report an outbreak of rinderpest among his herds. It seems unfair to blame the chief for not reporting a disease he had never heard of; this was the first rinderpest breakout in the country. No one knew how it mutated or what caused it (BSAC Report 1896/7)

The arrest of Nehanda

The African Triumvirate was very successful in most of its efforts. Their most important achievement was achieving union between the Shona and the Ndebele. The collective actions of the freedom fighters caused irreparable damage to BSAC property and many more settlers were killed than Selous cared to report in his diaries (Selous, 1899). More British reinforcements were arriving by rail from Beira. Those that came before 1896 were ambushed in the Mvumba Mountains by Chingayira Makoni and his commandoes. Those who came by way of the Hunters' Road over the Limpopo River were ambushed by Chivi, Mazorodze, and Nyajena commandoes, who remained vigilant when the Chimurenga broke out in 1883. This chapter draws its interpretation of the capture and trial of the African Triumvirate members Nehanda Charwe and Gumboreshumba Kagubi, as well as others from Charumbira (2008), Beach (1998), and Kazembe (2011).

The trial of the freedom fighters

Beach (1998) wrote:

"Yet it is ironic that the life of Charwe is still not clearly known in spite of some 35 years of research into the two periods by professional historians. Essentially, we have only two short periods of relative clarity, in late June 1896 and in early 1898. Around these two periods and in what lay before and between them is a mixture of fact, legend, and myth, much confused by views that developed from her death onwards." (1998:2).

Beach points out that a medium could be possessed by one or two spirits, giving the medium three personalities. It then becomes important to state which personality is present at any given time. It seems likely that Nehanda was possessed by at least two spirits. During her trial, she displayed impressive astuteness by denying the accusations that she had murdered Native Commissioner Henry Pollard. The court implicated Nehanda because it alleged that she had given the order to execute Pollard. It is arguable whether ordering someone to commit a crime and actually committing a criminal offence are the same thing.

The applied English legal system

Murder is the single most serious criminal offense in African, English, or Roman Dutch Law. Depending on the circumstances surrounding the killing, in English and Dutch Law, a person convicted of murder may be sentenced to many years in prison, a prison sentence with no possibility of parole, or death. In African Law, the penalty depends on the situation and circumstances, but whatever the motive for murder, the accused must compensate the bereaved family. Rozvi traditional customs require the compensation of the bereaved family because the deceased could turn into ngozi (undesirable) spirit that will haunt the accused and his family until an amicable compensation is reached. However, African Law was not used in the trial of Nehanda. She was at the mercy of the English legal system, in which witnesses play a critical role. As the judge could not find any credible witnesses, he was unable to reach a verdict. In Crais (2001), it is argued that conquest and state formation followed each other. The Company was running out of time and had not declared a dividend since its inception in 1889. The shareholders were becoming impatient. The defeat of the African Triumvirate as the main protagonist of the Company efforts to annex Zimbabwe meant the beginning of making progress. The Company introduced the rules and regulations that characterized the modus operandi for the next twenty years at the end of the royal charter in 1923. Crais suggested that the appropriation of African land and creating of the African Reserves took immediate priority. The traditional leaders were once again vetted to give appropriate rewards in terms of their contribution in the war. The entire African Tribal Trust Land, situated between Mwenje River and the foothills of Chawona Mountains, is named after Chiweshe, the policeman who falsified evidence to incriminate those who were hanged. Chiefs Nyachuru Mapondera and others were relegated and even made to report to the then new Chief Chiweshe. The structure had changed drastically. The chiefs were now reporting to the native commissioners. Crais (2001) viewed conquest as a cross-cultural encounter which often resulted in violence as the indigenous people resisted annexure The African Triumvirate were caught in this encounter. They failed to counteract the ballistics of the Company dominated by state-of-the-art fighting technology such as self-loading Winchester rifles of Hotchkiss machine guns.

Contaminated evidence

In around June 1897, the African Triumvirate returned to its hideout in the Mazowe Mountains to strategize and recuperate. Nehanda went into hiding, together with the commandoes Gutsa and Zindoga, who came from the same village as Nehanda. According to Mutswairo (1956) an individual who had been in Makope's Court found himself in a position to take revenge. This man, who was employed in the Native Commissioner's Office as a policeman, volunteered to incriminate Nehanda. First, he went to the police to report the whereabouts of Nehanda and her commandoes. He then gave an erroneous and dishonest account that implicated Nehanda in the murder of Native Commissioner Henry Pollard.

The BSAP proceeded to the hideout, which was a cave in the Shavarunzi Mountains. The police used dynamite to blow up the caves until Nehanda and the others came out. Kagubi presented himself to the police when he heard that Nehanda had been arrested. Mukwati Chaminuka was still at large and was never found. According to Charumbira (2008), Pollard's disappearance was blamed on Nehanda Charwe because she was the last person seen with him. That fact alone was not conclusive evidence. It was absurd to claim that a man could have been murdered by a woman with no gun or weapon to commit the heinous crime. Nyakupfuka (2012) has argued that the crime and accusations were primarily based on British superstition and witchcraft. Nehanda was one of the highest priestesses of the Rozvi Traditional Religion. This fact suggested that she advocated for an African form of spiritualism that offered a cosmological reference point to explain health, work, war, productivity, wealth, peace, and prosperity. The BSAC felt undermined by her position and sought to get rid of her (Selous, 1899: 236).

The charges amounted to murder

However, when Nehanda and others had been arrested, there was a jailbreak, in which potential key witnesses escaped. The native policemen worked tirelessly, even though they could easily have gone to Mozambique to join the Kadungure Chivaura Mapondera freedom forces. The court was left with no credible witnesses to convict Nehanda under English Criminal Law or Roman Dutch Law. The BSAC was registered first in England and later in South Africa at the two countries' respective stock exchanges. It had the privilege of being able to adapt the laws of either country for use in the colony of Southern Rhodesia. According to Lan (1985), the colonies did not recognize local customs or African Traditional Law for the following two reasons: first, the colonists assumed that, as they had conquered the land, the onus was on the Africans to learn about Europeans. The second reason involved language. The Europeans did not want to learn the Shona or Ndebele languages; instead, Africans had to learn English. They chose to create the Chiraparapa lingo, which was and is a fusion of Dutch, English, Ndebele, and Shona.

Conveyances of meaning

The court proceedings were conducted in English. Criminal proceedings relied on a jury to dispense justice. The dilemma the court faced was that many jury members did not speak English and had to rely on translations from English to Shona and vice versa. In conveying meaning from one language to another, the intended meaning can easily be lost. This could be one of the reasons why the judge ordered the case dismissed until credible witnesses could be found. The Chiraparapa language was spoken between masters and servants in domestic employment, agriculture, and the mining industry. It lacked the reciprocal meanings, context, and syntax to be relied on in a court of law where precise translations were critical to the dispensation of justice. On the other hand, the BSAC did not accept African Common Law. It left the interpretation of that law to the so-called native commissioners, who were not native—just colonists who created translations that echoed the sentiments of the BSAC (Chivanda, 1966).

Native Commissioner Pollard

Native Commissioner Pollard was a relative stranger in the Mazowe Valley. It was a valley infested with wildlife that was completely new to Pollard. Wild animals, such as hyenas and lions, roamed the valleys. It was no place for a European settler to travel alone on horseback at night (Beach, 1984). Pollard had relied on the old Mazowe road to return to his base at Mt. Hampden. He could have been lured by Nehanda to the place where her people mined gold, as they were business partners. Pollard could have tried to assault her, as Nehanda was a young woman in her early thirties, although she wielded enormous power and respect among her people (Lan, 1985). Alternatively, Pollard could have timidly offered to have relations. His compatriot, Frederick Selous, was polygamously married to three African women (Selous, 1899). Nehanda and Pollard were both single. This is just speculation. After 1897, Nehanda was captured and charged with the murder of Native Commissioner Pollard. She was found guilty, after an eyewitness testified against her. The story is that the man who accused Chief Makope of mistreating him when he married the chief's daughter volunteered, in his new role as a policeman employed by the BSAC, to bear false witness against Mbuya Nehanda (Mutswairo, 1983). The policeman claimed that Nehanda ordered an associate (whom he could not identify in court) to cut off Pollard's head. The judge, tired of the case, took the African policeman's statement at face value. He just wanted the whole thing to end. Both Beach (1998) and Charumbira (2008) concur that the BSAC wanted Nehanda to be hanged because she was the ringleader of the revolt that started in the Mazowe area.

Gender discrimination

Charumbira (2008) introduces the issue of gender discrimination and problems with translations. Translations create statements that can be interpreted differently in English. In such cases, the translations are not consistent. For this reason, the judge concluded that there was no conclusive evidence. Only when the native policeman testified falsely against Nehanda Charwe was she convicted. The native policeman may have believed that Nehanda, as a woman, should not have been involved in the politics or administration of African affairs (Mutambirwa, 1980). The judge accepted the native policeman's testimony *in toto* because he wanted the case to end.

No direct evidence

According to Beach (1998:34), there was no direct evidence that Nehanda played an important role in launching the resistance. The Company rewarded everyone who helped to arrest Nehanda, including the Crown witness. As Beach explains:

"When the case of Charwe and Hwata came to court on 2 March 1898, Murphy ran into trouble: Charwe said that she had not ordered Pollard's killing. Gutsa Hwata admitted that he had done the act, but on Charwe's orders. Unable to obtain separate trials or to defend both prisoners when their evidence conflicted thus, and unwilling to choose one or the other, Murphy withdrew. Thus, neither had a defense counsel, unlike the rest of the rising prisoners. At the trial, Gutsa and Zindoga were not present: they had been a part of a mass jailbreak and had not been recaptured" (1998:44).

There was no conclusive evidence to condemn Nehanda Charwe to death. However, there was pressure from Cecil Rhodes, who had sent large amounts of money for the arrest and conviction of perceived troublemakers, such as Nehanda

Charwe. Consequently, Nehanda Charwe was charged with the murder of Henry Hawkins Pollard and hanged in March 1898. A certain Mutenhesanwa was offered the opportunity to become a chief (Thompson, 2006).

Thus, the African policeman, who had a bone to chew with Nehanda Charwe in her capacity as the counsel to Paramount Chief Makope, saw an opportunity to advance his own ambition to become a chief by incriminating Mbuya Nehanda in the death of Pollard in 1897. As soon as the judge was informed that a credible witness had been found, the dates for the trial were set. Although all other charges of treason were dropped, Nehanda was convicted of the murder and sentenced to death in 1898.

Many scholars have commented on Nehanda's unfair trial and accused the BSAC of multiple miscarriages of justice. For example, Galbraith (1970) notes that the BSAC supported the illegal invasion of the Transvaal Boer Republic. The same powerful company sought to impose its will on weaker states in Southern and Northern Rhodesia and Nyasaland and on the British Cape Colony. Nyakupfuka (2013) argues that the First Chimurenga broke out because Rhodes and his Company sought to claim the colony by way of conquest. It was obvious that BSAC aggression towards traditional chiefs was designed to provoke a military confrontation, in which the BSAC would prevail. Some of the Africans who had joined the BSAC as soldiers deserted to join the freedom fighters. According to Beach (1998), the Civil Commissioner and Magistrate of Salisbury, Rhodesia, Hugh Marshall Hole expressed his anger at deserters. However, the general context of Pollard's death only emerged at the 1898 trial. Long before that, rumors had been at work. On June 19, 1896, a "Zambezi" woman in men's clothes reached Salisbury, saying that she had seen Pollard tortured to death, and that Forbes' party had all been killed. Although she was not believed, on October 29th, Marshall H. Hole, the Civil Commissioner, repeated the rumor about Pollard being tortured, claiming that it had been carried out by his own African police near Mt. Darwin (1998:14).

This was probably a combination of the July rumor and the fact that Pollard had last been seen by whites with his police in the Mt. Darwin area. By February 1897, W.L. Armstrong, an over-imaginative self-proclaimed expert on the Northern Shona, was claiming that Pollard had been kept alive for fifteen days, fed partly on the flesh of his own arms and legs, and then clubbed. This time, the rumor was linked to the name of Nehanda. Although there was no truth to it, such a rumor can feed on rumor until it becomes a fact (University of Michigan, 2014).

Thus the BSAC charged Nehanda with the murder of Henry Pollard because the other charges of treason could not be proved. The witnesses to the murder of Henry Pollard were unreliable: nobody saw Nehanda murder Henry Pollard. Bouchard (2013) has suggested that the evidence that Nehanda Charwe had committed treason was very thin, and that this was the reason the BSAC decided to charge her with the murder of Native Commissioner Henry Hawkins Pollard. Clearly, no one minded relying on contaminated or inadmissible evidence, given by a witness with a grudge against Nehanda. Thus, Nehanda was found guilty of the murder of Native Commissioner Henry Pollard. The oracles had predicted that both the Chaminuka and Nehanda would die violent deaths, as they did. Her brother Gutsa, along with Gumboreshumba Kagubi and others, were hanged at the High Court jail in Salisbury in 1898 (University of Michigan, 2014).

The legacy of Nehanda

The story of Nehanda reveals the injustices perpetrated by the BSAC. Ultimately, a miscarriage of justice led to her conviction. Zimbabweans lost the land between the Limpopo and Zambezi Rivers and between the Eastern Highlands and the Estosha Pans in Namibia. The chiefs were relegated to headman and the title of king could no longer be applied to any authority, including Chaminuka. Instead, Queen Victoria became the head of a new country named Rhodesia. Nehanda will live on in history as the Royal Mhondoro whose ancestral line went back to Nyamhika, the daughter of Nyatsimba Mutota, the first leader of the Munhumutapa Empire. She will remain one of the most revered revolutionary leaders and the best "Aunt" Zimbabweans ever had.

A discussion of economic development under apartheid followed, after 1898. This was a war situation, in which both sides aimed to win. No systems of governance are perfect. Most Britons underestimated the dangers they would face in that part of the world.

When the Pioneer Column arrived, Nehanda encouraged the local people to give them food and water. She wanted the villagers to get close enough to learn about the knee-less people's technology. "Get closer to learn their language and technology" she would say. The Pioneer Column brought missionaries, whose role in the new system was to introduce formal education and a health care system. Settlers who were injured or killed during the Ndebele or Shona attacks were treated in what became the first hospitals in Salisbury and Bulawayo.

The first schools for Africans were at the Salvation Army Pearson Farm, the Chishawasha Catholic Mission, and the Kutama Mission at Makwiro in 1892. The outbreak of the Matabele uprising in 1893 interfered with progress at these schools. Today, Zimbabwe's literacy rate is the highest in the Southern African Development Community (UNESCO, 2015).

The colonists had a tough time settling in Zimbabwe, given the cultural barriers that existed between them and the local communities. After their arrival, many local people began to migrate towards the urban, mining, and commercial farm settlements to search for work. The clear majority of Zimbabwe's migration continues to be internal—a rural-urban flow. When it comes to international migration, over the last 40 years, Zimbabwe has gradually shifted from being a destination country to one of emigration and, to a lesser degree, transit (for East African illegal migrants traveling to South Africa).

Paving the way for equality

Women in the Mutapa states were not treated as equal to men during that time. Traditional authorities viewed women as property and chattel belonging to their fathers, and later their husbands. They were transferred to husbands after their lobola was paid. Nehanda did not advocate for women, but her leadership during the Chaminuka's wake and organizing and developing the resistance (including the fighting) was exemplary. It paved the way for women to become partners in their households. Women played a critical role as business partners in cash crop production, stimulating the growth of relatively prosperous peasantry economies. Where they retained control of production, they experienced an increase in household income and family status. According to Mupepi (2017a), as men migrated to work on the Kimberly Reef and Rand and Great Dyke diamond and gold fields, women conducted successful household enterprises. Nehanda had encouraged the local people to learn the ways of the knee-less people. When the missionaries in 1899 established schools such as the Chishawasha St. Dominic Girls High School, St. David's Bonda Mission, the Usher Institute, and the Monte Cassino Mission, the first students were girls. These schools produced the first cohorts of teachers and nurses, who were quickly given jobs in the mushrooming Christian education system that was spreading throughout the African Tribal Trust Lands. After WW1, boys' and coed schools sprang up throughout the country. The Anglican Church built St. Augustine's Mission at Penhalonga, and the American United Methodists constructed a primary and secondary school, as well as a teachers' college, at Old Umtali.

Collectively, the missionaries produced the country's artisans, teachers, nurses, agronomists, medical orderlies, and public health assistants. When these qualified Africans went out to work in the communities, they were emulated by people who were still at home, but who saw that their educated neighbors had started to improve their standard of living in many ways. Some were able to build brick and mortar homes, complete with running water. Others bought cars and could drive around to get to know their country.

The work of the missionaries was priceless in the economic development of Southern and Northern Rhodesia and Nyasaland. It was critical in the design and implementation of a Christian education system that led to high literacy rates in Sub-Saharan Africa. In the Mazowe Valley, the death of Captain Edward Cass and others laid the foundation for the work of the Salvation Army, which had been allocated a stand in Salisbury Township on Montague Avenue. From this base, the Salvation Army was able to launch corps and centers in places such as the Howard Institute, the Usher Institute, the Bradley Institute, and Mazowe High School. It incubated and grew a formidable membership from its Pearson Farm and Montague Avenue bases.

As a British colony, Zimbabwe attracted significant numbers of permanent immigrants from the UK and other Western countries, as well as within Africa. Although Zimbabweans have migrated to South Africa since the beginning of the 20th century to work as miners, the first major exodus from the country occurred in the years before and after independence in 1980. The immigrants brought the talent, technology, and know-how needed to grow the colony. Adam Smith's concept of the division of labor was initially used to expand production in agriculture and the mining industry, and later in manufacturing and the service sector. The colonists followed David Ricardo in focusing on comparative costs in developing export markets.

Outward migration was politically and racially influenced, especially after 1980. A large number of people of European descent chose to leave, rather than live under a new black-majority government.After Mbuya Chief Hwata, Gutsa, Nyangombe, Gumboreshumba Kaguvi, and others were killed, the principal native commissioner of Mashonaland eventually had to recognize the local authorities. Many of the chiefs, such as Hwata and Nyachuru, were reassessed. They lost a significant amount of land in the

213

creation of commercial farms and mining settlements. Low labor costs made it possible for the exporters to have wider profit margins. The colonists kept abreast of technological developments and were innovative in creating their own animal breeds, such as Afrikander heifers and Rhodesian ridgeback guard dogs.

Shifting the balance of power

Ballistics technology, such as the Maxim machine gun, helped to shift power from the traditional rulers to the colonists. None of the traditional authorities were technologically savvy. Maxim guns were at the cutting edge of warfare and could annihilate thousands of musket, spear, and bow and arrow warriors within minutes. Nehanda encouraged her people to learn about European technology. Legend has it that when she was about to be executed, she said: *My bones will rise again, but you must take the Maxim gun if you want to rule yourself.* Realizing that they had lost their land, the Hwata and many other ethnic groups dispersed further into the interior, where they recreated themselves. Some remembered what Nehanda Charwe had said about the settlers and their technology. She had urged them to study the settlers and understood their language, customs, and weapons, including machine guns and dynamite. In the words of George Washington, experience taught the traditional authorities to secure their country first from Ndebele raids. Any future attacks or invasions could also be prevented. Washington suggested that once the enemy had secured himself inside, it would be difficult to dislodge him (The Founding Fathers, 2017). Many of the traditional authorities reconstructed their communities and lived to fight again in the Second Chimurenga.

References

Aldrich, Robert, and Garry Wotherspoon (2001). Who's Who in Gay and Lesbian History. London, UK: Routledge ISBN 0-415-15982-2

Andrews, Kenneth R. (1985). *Trade Plunder and Settlement: Maritime Enterprise and the Genesis of the British Empire 1480–1630.* Cambridge, UK: Cambridge University Press.

Barthorp, Michael (2002). The Zulu War: Isandhlwana to Ulundi. Weidenfeld & Nicolson. ISBN 0-304-36270-0.

Beach, D.N. (1998). An Innocent Woman, Unjustly Accused? Charwe, Medium of Nehanda Mhondoro Spirit and the 1896–97 Central Shona Rising in Zimbabwe. *History in Africa* 25 (27–54).

Beach, D.N. (1979). Chimurenga: The Shona Rising of 1896–97. *Journal of African History* 20, 3:395–420.

Beach, D.N. (1977). The Shona Economy: Branches of Production. In *The Roots of Rural Poverty in Central and Southern Africa.* Edited by Robin Palmer and Neil Parsons. London, UK; Heinemann.

Beach, D.N. (1974). Ndebele Raiders and Shona Power. *Journal of African History* 15, 4 (633–651).

Bourdillon, M.F.C. (1979). Religion and Authority in a Korekore Community. *Africa* 49, 172–181.

Bourdillon, M.F.C. (1978). The Cults of Dzivaguru and Karuva amongst the North-Eastern Shona People. In *The Guardians of the land; Essays in Central African Territorial Cults.* Edited by J.M. Schoffeleers. Gweru: Mambo Press, pp. 235–255.

Bourdillon, Michael (1982). *The Shona Peoples; An Ethnography of the contemporary Shona, with special reference to their religion. 2nd Edition.* Gweru: Mambo Press.

Bouchard, Gerald (2013). *National Myths: Constructed pasts, contested presents.* New York: Routledge.

British Medical Journal (1953). Cecil Rhodes. *The British Medical Journal* 2, No. 4826 pp. 29–30.

British South Africa Police (2017). *The War campaigns of the British South Africa Police.* Accessed 12/13/17 http://bsap.org/hiscampaigns.html#Mashona%20Rebellion2 018961897.20.

British South Africa Company Report (1975). *Reports on the native disturbances in Rhodesia 1896–1897.* Salisbury, Rhodesia: The British South Africa Company.

British South Africa Police (March 1898) [2017]. *Native Disturbances in Rhodesia 1896-97.* Bulawayo: Books of Rhodesia

Buchan, James (2006). *The Authentic Adam Smith: His Life and Ideas.* London, UK: W. W. Norton and Company. ISBN 0-393-06121-3.

Burton, Clive (1971). *Settlers to the Cape of Good Hope; Organization of the Nottinghamshire Party, 1819–1820.* Port Elizabeth: Port Elizabeth Series

Catholic Church (2015). *The Catholic Church in Zimbabwe.* Accessed 04/11/2015. http://www.catholic-hierarchy.org/country/zw.html

Chakaipa, Patrick (1959). *Karikoga Gumiremiseve (the Ten Arrows).* Salisbury, Southern Rhodesia: Addison-Wesley Longman Limited.

Charumbira, Ruramisai (2008). Nehanda and the Gender Victimhood in the Central Mashonaland 1896–97 Rebellions: Revisiting the Evidence. *History in Africa* 35 (103–131).

Chavunduka, G.L. (1980). *Traditional healers and the Shona patient.* Gweru: Mambo Press.

Chibanda, C.G. (1966). *The Mashonaland Rebellion in oral tradition: Mazowe District.* Unpublished Bachelor of Arts seminar paper, Department of History, University of Zimbabwe.

Chikuse, K. (2014). Mwari. Accessed 01/17/18 http://shona.website/2014/07/26/mwari/

Coelho, Teresa Pinto (2006). *Lord Salisbury's 1890 Ultimatum to Portugal.* Accessed 08/19/13http://www.mod,langs.ox.ac.uk/files/windsor/6_pintocoelho.pdf

Crais, Clifton C. (2001).The Culture of Power in Southern Africa: Essays on State formation and the political imagination. Portsmouth, NH; Heinemann

Davidson, Basil (1997). *Africa in History, Revised and Expanded Edition.* New York: Touchstone Books ISBN 0-684-82667-4

Dodds, Glen Lyndon. (1998). *The Zulus and Matabele, Warrior Nations.* London, UK: Arms and Armour Ltd.

Dominican Missionary Sisters (2015). *Our story since 1877: Our moves.* http://www.dominicanmissionarysisters.org/index.php?page=our-story-2

Eckstein, Arthur M. (2009). *Mediterranean Anarchy, Interstate War, and the Rise of Rome.* Davis: University of California Press.

Evans-Pritchard, E.E. (2010). The notion of Witchcraft Explains Unfortunate Events. In Richard Grinker Stephen C. Lubkemann and Christopher B. Steiner (Eds.), Perspectives on Africa. Second Edition. Wiley and Blackwell London, UK .Pp249-256

Ferguson, Niall (1999). *The House of Rothschild: The World Banker, 1849–1999.* Berkerley: University of California Press.

Ferguson, Niall (2004). *Empire, The rise and demise of the British world order and the lessons for global power.* New York: Basic Books. ISBN 0-465-02328-2.

Floyd, B.N. (1962). Land Apportionment in Southern Rhodesia. *Geographical Review* 52, No. 4.

Founding Fathers, the (2017). *American Collector's Special Issue.* Washington DC: Centennial Publishers.

Galbraith, John S. (1970). The British South Africa Company and the Jameson Raid. *The Journal of British Studies* 10 (1), 145–161.

Galbraith, J. S. (1974). *Crown and Charter: The early Years of the British South Africa Company.* Berkeley University of California Press. ISBN 978-0-52002-693-3.

Gann, Lewis H. (1965). *A history of Southern Rhodesia; early days to 1934.* First Edition. London, UK: Chatto and Windus, p. 118. ISBN 978-0-85664-771-0

Gann, Lewis H. and Peter Duignan (1969). *Colonialism in Africa, 1870–1960.* Washington DC: Hoover Institute Publication.

Gelfund, Michael (1959). *Shona Ritual: with special reference to the Chaminuka cult.* Cape Town: Juta and Company Limited.

Gelfund, Michael (1966). *An African's religion: The Spirit of Nyajena, Case History of a Karanga People.* Cape Town: Juta and Co.

Gibbs, P., and Phillips, H., (2000). *The History of the British South Africa Police.* Victoria, Australia: Something of Value Publications.

Darlene Clark Hine, Darlene Clark, (2011).The African-American Odyssey. (New York: Prentice Hall

Harcourt, Geoff, and Riach, Peter (1997). *A 'Second Edition' of the General Theory.* London, UK: Routledge.

Hanson, Neil (2001). *The Dreadful Judgment: the True Story of the Great Fire.* London, UK: Doubleday.

Hodder-Williams, Richard (1983). *White farmers in Rhodesia 1890–1965; A History of Marondera District.* London, UK: MacMillan.

Jesuits, the (2018) saints and martyrs: Servant of God (SG), Goncalo daSilveira,SJ.Accessed1/27/18
        http://www.jesuit.org.sg/html/companions/saints.martys/March/g oncalo.silveira.html

Kazembe (2011). Divine Angels and Vadzimu in Shona Religion. *The Rose Croix Journal* 8, 96–98.

Keppel-Jones, A. (1983). *Rhodes and Rhodesia: The White Conquest of Zimbabwe, 1884–1902.* Toronto: McGill-Queen's University Press. ISBN 978-0-7735-0534-6

Keynes, Maynard John (2007). *The General Theory of Employment, Interest and Money.* Reprint Edition. London, UK: Macmillan.

Knight-Bruce, George (1895). Project Canterbury. Canterbury, UK; *Society for the Propagation of the Gospel in Foreign Parts.* Accessed 08/19/13http://anglicanhistory.org/africa/knight-bruce_mashonaland1892

Koch, Robert and Remy Koch (1984). Christianity: New Religion or Sect of Biblical Judaism? Palm Beach, Florida; Messenger Media

Lane. Timothy (2001). Witchcraft, chiefs and state in the northern Transvaal 1900–1930. In Clifton C. Crais (Ed), The Culture of Powerin Southern Africa: Essays on State Formation and the Political Imagination, Portsmouth, NH; Heinemann Pp121–149

Levi-Strauss, Claude (1949). *The Elementary Structures of Kinship.* New York: Beacon Press.

Limpit law, D. (2011). Nationalization and mining: Lessons from Zambia. *Metall* 111 (10) ISSN 2411–9717

Mandiringana, E.; Stapleton, T. J. (1998). The Literary Legacy of Frederick Courteney Selous. *History in Africa.* 25, 199–218.

Madzivanzira, Alan (2017). The Rise and fall of the Hwata Chieftaincy. Accessed 12/14/17 Http://www. Thepatriot.co.zw/old_posts/rise-and-fall-of-Hwata-chieftaincy

Mazarire, Gerald Chikozho (2006). *Memory and contestation for the Scramble of Zimbabwe: Chivi (Mashonaland) c. 1870–1892.* Harare: National Research Database of Zimbabwe.

Mazarire, Gerald Chikozho (2000). *Where civil blood made soldiers' hands unclean.* Harare: National Research Database of Zimbabwe.

Meredith, Martin (2007). *Diamonds, Gold, and War.* New York: Public Affairs.

Moore, R.I. (1984). Atlas of World History. Sheffield, England; Rand McNally

Mudenge, S.I. (1974). Role of Foreign Trade in the Rozvi Empire: A Reappraisal. *The Journal of African History* 15 (3), pp. 373–391.

Mudenge, S.I.G. (1988). *A Political History of Munhumutapa c.1400–1902*. Harare: Zimbabwe Publishing House.

Mudenge, Stan (2011). *A Political History of Munhumutapa*. Harare: Zimbabwe Publishing House

Mupepi, M. (2017). Diamonds Are Not for Forever: Talent Development at De Beers. In M. Mupepi (Ed.), Effective Talent Management Strategies for Organizational Success (pp. 134–159). Hershey, PA: IGI Global. doi:10.4018/978-1-5225-1961-4.ch010

Mupepi, Mambo (2015). *British Imperialism in Zimbabwe: Narrating the Organization Development of the First Chimurenga 1883–1904*. San Diego: Cognella.

Mupepi, Mambo (2014). *Can the division of labor be re-engineered to advance organizational dynamism?* SAGE Open April–June 2014, pp. 1–6.

Murdoch, Norman H. (2015). *Christian Warfare in Rhodesia: The Salvation Army and African Liberation 1891–1991*. London, UK: Lutterworth Press

Mutambirwa, James A. (1980). *The rise of Settler power in Southern Rhodesia 1898–1923*. Rutherford: Fairleigh University Press.

Mutswairo, Solomon M., Emmanual Chiwome, Nhira Edgar Mberi, Albert Musarire and Munashe Furusa (1996). *Introduction to Shona Culture*. Harare: Zimbabwe Publishing House.

Mutswairo, Solomon M. (1983). *Mapondera, Soldier of Zimbabwe*. Harare: Longmans.

Mutswairo, Solomon M. (1956). *Feso*. Gweru, Southern Rhodesia: Mambo Press.

Nyandoro, Misheck (1995). A Flame of Sacred Love: The Salvation Army in Zimbabwe. Harare: Salvation Army Territorial Headquarters Zimbabwe.

Isak Niehaus with Eliazaar Mohlala and Kally Shokane (2001). Witchcraft, Power and Politics: exploring the occult in the South African lowveld. Ann Arbor: University of Michigan University Press

Nicolaides, A. (2011). Early Portuguese imperialism: Using the Jesuits in the Mutapa Empire of Zimbabwe. *International Journal of Peace and Development Studies* 2(4), pp. 132–137.

Noll, Mark A.; Nystrom, Carolyn (2011). *Clouds of Witnesses: Christian Voices from Africa and Asia.* InterVarsity Press. ISBN 978-0-8308-6861-2.

Northern Rhodesian Government (1964). Northern Rhodesia (Zambia) White Paper on British South Africa Company's Claims to Mineral Royalties. *Legal Materials* 3 (6), pp. 1133–1170.

Nyakupfuka, Andrew (2013). *Superstition and Diversity: Witchcraft, taboos, and legends.* Bloomington, Indian: Balboa Press.

Owomoyela, Oyekan (2002). Culture and customs of Zimbabwe. Westport: Greenwood Publishing Group. p. 163. ISBN 0-313-31583-3.

Onslow, Sue, and Annie Berry (2010). *Why did you fight? Narratives of Rhodesian identity during the insurgency 1972–1980; an oral history project.* Bristol, UK: The University of the West of England.

Parsons, Neil (1993). *A New History of Southern Africa, Second Edition.* London: Macmillan.

Pikirayi, Innocent (2011). *The true story of great Zimbabwe.* Accessed 08/19/13
http://www.newzimbabwe.com/news/printVersion.aspx?newsID=6122

Poland, M., Hammond-Tooke, D. and Voigt, L. (2003). *Abundant Herds.* Winnipeg: Fernwood Press.

Ranger, Terence (1982a). The Death of Chaminuka: Spirit Mediums, Nationalism, and the Guerilla War in Zimbabwe. *African Affairs* 81 (324), 349–369.

Ranger, T. O. (1982b). Literature and Political Economy: Arthur Shearly Cripps and the Makoni Labor Crisis of 1911. *Journal of Southern African Studies* 9 (1), pp. 33–53.

Ranger, Terence (1967). *Revolt in Southern Rhodesia, 1896–97.* Evanston, Illinois: Northwestern University.

Ranger, Terence (1987). Taking Hold of the Land: Holy Places and Pilgrimages in Twentieth-Century Zimbabwe. *Past and Present No. 117 pp158–194*

Robert, Dana L. (2011). Christian Mission: How Christianity Became a World Religion. London, UK; John Wiley & Sons. ISBN 978-1-4443-5864-3.

Reboussin, Dan (2015). A Guide to the George Fortune Papers. Accessed 1/27/18

http://web.uflib.ufl.edu/spec/manuscript/guides/fortune.htm

Rotberg, Robert I. (1988). *The Founder: Cecil Rhodes: The Pursuit of Power.* Cambridge, UK: Cambridge University Press.

Rothenberg, Gunther E. (1978). *The art of warfare in the age of Napoleon.* Bloomington: Indiana University Press.

Rusare, Patience (2015). The Untold Story of First Chimurenga Heroes. Accessed 04/11/15 *the Zimbabwe Patriot January 14, 2015*

Samkange, Stanlake (1967). *On trial for my country.* New York: Heinemann African Series

Schmidt, Elizabeth (1992). *Peasants, Traders and Wives: Shona Women in the History of Zimbabwe.* Harare: Baobab Publishers.

Selous, Frederick C, (1969). *Sunshine and storm in Rhodesia.* New York: Negro Press.

Shillington, Kevin (2005). *History of Africa, Revised 2nd Edition.* New York: Palgrave Macmillan.

Sibanda, M, and H. Moyana (1992). *The African Heritage. History for Junior Secondary Schools. Book 1.* Harare: Zimbabwe Publishing House. ISBN 978-0-908300-00-6

Stone, Daniel (2017). Grown home: sustainability. *National Geographic Vol. 232 No. 5 (3pages).*

Stott, Anne (2012), *Wilberforce: Family and Friends.* New York: Oxford University Press, ISBN 978-0-19-969939.

Staff Reporter (1964). Northern Rhodesia Promises Copper Firms Royalty Terms better than the British Provide. *The Wall Street Journal Eastern Edition September 21, 1964.*

Steel, David (2002). *Lord Salisbury: A Political Biography* London, UK; Routledge

Steere, Douglas V. (1973). *God's irregular: Arthur Shearly Cripps.* London: Great Britain. SPCK SBN 281-02675-0

Tabler, Edward (1972). Pioneers of Rhodesia Accessed 1/22/2018   *https://www.geni.com/projects/Pioneers-of-Rhodesia-Individuals/14703*

Tambi, E.N., Maina, O.W., Mukhebi, A.W., Randolph, T.F. (1999). Economic impact assessment of rinderpest control in Africa. *Review of Science Technology* 18 (2), pp. 458–77.

Thompson, P. S. (2006). *Black Soldiers of the Queen: The Natal Native Contingent in the Anglo-Zulu War.* Atlanta: University of Alabama Press. ISBN 978-0-8173-5368-1.

Tvedten, Inge (1997). Angola: Struggle for Peace and Reconstruction Boulder, CO; Westview Press

UNESCO (2015). Education in Africa. Accessed 12/18/17 http://uis.unesco.org/en/topic/education-africa

University of Michigan (2014). *The British South Africa Company Reports 1890–1899.* Ann Arbor: UM Press.

Vambe, Laurence (1972). *An ill-fated people: Zimbabwe Before and after Rhodes.* Pittsburgh: University of Pittsburgh Press.

Van Vuuren, Hennie (2017). *Apartheid guns and money: A tale of profit.* Johannesburg: Jacana Media.

Von der Heyde, Nicki (2017). *Guide to Sieges of South Africa: Anglo-Boer Wars; Anglo-Zulu War; Frontier Wars; Basuto Wars.* Cape Town: Penguin Random House.

Peter Warwick, (2004). *Black People and the South African War 1899–1902* London, UK; Cambridge University Press

Welsh, Pamela (2009). *Church and Settler in Colonial Zimbabwe: A Study in the History of the Anglican Diocese of Mashonaland/Southern Rhodesia, 1890–1925.* Boston, MA: Brill Publications.

Williams, Chancellor (1990). *The Destruction of the Black Civilization: Great Issues of a race from 4500BC to 2000AD.* Chicago: Third Press

Worby, Eric (2001). Tyranny parody and ethnic polarity: Ritual engagement with state in northwestern Zimbabwe. In Clifton C, Crais (Ed), Conquest, State, Formation and

Subaltern Imagination. Portsmouth, NH; Heinemann Pp 27-28

Zulu Wars (1879). Colonel Edwaed Graham Pennfarthing. Accessed 01/15/18 http://www.1879zuluwar.com/t1251-lieutenant-colonel-edward-graham-pennefather

Zvobgo, Chengetai J. M. (2009). *A History of Zimbabwe, 1890-2000 and Postscript, Zimbabwe, 2001-2008.* Cambridge Scholars Publishing. ISBN 978-1-4438-1599-4.